SQL
for
Microsoft® Access
2nd Edition

Cecelia L. Allison
& Neal A. Berkowitz

Wordware Publishing, Inc.

0 9 2 6 5 3

Library of Congress Cataloging-in-Publication Data

Allison, Cecelia L.
    SQL for Microsoft Access / by Cecelia L. Allison and Neal A. Berkowitz. -- 2nd ed.
      p.   cm.
    Includes index.
    ISBN-13: 978-1-59822-060-5
    ISBN-10: 1-59822-060-8 (pbk.)
    1. SQL (Computer program language).   2. Microsoft Access.   I. Berkowitz, Neal.
    II. Title.
    QA76.73.S67A44 2008
    005.75'65--dc22   2008016899
                                                                   CIP

ISBN-13: 978-1-59822-060-5
ISBN-10: 1-59822-060-8
10 9 8 7 6 5 4 3 2 1
0805

All inquiries for volume purchases of this book should be addressed to Wordware
Publishing, Inc., at the above address. Telephone inquiries may be made by calling:

(972) 423-0090

Contents

Contents ▶

Contents ▷

Contents ▶

Acknowledgments

I'd like to thank God for giving me the strength, perseverance, and guidance to complete another edition of this book. I'd like to send a special thanks to my sisters and brothers: Tanya Levin, Panzina Hill and her husband, Dudley Hill, Reginald Coney, and Timothy Coney. I'd also like to send a special thanks to Tim McEvoy and the staff at Wordware Publishing; I am grateful for another opportunity to work with you. I'd like to thank Neal Berkowitz for your hard work and expertise. I'd also like to thank the following special people: Thomas and Debra Brown, Leonard and Yolanda Cole, Teik-Seng Yu (aka Cowboy), the members of Northside Church of Christ (Tampa), Richard and Gayle Finch, Sandy Stephenson, Dion and Stephanie Dixon, Mary Carias, Demetrius Thompson, Otis Coney, Low and Ann Coney, Vernon and Yvonne Spellman, Odessa Browne, Obit F. and Yvonne O. Allison, Yolanda D. Love, and Lashawn Jackson.

Cecelia L. Allison

The computer field is one in which many people freely give of their knowledge and expertise. Chuck, Larry, David, Michael, Charlie, Steve, and everyone else — thanks for the help! Extra thanks goes to my coauthor, Cecelia, who has kept me on target, and Tim and Beth at Wordware, who keep pushing me to finish things.

Neal A. Berkowitz

Introduction

To get the most out of a book, it is usually a good idea to discover immediately what the authors plan to discuss in the book, how they plan to present the material, and how much knowledge of the subject the reader needs to have. So, to put things in a nutshell, this is a book about basic SQL and how to build SQL database queries in Microsoft Access. As an added plus, the final chapters of this book discuss the integration of SQL script in Visual Basic and ASP.

The primary targets are those people who have done some work in Access or a comparable program and who can build queries and tables using the tools, wizards, or query grids, but who are now ready to take the next big step into the underlying programming of SQL itself.

So, how do we go about presenting a topic like SQL in a simple, easy-to-understand format? Well, we have to start somewhere, so each chapter begins with a short introduction to highlight what we plan to discuss in that chapter. The next section of each chapter is a list of important definitions. Here you will find the keywords and terms that are to be used, explained, and expanded upon. This is also the perfect place to scan if you want to find where a specific keyword is introduced and how it is used in an SQL statement. This is not a replacement for the index or table of contents! Instead, it is for those who want a quick, concise answer.

The bulk of the chapters will contain all the little bits of facts and examples that are used to impart wisdom and fill up the rest of the pages in the book. We will be taking a two-pronged approach to the SQL language. First, we will present it from a "blank slate" approach. Here we will build on one reserved word at a time until we cover the ins and outs of the language. Since we expect everyone to know a bit of Access, we will also be flipping between the three major layouts of the

Access query screen. We expect the user to be familiar with both the query grid of the Design view and the results screen of the Datasheet view. We suspect that you have at least accidentally selected SQL view once or twice. We will use the power of Access to show the results of Design view queries in SQL view and illustrate both the good and bad of the Access interpreter. The power of SQL view extends the capabilities of Access tremendously. It also presents to the programmer what is really happening in the case of complex queries.

The Importance of SQL in Microsoft Access

Some people will say that they do not need SQL to program in Access. They are correct. But to use an analogy (you are hereby warned that one of the authors loves analogies), not using SQL is like not using any gear but first to drive a car. It can be done, but the car has to work a lot harder and you waste a lot of energy.

Let's begin with one of the more mundane uses of the SQL format of a query. You need to send a copy of a query to a friend who is using one of your databases. He can get around in Access. You have this great new wonderful query you want him to use but you don't want to have to send him the entire database. You have two options. You can create a new database that only contains your one query and the needed tables to keep it from blowing up if he accidentally tries to edit it in place. You can then e-mail the new database, and he can copy the query into his database.

The other method is to use SQL, which makes the entire process much simpler. First, change the view of the query to SQL view. This produces a block of text that is the SQL statement. Copy it to the clipboard and paste it in the text field of an e-mail message. Send it. Have your friend open up Access and build a new query and then change to SQL view, paste the contents of the e-mail message you sent as the SQL value of the query, then change to Design view. Voilà! You have just sent a query without the overhead or hassles of an Access file.

SQL will prove to be as useful in lots of other ways as you will see in later chapters.

Code Interpretations

Throughout the chapters of this book you will also come across many syntax (a series of rules that state how SQL script must be scripted) models that show you the proper format to follow when creating a specific query. When interpreting SQL syntax models, note the following:

- Keywords are typed in all uppercase.
- Items enclosed in brackets [ ] represent optional items.
- A | symbol means or.
- Parentheses should be included in the actual query.

Companion Files

The companion files can be downloaded from www.wordware.com/files/sql-access2ed. There are two files: database.zip and wordwarebook.zip.

Database.zip contains the database used in the examples, and wordwarebook.zip includes the files used in the ASP examples in Chapter 15. The wordwarebook.zip files must be installed on a web server (see Chapter 15 for instructions).

Chapter 1

The Relational Database Structure

Introduction

In this chapter you will learn about the structure of the relational database. You will also learn about database modeling and a database design technique called normalization. Read over the chapter definitions before you begin.

Definitions

Attribute — The characteristics of an entity.

Client — A single-user computer that interfaces with a multiple-user server.

Client/server database system — A database system that divides processing between client computers for data input and output, and a database server, used for data inquiries and manipulations.

Column — A field within a table.

Data modeling — The process of organizing and documenting the data that will be stored in a database.

Database — A collection of electronically stored organized files that relate to one another.

Database management system (DBMS) — A system used to create, manage, and secure relational databases.

Entity — Any group of events, persons, places, or things used to represent how data is stored.

ERD model — The Entity Relationship Diagram model is a representation of data in terms of entities, relationships, and attributes.

File — A collection of similar records.

Foreign key — A column in a table that links records of the table to the records of another table.

Keys — Columns of a table with record values that are used as a link from other tables.

Normalization — A three-step technique used to ensure that all tables are logically linked together and that all fields in a table directly relate to the primary key.

Primary key — A column in a table that uniquely identifies every record in a table.

Referential integrity — A system of rules used to ensure that relationships between records in related tables are valid.

Relational database — A collection of two or more tables that are related by key values.

Relationship — An association between entities.

Row — A record within a table.

Server — A multiple-user computer that provides shared database connection, interfacing, and processing services.

Table — A two-dimensional file that contains rows and columns.

Before we begin exploring SQL we need to step back a bit and discuss the basics of databases. Yes, much of this will be old hat to most of you, but we hope that with this short discussion we can fill a few knowledge holes before they become obstacles so everyone is on the same footing.

Early Forms of Data Storage

Before the existence of the computer-based database, information was transcribed on paper and stored in a physical file. Ideally, each file contained a separate entity of information, and was most commonly stored in either a file cabinet or card catalog system.

An organization that stored files in this manner may have, for example, had one file for personal employee information and another file for employee evaluations. If the organization needed to update an employee name, each individual file for the employee needed to be updated to maintain consistent data.

Updating files for one employee was not a big deal, but if several employee names needed to be updated, this process was very time consuming. This method of storage not only called for multiple updates among individual files, but it also took up a great deal of physical space.

With the advent of computers, the information in the files moved to databases, but the format for the databases continued to mirror the hard copy records. In other words, there was one record for each piece of information. The problems with associated hard copy records were also mirrored. Using the example above, if an employee's name needed to be updated, each individual file of the employee had to be updated. On the other hand, searching for information was considerably faster and storage was more centralized. Files of this type are referred to as "flat" files since every record contains all there is about the entity.

As a side note, for many years Microsoft tried to sell Excel as a basic database program in addition to its primary use as a spreadsheet. All the information was stored in a single place, with each Excel row containing all the information. Columns corresponded to fields, with every record containing every field that was used. Referring to Excel as a database program ceased when Microsoft bought FoxPro and acquired a "real" database program.

The Relational Database Structure

A modern database, on the other hand, alleviates the problem of multiple updates of individual files. The database enables the user to perform a single update across multiple files simultaneously. A *database* is a collection of organized files that are electronically stored. The files in a database are referred to as tables.

We come in contact with databases every day. Some examples of databases include ATMs, computer-based card-catalog systems at a library, and numerous Internet features including order forms and catalogs of merchandise.

The most popular and widely implemented type of database is called a relational database. A *relational database* is a collection of two or more tables related by key values.

Tables

We refer to the *tables* in a database as two-dimensional *files* that contain rows (records) and columns (fields). The reason we say that tables are two-dimensional is because the rows of a table run horizontally and the columns run vertically, hence two dimensions. Take a look at Figure 1-1.

Column1 ▾	Column2 ▾	Column3 ▾	Column4 ▾	Column5 ▾
*				

Figure 1-1. A blank table

Figure 1-1 shows an unpopulated (empty) table with five columns and six rows. Each *row* in the table represents an individual record and each *column* represents an individual entity of information. For example, a table named Customers could have the following seven entities (columns) of information: First Name, Last Name, Address, City, State, Zip, and Phone. Each customer entered into the Customers table represents an individual record.

Keys

To create a relationship between two tables in a relational database you use keys. *Keys* are columns in a table that are specifically used to point to records in another table. The two most commonly used keys during database creation are the primary key and the foreign key.

The *primary key* is a column in a table that uniquely identifies every record in that table. This means that no two cells within the primary key column can be duplicated. While tables usually contain a primary key column, this practice is not always implemented. The absence of a primary key in a table means that the data in that table is harder to access and subsequently results in slower operation. On the other hand, tables with very few entries will often not be indexed. This is especially true if the value is not used for searches or lookups. A table with three values of single, married, and divorced might not be indexed, although a table that uses this information, like an employee table, would definitely index on this field.

SocialSecNum ▾	Firstname ▾	Lastname ▾	Address ▾	Zipcode ▾	Areacode ▾	PhoneNumber ▾
111-10-1029	Tanya	Levin	2001 40th Ave S Honolulu, HI	96822	808	423-5671
165-35-4892	Willie	Coney	3900 35th Ave S. St. Pete, FL	33700	727	321-1111
444-57-3892	John	Allison	1400 22nd Ave N Atlanta, GA	98700	301	897-1600
452-72-0123	Yolanda	Cole	9021 Peachtree St N Tampa, FL	33622	813	827-4411
666-15-3392	Rosa	Coney	4399 Center Loop Tampa, FL	33677	813	898-0001

Figure 1-2. Employees table

Figure 1-2 shows a table named Employees. The SocialSecNum column is the primary key column in the Employees table. Since no two people can have the same social security number, social security numbers are commonly used as a primary key. As you can see, the SocialSecNum column uniquely identifies every employee in the Employees table.

The *foreign key* is a column in a table that links records of one type with those of another type. Foreign keys create relationships between tables and help to ensure referential integrity. *Referential integrity* ensures that every record in a database is correctly matched to any associated records. Foreign keys help promote referential integrity by ensuring that every foreign key within the database corresponds to a primary key.

Every time you create a foreign key, a primary key with the same name must already exist in another table. For example, the SocialSecNum column is used to link the Employees table in Figure 1-2 to the Departments table in Figure 1-3.

DepartmentID ▾	SocialSecNum ▾	DepartmentName ▾
1	444-57-3892	Human Resources
2	666-15-3392	Finance
3	165-35-4892	Information Systems
4	111-10-1029	Customer Service
5	452-72-0123	Human Resources

Figure 1-3. Departments table

The SocialSecNum column is a primary key column in the Employees table and a foreign key column in the Departments table. Notice that the Departments table in Figure 1-3 also contains its own primary key column named DepartmentID.

The Planning Stage

Before creating a database, careful planning must go into its design. Careful planning in the beginning can save you many headaches in the future such as major restructuring of the tables or a total redesign! You should begin by asking yourself and the users several key questions concerning the database system. Among other questions, find out who will use the database, what the users need from the database, and what information the database will store.

⊃ **Side Note:**   Actually it is not really a good idea to use a social security number as a primary key, as one of the authors discovered during two different database projects. One of the qualities of a primary key is that the value should not change. In the case of one employee database, the client had employees who would periodically show up with a new, different social security card and request that all of their records be changed! Since the social security number was used in multiple tables as the linking field, the user had to carefully go through the entire database and make changes. One slipup and database integrity went out the window. In another case, a database of patients was created, only to find that many of the patients did not have social security numbers. We had to artificially generate special, unique numbers to compensate for the lack of social security numbers.

Data Modeling

You should also utilize data modeling techniques to better understand how the data will be represented in the database. *Data modeling* organizes and documents the data that will be stored in the database. It provides a graphical representation of the structure of the database and how data will be represented in the database. Understanding how data will be represented in the database will help you avoid storing redundant or insufficient data. Data modeling can be done either on a plain sheet of paper or with specialized software.

Entities and Relationships

One widely implemented data model is called the Entity Relationship Diagram, or ERD model. The *ERD model* represents data in terms of entities and relationships. An *entity* is any group of events, persons, places, or things used to represent how data is stored. You can think of an entity as a table stored in a database. A *relationship* is an association between entities. Additionally, the model demonstrates the *attributes*, or the characteristics, of the entities. You can think of attributes as the columns in a table. For example, the entity Employee can have the following attributes: Name, Address, Phone Number, and Email.

There are four types of relationships among entities: one-to-one relationship, one-to-many relationship, many-to-one relationship, and many-to-many relationship.

An ERD model graphically depicts relationships by use of shapes, numbers, letters, and lines. Rectangles represent entities. Diamonds combined with letters above lines that connect to the rectangles represent relationships. Using the most basic style of relationship notation, the number 1 represents one and the letter M represents many. Attributes in an ERD are represented by ovals.

Figure 1-4 represents a one-to-one relationship within an organization. It illustrates that one computer is assigned to a single employee. A single employee has one computer.

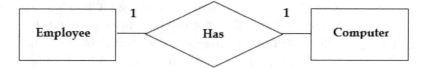

Figure 1-4. One-to-one relationship

Figure 1-5 represents a one-to-many relationship within an organization. The diagram illustrates that many customers conduct business transactions with the same employee. Each employee has many customers while every customer has a single employee to work with.

Figure 1-5. One-to-many relationship

Figure 1-6 represents a many-to-one relationship within an organization. The diagram illustrates that one department contains many employees. Many employees belong to one department.

Figure 1-6. Many-to-one relationship

Probably the most common and most useful relationship is the many-to-many, where multiple items of one group are associated with multiple items of a second group. Think in terms of a school with many classes and many students, which is illustrated in Figure 1-7. Each student is a member of many classes. Each class has many students. You can achieve the same overall result with two one-to-many relationships (many students to one class and many classes for each student), but the data is far more useful when viewed as a single relationship. By thinking of the information as a single relationship, you eliminate the need for multiple storage receptacles for the information and you improve on the ways you can look at the data.

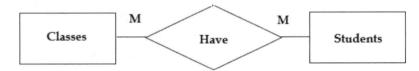

Figure 1-7. Many-to-many relationship

Normalization

Another widely implemented technique used in the planning stage of database creation is called normalization. *Normalization* is a three-step technique used to ensure that all tables are logically linked together and that all fields in a table directly relate to the primary key.

In the first phase of normalization, you must identify repeating groups of information and create primary keys. For example, the following column names represent columns in a table named Products: Cashier ID, Product Name, Product Description, Product Price, Order ID, Order Date, and Cashier Name. Notice that the column names contain repeating groups of information and there is no primary key assigned. To complete the first form of normalization, eliminate the Cashier ID and Cashier Name columns since they represent a separate group of information and would be better suited in another table. Additionally, assign a primary key to the Products table. Now the columns for the Products table would look something like the following: Product ID, Product Name, Product Description, Order ID, Order Date, and Product Price.

In the second phase of normalization, you need to take another look at your column names to make sure that all columns are dependent on the primary key. This involves eliminating columns that may be partially in the same group, but not totally dependent on the primary key. Since the Order ID and Order Date columns are concerned with a customer's order as opposed to the actual product information, they are not dependent on the primary key. These columns should be removed and placed in another table, perhaps one named Orders. Now the Products table should contain the following columns: Product ID, Product Name, Product Description, and Product Price.

In the third phase of normalization, you need to reexamine your columns to make sure each column is dependent on the primary key. Consider creating additional tables to eliminate non-dependent primary key columns, if necessary. Since the

Products table contains columns that are all dependent upon the primary key, there is no need to further alter the columns for the Products table. Once all of your tables are normalized, you can begin to link tables by assigning foreign keys to your tables.

Client/Server Databases

As stated earlier in the chapter, databases alleviate the need to have multiple updates of individual files. Another great aspect of the database is that data can also be accessed simultaneously by more than one user. This is called a client/server database. A *client/server* database system divides processing between client computers and a database server, enabling many users to access the same database simultaneously. In addition, each machine in the system can be optimized to perform its specific function. This results in far greater efficiency, speed, and database stability.

The *client* is a single-user computer that interfaces with a multiple-user server. The *server* is a multiple-user computer that stores the database and provides shared database connection, interfacing, and processing services. You can think of a client as any of the many single-user computers that access the Internet. A server can be thought of as America Online's server, which thousands of people access to connect to the Internet.

Database Management Systems

Databases are created using software programs called database management systems (DBMSs). *DBMSs* are specifically used to create, manage, and secure relational databases. The specific duties of a DBMS include the following: create databases, retrieve data, modify data, update data, generate reports, and provide security features. The most widely used DBMSs are Microsoft Access, Oracle, Microsoft SQL Server, DB2, Sybase,

FileMaker, and MySQL. Most DBMSs employ a nonprocedural database programming language called SQL to help in the administration of databases. Chapter 2 discusses SQL in greater detail.

Summary

In this chapter, you learned about the early forms of data storage and the relational database structure. You learned about primary and foreign keys and about implementing data modeling techniques and normalization in the planning stage of database design. You also learned about client/server databases and about database management systems (DBMSs).

Quiz 1

1. True or False. Normalization is a three-step technique used to ensure that all tables are logically linked together and that all fields in a table directly relate to the primary key.

2. True or False. A relational database is a collection of one or more tables that are related by key values.

3. True or False. A table is a two-dimensional column that contains files and fields.

4. True or False. A foreign key is a column in a table that links records of one database with those of another database.

5. True or False. A primary key is a column in a table that uniquely identifies every record in that table.

Project 1

Use the ERD model to diagram a one-to-many relationship showing one student who takes many courses and a many-to-one relationship showing many students in a single course. Compare this to the many-to-many model.

Chapter 2

Structured Query Language and Microsoft Access

Introduction

In this chapter, you will learn about Structured Query Language (SQL) and the Microsoft Access database management system. You will also learn how to open Microsoft Access and how to locate SQL view within Microsoft Access. Be sure to read over the definitions for this chapter before you begin.

Definitions

Clause — A segment of an SQL statement that assists in the selection and manipulation of data.

Keywords — Reserved words used within SQL statements.

Microsoft Access — A desktop database management system used to create, manage, and secure relational databases.

Query — A question or command posed to the database.

Statements — Keywords combined with data to form a database query.

Structured Query Language (SQL) — A nonprocedural database programming language used within DBMSs to create, manage, and secure relational databases.

Syntax — A series of rules that state how SQL script must be written.

Structured Query Language

SQL is a nonprocedural database programming language used to create databases, manipulate and retrieve data, and provide security to relational database structures. SQL is often referred to as nonprocedural because of the way it processes instructions. In contrast to high-level procedural computer languages such as Visual Basic and C++, which process instructions based on how to perform an operation, SQL processes instructions based on what operation to perform. For example, "what to retrieve," "what to insert," or "what to delete."

SQL stands for Structured Query Language and was first created in 1970. It used to be called SEQUEL, which stands for Structured English Query Language.

SQL is implemented in a number of database management system platforms, and the rules for SQL vary slightly from one DBMS to another. Because of the variations of SQL, each DBMS refers to SQL using a distinct name that is specific to the DBMS. For example, the Oracle DBMS refers to SQL as PLSQL (Procedural Language extensions to SQL), Microsoft SQL Server refers to SQL as Transact-SQL, and Microsoft Access refers to SQL as Access SQL.

SQL Versions

There are also different versions of SQL. There are currently two versions of the SQL language, and a third version is in the works. The two current versions of SQL are referred to as SQL-89 and SQL-92. SQL-92 is the latest version and functions at a more advanced level because it contains more features than SQL-89.

Currently, most versions of Microsoft Access come with version SQL-89 installed. In Microsoft Access 2002 and higher you can set the SQL version through the user interface for the current database and as the default setting for new databases.

Switching to Version SQL-92 in Microsoft Access 2007

To switch to SQL-92 in Microsoft Access 2007, open your database and click the **Office** button in the top-left corner of the screen. Next, click the **Access Options** button and then click the **Object Designers** heading. You have the option to check the This Database box, the Default for New Databases box or both boxes. Choose an option and click **OK**.

Switching to Version SQL-92 in Microsoft Access 2003

For a Current Database

To set the SQL version in Microsoft Access 2003 for the current database, select the **Tools** menu and click **Options**, then click the **Tables/Queries** tab. Select the **This Database** check box to set the query mode to ANSI-92 SQL or clear the check box to set the query mode to ANSI-89 SQL.

Default Setting for New Databases

To set the default to the SQL-89 version, select the **Tools** menu and click **Options**, then click the **Tables/Queries** tab. Clear the **Default for new databases** check box.

To set the default to the SQL-92 version, select the **Tools** menu and click **Options**, then click the **Advanced** tab. Select **Access 2002 - 2003** from the Default File Format list box. Click the **Tables/Queries** tab. Select the **Default for new databases** check box.

SQL Components

The Structured Query Language is broken up into three components: DDL, DML, and DCL.

The Data Definition Language (DDL) component is used to create tables and establish relationships among tables.

The Data Manipulation Language (DML) component is used to manage the database by performing such operations as retrieving data, updating data, deleting data, and navigating through data.

The Data Control Language (DCL) component is used to provide security features for the database.

SQL Syntax

In order to implement SQL, you must follow a series of rules that state how SQL script must be written. These rules are referred to as *syntax*. When a syntax rule is violated, the DBMS will return a system-generated error message to the screen. Stick to the syntax and you can reduce the probability of seeing these unpleasant messages.

The SQL language is made up of a series of keywords, statements, and clauses. The keywords, statements, and clauses are combined to enable users to create queries that extract meaningful data from the database. A *query* is a question or command posed to the database, and *keywords* are reserved words used within queries and SQL statements. Keywords are considered reserved because they cannot be used to name parts of the database. For example, you cannot use a keyword to name the database, tables, columns, or any other portion of the database.

A *clause* is a segment of an SQL statement. Think of a clause as a prepositional phrase that modifies the data in some way. A WHERE clause, for example, restricts where the data comes from. An ORDER BY clause orders the data. Clauses combine to form the entire SQL *statement*, which combines keywords with data to form a database query. Since you cannot have an actual conversation with the database like you would a person, keywords, statements, and clauses help you convey what you need to accomplish. Within the next few chapters, you will learn how to implement keywords, statements, and clauses in Microsoft Access.

The Power of SQL in Microsoft Access

Microsoft Access is the industry standard desktop (not required to be connected to a server) database management system. It is used to create, manage, and secure relational databases. The user interface in Microsoft Access is easy to comprehend and enables a person with no prior knowledge of SQL to create databases quickly and easily.

Although you don't actually need to know SQL to create and maintain databases in Microsoft Access, knowing SQL gives you an extra edge that many users overlook.

Understanding the SQL language gives you more power and control over your database. You can create more powerful queries using SQL. For example, with SQL you can create tables, queries that pass through Access to an external server (pass-through queries), combined queries (unions), and nested queries (subqueries). Additionally, you'll understand system-generated queries more fully, enabling you to manually edit Access-generated queries to create your own customized queries.

The Query Wizard

Microsoft Access provides several tools to enable you to create queries. Probably the most popular and simplest query tool to use is called Query Wizard. The Query Wizard, shown in Figure 2-1, enables the user to create simple queries by simply answering a series of questions. The questions pinpoint which columns you want to display and how you want to display the results from a query.

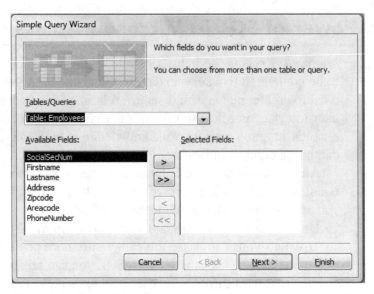

Figure 2-1. Query Wizard

The Query Design Tool and SQL View

Another straightforward query tool that is simple to use is referred to as Query Design view or Design view. The Query Design tool, shown in Figure 2-2, enables users to create queries by selecting table and column names and specifying conditions on the data they want to retrieve. The Query Design tool is a little more powerful because of the extra added feature of being able to set conditions on data. It also contains an SQL view that displays the SQL script from the queries created in Query Design. The SQL Query Design tool is so useful that Microsoft incorporated it into their SQL Server product a few years ago. Most people who develop in Access find that it is all that they need to write queries, and for many people this is true. (But you want to become a real power user, so we leave the Query Design view and move on to true SQL.)

SQL view is useful because you can use it to examine and learn SQL script so that you can eventually create your own customized queries. Microsoft Access makes it easy for you to switch back and forth between Query Design and SQL view by simply clicking the View button to choose which tool you want. Figure 2-2 points out the View button.

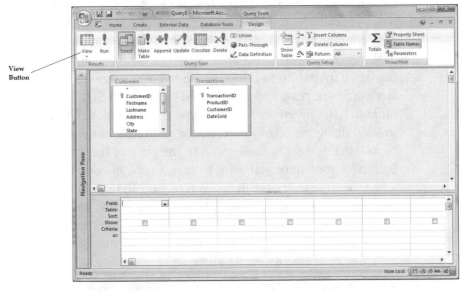

Figure 2-2. Query Design tool

Opening Microsoft Access and Switching to SQL View

Although SQL script can be implemented in several portions of Microsoft Access, the bulk of the SQL statements in this book will be implemented in SQL view.

Opening Microsoft Access

To create a new database in Microsoft Access, open Microsoft Access and click **Blank Database** under the New Blank Database heading.

At this point you must give your database a name. All databases must be named at the time they are created. You may name your database whatever you want, although it is generally a good idea to give it a short, descriptive name. While a database name can contain characters other than text or numbers, it is generally preferable to avoid these characters since they may confuse the SQL parser. Also, it is not a good idea to use SQL reserved words when naming your database since this, too, is an invitation to future problems. Remember, SQL keywords are reserved words used only within SQL statements. To name your database, type the name of your database in the File Name box located on the right side of the screen. Next, click the small folder icon to the right of the File Name box to locate where you want to save a copy of your database. The File New Database dialog will pop up so that you can browse for a location for your database. After you choose a location, click **Create** to save your database. Figure 2-3 illustrates the Microsoft Access window used to open an existing database or create a new database.

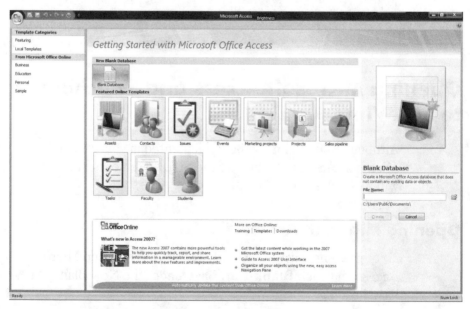

Figure 2-3. Microsoft Access Getting Started screen

Switching to SQL View in Microsoft Access 2007

Now that you have created a database, let's go to the area (SQL view) where most of the SQL script in this book will be implemented. To switch to SQL view, click **Create** from the menu running across the top of the screen. Next, click the Query Design button near the top-right side of the screen. This will cause the Show Table dialog box to appear. Click **Close** in this dialog box without selecting any tables. Take a look at Figure 2-4.

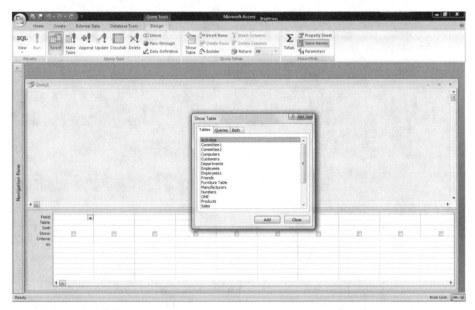

Figure 2-4. Show Table dialog box

Next, locate the View drop-down button near the top left of the screen. To see the name/description of any button or tool, simply place your cursor over it. Figure 2-5 shows the View button in Query Design view.

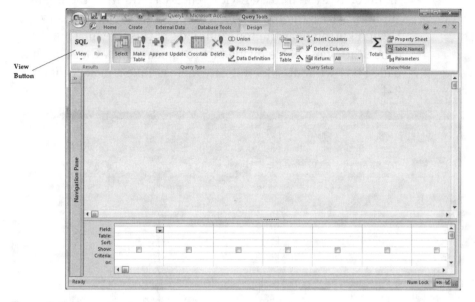

Figure 2-5. Query Design view

To switch to SQL view, use the View button and select **SQL View**. (Click the down arrow and scroll to the SQL View option.) This is the view in which you will type most of the SQL script in this book. You must use the Run button to execute SQL script typed in SQL view. Figure 2-6 shows the Run button in SQL view.

Figure 2-6. SQL view

Switching to SQL View in Microsoft Access 2003

If you are using a version of Microsoft Access that was released earlier than Microsoft Access 2007 (e.g., Microsoft Access 2003), the process for locating SQL view will differ slightly.

To locate SQL View in Microsoft Access 2003, open Microsoft Access and either create a new database or select an existing database. Next, click **Queries** on the left, and then click the **New** button located near the top of the screen. When the New Query dialog box appears, select **Design View** and click **OK**. Take a look at Figure 2-7.

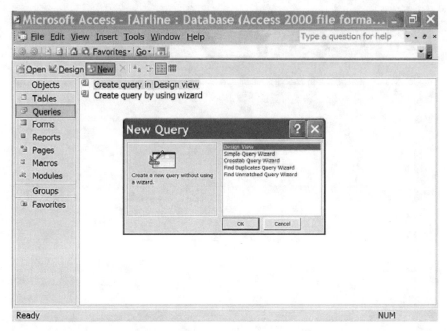

Figure 2-7. Microsoft Access 2003 New Query dialog with Design View selected

Click **Close** in the Show Table dialog box (do not select any tables). You are now in Query Design view. Next, locate the View button near the top of the screen. Figure 2-8 shows the View button in Query Design view.

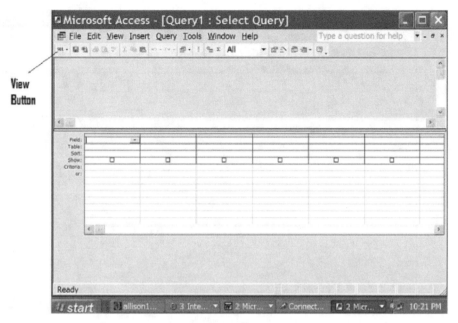

View
Button

Figure 2-8. Microsoft Access 2003 Query Design view

To switch to SQL view, use the View button and select **SQL View**. (Click the down arrow located on the View button to find the SQL View option.) You must use the Run button to execute script typed in SQL view. Figure 2-9 shows the Run button in SQL view.

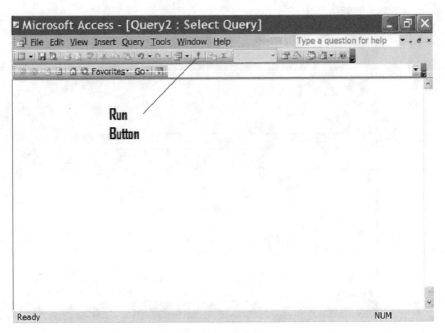

Figure 2-9. Microsoft Access 2003 SQL view

Summary

In this chapter, you learned about Structured Query Language (SQL) and Microsoft Access. You learned about the different versions and components of SQL and about SQL syntax and the power of SQL in Microsoft Access. You also learned about the Query Wizard, Query Design tool, and SQL view in Microsoft Access.

Quiz 2

1. What does SQL stand for?

2. What was SQL called before it was called SQL?

3. Which SQL component is used to create tables and establish relationships among tables?

4. True or False. SQL is a procedural database programming language used within DBMSs to create, manage, and secure relational databases.

5. True or False. Microsoft Access refers to SQL as PLSQL.

Project 2

Practice locating SQL view without looking at the instructions for doing so.

Creating Tables and Inserting Records

Introduction

In this chapter, you will learn how to create a table and insert records into a table. You will learn about data types, field sizes, and constraints. You will also learn how to update and delete records in a table. Read the definitions for this chapter before you begin.

Keywords

ALTER TABLE	INSERT INTO
CREATE TABLE	SELECT INTO
DELETE	UPDATE

Definitions

ALTER TABLE — Keywords that are used to modify columns and constraints in an existing table.

Constraints — Used to restrict values that can be inserted into a field and to establish referential integrity.

CREATE TABLE — Keywords that are used to instruct the database to create a new table.

Data type — Specifies the type of data a column can store.

DELETE statement — Used to remove records from a table.

Field — Equivalent to a column.

Field size — Specifies the maximum number of characters that a field can hold.

INSERT statement — Used to add records to a table.

NULL — Used to indicate no value.

SELECT statement — Used to retrieve records from the database.

UPDATE statement — Used to update records in a table.

The Data Definition Language Component

In Chapter 2, you learned that the SQL language is broken up into three components: Data Definition Language, Data Manipulation Language, and Data Control Language. Recall that the Data Definition Language (DDL) component is used to create tables and establish relationships among tables, and the Data Manipulation Language (DML) component is used to manage the database by performing such operations as retrieving, updating, deleting, and navigating through data. The Data Control Language (DCL) component is used to provide security to data in a database. The commands within each of these components are as follows:

Table 3-1

DDL	DML	DCL
CREATE TABLE	INSERT INTO	ALTER DATABASE
DROP TABLE	SELECT INTO	CREATE GROUP
ALTER TABLE	UPDATE	DROP GROUP
CREATE INDEX	DELETE	CREATE USER
	SELECT	ALTER USER
	UNION	DROP USER
	TRANSFORM	ADD USER
	PARAMETER	GRANT PRIVILEGE
		REVOKE PRIVILEGE

➲ **Note:** The DCL commands can only be executed in the Visual Basic environment of Microsoft Access. An error message will be returned if used through the Access SQL view user interface. Visual Basic is the host language for the Jet DBMS, which handles the translation of database queries into Access SQL.

In this chapter, we will focus on the implementation of the CREATE TABLE, ALTER TABLE, INSERT INTO, SELECT INTO, UPDATE, and DELETE statements. Let's begin by learning how to create a table.

Enable a Blocked Query in Microsoft Access

Before we begin to create and populate tables with records, let's ensure that your database is not in Disabled mode. Disabled mode is a security feature designed to block specific types of SQL queries.

Microsoft Access 2007 defaults to Disabled mode when you open a database that is not saved in a trusted location or if you chose not to trust the database. When Microsoft Access is in Disabled mode you will not be able to run action, append, update, delete, or make-table queries.

To disable Disabled mode, look for messages similar to the following in the Access status bar:

■ This action or event has been blocked by Disabled mode.

■ Certain content in this database has been disabled.

Take a look at Figure 3-1, which shows one of the above messages in the Access status bar.

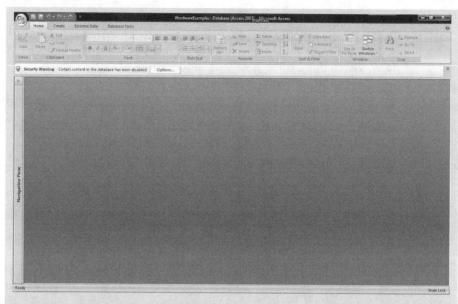

Figure 3-1. Microsoft Access in Disabled mode

To enable blocked content, click **Options** on the Access status bar. The Microsoft Office Security Options dialog box will appear. Click **Enable this content**, and then click **OK**.

⊖ **Note:** If you don't see a security message on the Access status bar, click the Database Tools tab, and in the Show/Hide group, click Message Bar.

CREATE TABLE Syntax

```
CREATE TABLE Tablename
(
Columnname Datatype Field Size, [NULL | NOT NULL]
    [optional constraints]
);
```

To create a table, you must define a table name, column names, data types, and field sizes. In the preceding syntax, the CREATE TABLE keywords are used to instruct the database to create a new table and must be followed by the name of the table. The CREATE TABLE syntax also requires opening and closing parentheses. The open parenthesis follows the name of the table and the close parenthesis is located at the end of the CREATE TABLE script. The closing semicolon tells Microsoft Access where the query ends. The closing semicolon is optional in Access, although getting into the habit of using it will be helpful when you start building complex SQL statements consisting of multiple declarations. The following SQL script creates a table named Toys:

```
CREATE TABLE Toys
(
);
```

While this is a good example of a table, there is a critical element missing. A table is not useful unless it has fields to hold data, so let's add a few fields to the SQL script.

```
CREATE TABLE Toys
(
ToyID INTEGER,
ToyName CHAR (30),

Price MONEY,
Description CHAR (40)
);
```

Notice that in the preceding script, the SQL keywords are typed in all caps. While SQL script is not case sensitive, it is accepted practice to capitalize keywords. Keywords in all caps stand out better and make your SQL script more readable. We highly recommend the capitalization of keywords.

Another widely implemented practice that is not required in SQL programming is to format the code. SQL commands execute without errors if placed on the same line, but again your SQL script is much easier to read and, more important, to debug when you break it up into several lines.

⟲ **Note:** When you create table and column names that contain spaces, enclose the names in brackets ([ ]). For example, the following script creates a table named Furniture with column names that contain spaces:

```
CREATE TABLE Furniture
(
[Furniture ID] INTEGER,
[Furniture Name] CHAR (30),
[Furniture Price] MONEY
);
```

Data Types

When you create column names for a table, each column must contain a data type. A *data type* specifies the type of data a column can store. For example, if you create a column that can only store numbers, you must assign it a specific data type that will only allow numbers to be stored in the column. SQL view supports a variety of different data types. Tables 3-2 and 3-3 list data types used in Microsoft Access.

Table 3-2. Common Microsoft Access data types

Data Type	Description
Numeric:	
DECIMAL	An exact numeric data type that holds values from $-10^{28}-1$ to $10^{28}-1$.
FLOAT	Stores double-precision floating-point values.
INTEGER	Also called INT. Stores long integers from $-2,147,483,648$ to $2,147,483,647$.
REAL	Stores single-precision floating-point values.
SMALLINT	Stores integers from $-32,768$ to $32,767$.
TINYINT	Stores integers from 0 to 255.
String:	
CHAR	A fixed-length data type that stores a combination of text and numbers up to 255 characters.

Data Type	Description
TEXT	A variable-length data type that stores a combination of text and numbers up to 255 characters. The length is determined by the Field size property. The string can contain any ASCII characters including letters, numbers, special characters, and nonprinting characters.
Miscellaneous:	
BINARY	Enables you to store any type of data in a field. No transformation of the data is made in this type of field.
BIT	Used to store one of two types of values. For example, true/false, yes/no, or on/off.
COUNTER	Stores a long integer value that automatically increments whenever a new record is inserted.
DATETIME	Stores date and time values for the years 100 to 9999.
IMAGE	Used to store Object Linking and Embedding (OLE) objects. For example, pictures, audio, and video.
MONEY	Stores currency values and numeric data used in mathematical calculations.
UNIQUEIDENTIFIER	A unique identification number used with remote procedure calls.

Table 3-3. Additional Microsoft Access data types

Data Type	Description
Currency	Used for monetary calculations.
Memo	Variable-length text field from 1 to 65,536 characters in length.
Number	Numerical data that can be used in all forms of calculations except those dealing with money. The Field size property determines the number of bytes that are used to store the number and, subsequently, the number range.
OLE Object	Any linked or embedded object including such things like images, Excel spreadsheets, Word documents, or virtually anything else.
Yes/No	Boolean values, which have only two states like yes/no, true/false, or on/off.

⇒ **Note:** Some data types do not require a field size.

Looking at the list of above data types the astute reader will ask "How does this list of data types compare to the standard Access data types that appear when building a table manually?" The answer is Microsoft has a very elegant solution to the different types — a list of synonyms (Table 3-4). In other words, when you manually build a table you are actually using the data types listed above, but you are using the old Access naming conventions.

Table 3-4. Microsoft Access data types and synonyms

ANSI SQL Data Type	Microsoft Access SQL Data Type	Synonym
BIT, BIT VARYING	BINARY	VARBINARY, BINARY VARYING, BIT VARYING
Not supported	BIT	BOOLEAN, LOGICAL, LOGICAL1, YESNO
Not supported	TINYINT	INTEGER1, BYTE
Not supported	COUNTER	AUTOINCREMENT
Not supported	MONEY	CURRENCY
DATE, TIME, TIMESTAMP	DATETIME	DATE, TIME
Not supported	UNIQUEIDENTIFIER	GUID
DECIMAL	DECIMAL	NUMERIC, DEC
REAL	REAL	SINGLE, FLOAT4, IEEESINGLE
DOUBLE PRECISION, FLOAT	FLOAT	DOUBLE, FLOAT8, IEEEDOUBLE, NUMBER
SMALLINT	SMALLINT	SHORT, INTEGER2
INTEGER	INTEGER	LONG, INT, INTEGER4
INTERVAL	Not supported	
Not supported	IMAGE	LONGBINARY, GENERAL, OLEOBJECT
Not supported	TEXT	LONGTEXT, LONGCHAR, MEMO, NOTE, NTEXT

ANSI SQL Data Type	Microsoft Access SQL Data Type	Synonym
CHARACTER, CHARACTER VARYING, NATIONAL CHARACTER, NATIONAL CHARACTER VARYING	CHAR	TEXT(n), ALPHANUMERIC, CHARACTER, STRING, VARCHAR, CHARACTER VARYING, NCHAR, NATIONAL CHARACTER, NATIONAL CHAR, NATIONAL CHARACTER VARYING, NATIONAL CHAR VARYING

Example 1

In this example, we'll create a table that demonstrates three data types described above. The following SQL script creates a table named TableOne with three columns (Field1, Field2, and Field3). Each column specifies a different data type (COUNTER, TEXT, and CURRENCY).

```
CREATE TABLE TableOne
(
Field1 COUNTER (4),
Field2 TEXT,
Field3 CURRENCY
);
```

In this SQL script, the Field1 column contains a COUNTER data type. The COUNTER data type stores a long integer value that automatically increments whenever a new record is inserted. Notice the number 4 is defined immediately following the COUNTER data type. This number causes the Field1 column to default to 4 and increment thereafter. If you do not specify a number with the COUNTER data type, the column will begin incrementing with the number 1.

The Field2 column contains a TEXT data type. The TEXT data type is a variable-length data type that stores a combination of text and numbers up to 255 characters.

The Field3 column contains a CURRENCY data type.

Constraints

Constraints enable you to further control how data is entered into a table and are used to restrict values that can be inserted into a field and to establish referential integrity. Recall that referential integrity is a system of rules used to ensure that relationships between records in related tables are valid. Table 3-5 explains the constraints available in Microsoft Access.

Table 3-5. Microsoft Access constraints

Constraint	Description
NULL/NOT NULL	Used to indicate if a field can be left blank when records are entered into a table.
PRIMARY KEY	Used to uniquely identify every record in a table.
FOREIGN KEY	Used to link records of a table to the records of another table.
UNIQUE	Used to ensure that every value in a column is different.
CHECK	Used to set criterion for the data entered into a column.

Now take a look at the following examples, which implement the constraints described in Table 3-5.

Example 2

Say you want to alter the Toys table script created earlier in the chapter. You want to add constraints that will ensure that every Toy ID is unique and that the ToyID, ToyName, and Price columns always contain values when new records are entered into the Toys table. Look at the following script:

```
CREATE TABLE Toys
(
ToyID INTEGER CONSTRAINT ToyPk PRIMARY KEY,
ToyName CHAR (30) NOT NULL,
Price MONEY NOT NULL,
```

```
Description CHAR (40) NULL
);
```

This script creates a new table named Toys with four columns (ToyID, ToyName, Price, and Description). A primary key constraint is defined for the ToyID column and the NOT NULL constraint is defined for the ToyName and Price columns. The Description column contains a NULL constraint. Following is an explanation of the NULL/NOT NULL and primary key constraints.

NULL/NOT NULL Constraint

The NULL/NOT NULL constraints are used to indicate whether or not a field can be left blank when records are entered into a table. You can also specify whether or not specific columns for a table may be left blank when a user enters a new record. *NULL* means no value. When NULL is specified in the creation of a table, it indicates that a field can be left blank when records are entered into a table. *NOT NULL* indicates that a field cannot be left blank when records are entered into a table.

In the Toys table script, the NOT NULL constraint is used to ensure that the ToyName and Price columns are not left blank when data is entered into the Toys table. The NULL keyword is specified for the Description column, which means this column can be left blank when entering records.

⊃ **Note:** In Microsoft Access, when you do not state NULL or NOT NULL during the creation of a column, it is automatically set to NULL.

PRIMARY KEY Constraint

The PRIMARY KEY constraint is used to uniquely identify every record in a table. The specification of a primary key ensures that there are no duplicate values in a column. Additionally, primary key fields are stored in ascending order and default to NOT NULL.

In the Create Toys script, the ToyID column contains a PRIMARY KEY constraint. The CONSTRAINT and PRIMARY KEY keywords are used to define the primary key. The name of the constraint (ToyPk) follows the CONSTRAINT keyword. Primary keys can also be defined using only the PRIMARY KEY keywords; however, this method does not enable you to assign a name to your primary key constraint. Assigning a name to your PRIMARY KEY constraint is vital because it makes it easier for you to update the constraint if necessary.

To view the new Toys table, type the following script:

```
SELECT *
FROM Toys;
```

This script uses a SELECT statement to retrieve records from a table. The SELECT keyword combined with an asterisk (*) instruct Microsoft Access to retrieve all the columns from a table. The FROM keyword instructs Microsoft Access to retrieve the records from the Toys table. You will learn more about the SELECT statement in Chapter 4.

Figure 3-2 shows the Toys table created from the Create Toys script.

ToyID	▾	ToyName	▾	Price	▾	Description	▾

Figure 3-2. Toys table

Example 3

Say you want to link the Toys table in Example 2 to a new table named Manufacturers. Additionally, you want to ensure that all phone numbers entered into the PhoneNumber column in the Manufacturers table are unique and that all updates and deletions made to the Manufacturers table affect corresponding records in the Toys table. Take a look at the following script:

```
CREATE TABLE Manufacturers
(
ManufacturerID INTEGER CONSTRAINT ManfID PRIMARY KEY,
ToyID INTEGER NOT NULL,
CompanyName CHAR (50) NOT NULL,
Address CHAR (50) NOT NULL,
City CHAR (20) NOT NULL,
State CHAR (2) NOT NULL,
PostalCode CHAR (5) NOT NULL,
AreaCode CHAR (3) NOT NULL,
PhoneNumber CHAR (8) NOT NULL UNIQUE,
CONSTRAINT ToyFk FOREIGN KEY (ToyID) REFERENCES Toys (ToyID)
ON UPDATE CASCADE
ON DELETE CASCADE
);
```

➲ **Note:** Make sure you have created the Toys table in Example 2 before you create the Manufacturers table since it contains the foreign key reference to the Toy table.

The preceding SQL script creates a table named Manufacturers with nine columns (ManufacturerID, ToyID, CompanyName, Address, City, State, PostalCode, AreaCode, PhoneNumber). A PRIMARY KEY constraint is defined for the ManufacturerID column, and the NOT NULL constraint is defined for all other columns. The PhoneNumber column contains a UNIQUE constraint and the ToyID column contains a FOREIGN KEY constraint. Following is an explanation of the ON UPDATE CASCADE and ON DELETE CASCADE keywords and the UNIQUE and FOREIGN KEY constraints used in Example 3.

FOREIGN KEY Constraint

The FOREIGN KEY constraint is used to link records of one table to the records of another. When you define a FOREIGN KEY constraint on a column, a column with the same name must exist as a primary key in another table. This enforces referential integrity since a foreign key value in one table cannot exist if it does not already exist as a primary key in another table. In the Create Manufacturers script, the foreign key column (ToyID) links the Manufacturers table to the Toys table. The CONSTRAINT, FOREIGN KEY, and REFERENCES keywords are used to define the foreign key. Although the ToyID column is defined near the top of the script, the definition of the ToyID foreign key can be placed at the end of the script. The name of the constraint (ToyFk) follows the CONSTRAINT keyword, and the name of the foreign key column (ToyID) follows FOREIGN KEY. The name of the linked table (Toys) and the primary key column (ToyID) from the linked table are defined after the REFERENCES keyword.

The ON UPDATE CASCADE and ON DELETE CASCADE keywords can be used with the FOREIGN KEY constraint to ensure that cascading updates and deletions occur. Cascading updates and deletions ensure referential integrity. For example, if you delete a manufacturer from the Manufacturers table, the manufacturer's product in the Toys table is deleted automatically.

The following script shows the specification of the FOREIGN KEY constraint from the Manufacturers table:

```
CONSTRAINT ToyFk FOREIGN KEY (ToyID) REFERENCES Toys (ToyID)
ON UPDATE CASCADE
ON DELETE CASCADE
```

○ Note: The ON UPDATE CASCADE and ON DELETE CASCADE keywords can only be used in SQL-92. If you use one of these keywords in earlier Access SQL versions, it will return an error message.

UNIQUE Constraint

The PhoneNumber column in the Manufacturers table contains a UNIQUE constraint. The UNIQUE constraint is used to ensure that every value in a column is different. The UNIQUE constraint is very similar to the PRIMARY KEY constraint; however, the UNIQUE constraint can be defined for more than one field in a table, and a column defined as unique does not automatically default to NOT NULL. A table can only have one primary key.

To view the Manufacturers table, type the following script:

```
SELECT *
FROM Manufacturers;
```

Figure 3-3 shows the Manufacturers table created from the Create Manufacturers script.

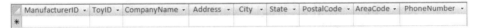

Figure 3-3. Manufacturers table

Adding Constraints to Existing Tables

Constraints can also be added to tables that have already been created. To add a constraint to an existing table you must use the ALTER TABLE statement. This statement is used to add or delete columns and constraints in an existing table. Following is the basic syntax to alter an existing table:

```
ALTER TABLE Tablename
ADD COLUMN ColumnName ColumnType (Size) ColumnConstraint |
DROP COLUMN ColumnName |
ADD CONSTRAINT ColumnConstraint |
DROP CONSTRAINT ColumnConstraint;
```

In this chapter, the ALTER TABLE statement is used to add and delete constraints to existing tables. In Chapter 11, you will learn how to use the ALTER TABLE statement to add a new column to a table and to delete a column from a table. Take a look at Example 4, which shows how to add the UNIQUE constraint to an existing table.

Example 4

Say you want to add a UNIQUE constraint to the ToyName column in the Toys table. Look at the following script:

```
ALTER TABLE Toys
ADD CONSTRAINT ToyNameUnique UNIQUE (ToyName);
```

This SQL script uses the ALTER TABLE statement to add the UNIQUE constraint to the ToyName column in the Toys table. The ALTER TABLE keywords are used to specify the table name (Toys). The ADD CONSTRAINT keywords are used to specify the constraint name (ToyNameUnique), the type of constraint (UNIQUE), and the name of the column (ToyName) to add the constraint to.

To delete the UNIQUE constraint from the ToyName column in the Toys table, simply type the following:

```
ALTER TABLE Toys
DROP CONSTRAINT ToyNameUnique;
```

In the script, the ALTER TABLE keywords are used to specify the table name (Toys), and the DROP CONSTRAINT keywords are used to specify the name of the constraint to delete (ToyNameUnique).

Example 5

Suppose you want to add a CHECK constraint that ensures that all prices entered into the Toys table are greater than 3. Look at the following script:

```
ALTER TABLE Toys
ADD CONSTRAINT CheckAmount
CHECK (Price > 3);
```

This script uses a CHECK constraint to ensure that all numbers entered into the Price column are greater than 3 (CHECK

(Price > 3)). The name of the constraint (CheckAmount) is specified after the CONSTRAINT keyword.

➲ **Note:** The UNIQUE constraint can only be used in SQL-92. If you use it in earlier Access SQL versions, it will return an error message.

To delete the CHECK constraint, type the following:

```
ALTER TABLE Toys
DROP CONSTRAINT CheckAmount;
```

Constraint Syntax

In Microsoft Access, the ALTER TABLE statement can be used to add any of the constraints discussed in this chapter to an existing table. The following shows the SQL syntax to add PRIMARY KEY, FOREIGN KEY, and NOT NULL constraints to an existing table:

```
ALTER TABLE Tablename
ADD CONSTRAINT ConstraintName PRIMARY KEY (ColumnName);
```

```
ALTER TABLE Tablename
ADD CONSTRAINT ConstraintName FOREIGN KEY (ColumnName)
REFERENCES LinkedTableName (PrimaryKey);
```

In the FOREIGN KEY constraint syntax, the table name and primary key column from the linked table are defined after the REFERENCES keyword.

```
ALTER TABLE Tablename
ALTER COLUMN ColumnName Datatype (Field size) NOT NULL;
```

The syntax to add the NOT NULL constraint to an existing table is slightly different from other constraints. To add a NOT NULL constraint to an existing table you use the ALTER COLUMN keywords, which are used to specify the column name, data type, field size, and the NOT NULL keywords.

Inserting Records

After you create a table, you can insert records into it using INSERT statements. Each INSERT statement inserts a single record into a table. Look at the following syntax for the INSERT statement:

```
INSERT INTO Tablename [(ColumnNames, ...)]
VALUES (values, ...);
```

Each INSERT statement contains the INSERT INTO and VALUES keywords. The INSERT INTO keywords are used to specify the table name and the column names to insert values into. The VALUES keyword is used to specify the values to insert into a table. Take a look at Example 6, which inserts five rows into the Toys table.

Example 6

This example inserts five records into the Toys table created earlier in the chapter.

```
INSERT INTO Toys (ToyID, ToyName, Price, Description)
VALUES (1, 'ToyTrain1', 11.00, 'Red/blue battery powered train');

INSERT INTO Toys (ToyID, ToyName, Price, Description)
VALUES (2, 'ToyTrain2', 11.00, 'Green/red/blue battery powered
        train');

INSERT INTO Toys (ToyID, ToyName, Price, Description)
VALUES (3, 'ElectricTrain', 15.00, 'Red/white AC/DC powered train');

INSERT INTO Toys (ToyID, ToyName, Price, Description)
VALUES (4, 'LivingDoll1', 12.00, 'Asian American Doll');

INSERT INTO Toys (ToyID, ToyName, Price, Description)
VALUES (5, 'LivingDoll2', 12.00, 'African American Doll');
```

The preceding INSERT statements insert five records into the Toys table. Since each INSERT statement contains a closing semicolon, it is easy to see where each statement begins and ends. Each INSERT statement inserts one record with four values.

As a side note, each time you execute an INSERT statement, Microsoft Access verifies the insertion of the new record by displaying a message/question that says:

"You are about to append 1 row (s). Once you click yes, you can't use the undo command to reverse the changes. Are you sure you want to append the selected rows?"

This feature can be turned off under Access options | Advanced | Confirm Action Queries, but for now leave it on as it will verify the actions taking place.

Each time you insert a new record, be sure to click Yes to this message.

Notice the INSERT statements that contain character strings enclosed in quotes. Whenever a table contains a column data type that accepts character strings, all character string values pertaining to the column must be enclosed in quotes. Since the ToyName and Description columns contain data types that accept character strings, the character string values in the INSERT statements are enclosed in quotes.

Type the following script to view the populated Toys table:

```
SELECT *
FROM Toys;
```

Figure 3-4 shows the populated Toys table.

ToyID	ToyName	Price	Description
1	ToyTrain1	$11.00	Red/blue battery powered train
2	ToyTrain2	$11.00	Green/red/blue battery powered
3	ElectricTrain	$15.00	Red/white AC/DC powered train
4	LivingDoll1	$12.00	Asian American Doll
5	LivingDoll2	$12.00	African American Doll

Figure 3-4. Populated Toys table

Inserting Data without Specifying Column Names

INSERT statements can also be executed without the specification of column names. To execute an INSERT statement without typing the column names, specify the values in the same order that the columns appear in the table. Look at Example 7, which inserts an additional record into the Toys table.

Example 7

Say you want to insert a complete record into the Toys table but you do not want to type the column names. Look at the following script:

```
INSERT INTO Toys
VALUES (6, 'DollHouse', 17.00, 'Grand Town House');
```

The preceding script inserts one record containing four values into the Toys table. Because the values are typed in the same order in which the columns appear in the table, it is not necessary to type the column names.

As a side note, if you want to insert values into specific columns only, specify only the column names you want to insert values into. Next, specify values in the same order as they appear in your INSERT statement.

Figure 3-5 shows the addition of the new record in the Toys table.

ToyID	ToyName	Price	Description
1	ToyTrain1	$11.00	Red/blue battery powered train
2	ToyTrain2	$11.00	Green/red/blue battery powered
3	ElectricTrain	$15.00	Red/white AC/DC powered train
4	LivingDoll1	$12.00	Asian American Doll
5	LivingDoll2	$12.00	African American Doll
6	DollHouse	$17.00	Grand Town House

Figure 3-5. Toys table showing six records

Inserting NULL Values

Example 8

Say you want to insert a record with a missing value. Take a look at the following script:

```
INSERT INTO Toys
VALUES (7, 'Doll/TownHouse', 15.00, NULL);
```

This script inserts one record containing three values into the Toys table. It inserts NULL for a missing value. Recall that NULL means no value. Figure 3-6 shows the Toys table after the insertion of the record containing the NULL value.

As a side note, you cannot insert NULL into columns that contain a NOT NULL constraint.

	ToyID	ToyName	Price	Description
⊞	1	ToyTrain1	$11.00	Red/blue battery powered train
⊞	2	ToyTrain2	$11.00	Green/red/blue battery powered
⊞	3	ElectricTrain	$15.00	Red/white AC/DC powered train
⊞	4	LivingDoll1	$12.00	Asian American Doll
⊞	5	LivingDoll2	$12.00	African American Doll
⊞	6	DollHouse	$17.00	Grand Town House
⊞	7	Doll/TownHouse	$15.00	

Figure 3-6. Toys table containing a NULL value

Copying Records from One Table to an Existing Table

Example 9

Sometimes it is necessary to populate a table with records from an existing table. Say, for example, you need to create a test table and you want to use data that is already stored in another table. Take a look at the following scripts. The first one creates a new table named ToysTest and the second one copies the records from the Toys table to the ToysTest table.

51

```
CREATE TABLE ToysTest
(
ToyID CHAR (7) CONSTRAINT ToyPk PRIMARY KEY,
ToyName CHAR (30) NOT NULL,
Price MONEY NOT NULL,
Description CHAR (40) NULL
);
```

This script creates a table named ToysTest. The ToysTest table contains the same data types and field sizes as the Toys table. The following script copies the records from the Toys table into the ToysTest table:

```
INSERT INTO ToysTest (ToyID, ToyName, Price, Description)
SELECT ToyID, ToyName, Price, Description
FROM Toys;
```

This script uses the INSERT INTO keywords to specify the table name and column names to insert records into. The SELECT and FROM keywords are used to specify the column names and table name from which to retrieve the records to insert. The SELECT keyword is used to specify the column names from the Toys table and the FROM keyword is used to specify the Toys table.

As a side note, the ToysTest and Toys tables do not have to have the same column names, but they do have to have similar data types and field sizes. Figure 3-7 shows the populated ToysTest table.

	ToyID	ToyName	Price	Description
⊞	1	ToyTrain1	$11.00	Red/blue battery powered train
⊞	2	ToyTrain2	$11.00	Green/red/blue battery powered
⊞	3	ElectricTrain	$15.00	Red/white AC/DC powered train
⊞	4	LivingDoll1	$12.00	Asian American Doll
⊞	5	LivingDoll2	$12.00	African American Doll
⊞	6	DollHouse	$17.00	Grand Town House
⊞	7	Doll/TownHouse	$15.00	

Figure 3-7. Populated ToysTest table

Copying Records from One Table to a New Table Simultaneously

Example 10

Say you want to create a new table and copy records from another table into your new table at the same time. Take a look at the following script:

```
SELECT ToyID, ToyName, Price, Description
INTO Toys2
FROM Toys;
```

This script creates a new table named Toys2 and copies the records from the Toys table into the new Toys2 table. It uses the SELECT and FROM keywords to specify the table name (Toys) and column names (ToyID, ToyName, Price, and Description) from which to retrieve the records to insert. The INTO keyword is used to create a table named Toys2 and to insert the records retrieved from the table (Toys) specified after the FROM keyword. Figure 3-8 shows the populated Toys2 table.

ToyID	ToyName	Price	Description
1	ToyTrain1	$11.00	Red/blue battery powered train
2	ToyTrain2	$11.00	Green/red/blue battery powered
3	ElectricTrain	$15.00	Red/white AC/DC powered train
4	LivingDoll1	$12.00	Asian American Doll
5	LivingDoll2	$12.00	African American Doll
6	DollHouse	$17.00	Grand Town House
7	Doll/TownHouse	$15.00	

Figure 3-8. Populated Toys2 table

Updating Records

The UPDATE statement is used to update records in a table. You can use this statement to change single or multiple records in a table. Look at the following syntax for updating a table:

```
UPDATE Tablename
SET ColumnName = Value
WHERE Condition;
```

Update a Record with a Text Value

Example 11

Say you want to add a value to one of the records in the Toys table. Look at the following script:

```
UPDATE Toys
SET Description = 'Town House'
WHERE ToyID = 7;
```

The preceding script inserts a value into one of the records stored in the Toys table. It uses the UPDATE keyword to specify the table (Toys) to update. The SET keyword is used to specify the column (Description) to update and the value (Town House) to insert into the column. The WHERE keyword is used to set conditions on retrieved data. It is commonly referred to as the WHERE clause. You will learn more about clauses and the WHERE clause in Chapter 5. In this example, the WHERE keyword is used to specify value 7 in the ToyID column. Figure 3-9 shows the Toys table containing the new value.

	ToyID	ToyName	Price	Description
⊞	1	ToyTrain1	$11.00	Red/blue battery powered train
⊞	2	ToyTrain2	$11.00	Green/red/blue battery powered
⊞	3	ElectricTrain	$15.00	Red/white AC/DC powered train
⊞	4	LivingDoll1	$12.00	Asian American Doll
⊞	5	LivingDoll2	$12.00	African American Doll
⊞	6	DollHouse	$17.00	Grand Town House
⊞	7	Doll/TownHouse	$15.00	Town House

Figure 3-9. Updated Toys table

Update a Record with a New Calculated Value

Example 12

In this example we will increase the price for an item in the Toys table. We will increase the price by 5 dollars:

```
UPDATE Toys
SET Price = Price + 5
WHERE ToyID = 7;
```

The preceding script uses the UPDATE keyword to specify the table (Toys) to update. The SET keyword is used to specify the column (Price) to update and is set equal to the Price plus 5 dollars (Price + 5). The WHERE keyword is used to set conditions on retrieved data. In this example, the WHERE keyword is used to specify value 7 in the ToyID column. It tells Microsoft Access to update the record containing a ToyID of 7. Figure 3-10 shows the Toys table containing the new value.

	ToyID	ToyName	Price	Description
⊞	1	ToyTrain1	$11.00	Red/blue battery powered train
⊞	2	ToyTrain2	$11.00	Green/red/blue battery powered
⊞	3	ElectricTrain	$15.00	Red/white AC/DC powered train
⊞	4	LivingDoll1	$12.00	Asian American Doll
⊞	5	LivingDoll2	$12.00	African American Doll
⊞	6	DollHouse	$17.00	Grand Town House
⊞	7	Doll/TownHouse	$20.00	Town House

Figure 3-10. Updated Toys table

Update Multiple Columns

Example 13

Say you want to update the ToyName and Description columns in the Toys table. Look at the following script:

```
UPDATE Toys
SET ToyName = 'ElectronicBlackTrain',
Description = 'Red/white electric powered train'
WHERE ToyID = 3;
```

The preceding script uses the UPDATE keyword to specify the table (Toys) to update. The SET keyword is used to specify two columns (ToyName, Description) to update. The WHERE keyword is used to specify value 3 in the ToyID column. It tells Microsoft Access to update the record containing a ToyID of 3. Figure 3-11 shows the Toys table containing the new value.

ToyID	ToyName	Price	Description
1	ToyTrain1	$11.00	Red/blue battery powered train
2	ToyTrain2	$11.00	Green/red/blue battery powered
3	ElectronicBlackTrain	$15.00	Red/white electric powered train
4	LivingDoll1	$12.00	Asian American Doll
5	LivingDoll2	$12.00	African American Doll
6	DollHouse	$17.00	Grand Town House
7	Doll/TownHouse	$20.00	Town House

Figure 3-11. Updated Toys table

Note: To update multiple columns, each column must contain the same WHERE clause value.

Note: The UPDATE statement does not generate a result set (records retrieved from the database). To see the result of an UPDATE statement, you have to open the table. Type the following statement to view the updated Toys table:

```
SELECT *
FROM Toys;
```

Update a Column that Contains a Date

Example 14

SalesID	ProductID	CustomerID	DateSold
1	BN200	2	3/3/2008
2	CT200	3	2/5/2008
3	ET100	5	2/6/2007
4	PO200	1	7/8/2008
5	TH100	3	2/8/2008
6	RX300	4	2/10/2007
7	CT200	2	2/22/2008
8	ET100	6	2/20/2008
9	LF300	6	2/18/2008
10	BN200	1	2/17/2008

Figure 3-12. Sales table

Suppose you want to update a column that contains a date. Take a look at the following script:

```
UPDATE Sales
SET DateSold = '04/03/2008'
WHERE SalesID = 1;
```

The preceding script uses the UPDATE keyword to specify the table (Sales) to update. The SET keyword is used to specify the column (DateSold) to update. The WHERE keyword is used to specify value 1 in the SalesID column. It tells Microsoft Access to update the record containing a SalesID of 1. Figure 3-13 shows the updated Sales table.

SalesID	ProductID	CustomerID	DateSold
1	BN200	2	4/3/2008
2	CT200	3	2/5/2008
3	ET100	5	2/6/2007
4	PO200	1	7/8/2008
5	TH100	3	2/8/2008
6	RX300	4	2/10/2007
7	CT200	2	2/22/2008
8	ET100	6	2/20/2008
9	LF300	6	2/18/2008
10	BN200	1	2/17/2008

Figure 3-13. Updated Sales table

⊃ **Note:** When an UPDATE statement contains a date value in the WHERE clause, the date value must be enclosed in pound signs, as shown below:

```
UPDATE Sales
SET DateSold = '04/03/2008'
WHERE SalesID = 1 AND DateSold = #02/03/2008#;
```

Deleting Records

The DELETE statement is used to remove records from a table. Look at the following delete syntax:

```
DELETE FROM Tablename
WHERE Condition
```

Example 15 shows how to delete a record from the Toys2 table.

Example 15

This example shows how to remove one record from the Toys2 table.

```
DELETE FROM Toys2
WHERE ToyID = 7;
```

The preceding script uses the DELETE and FROM keywords to specify the table (Toys2) from which to remove records. This WHERE clause is used to specify value 7 in the ToyID column. Figure 3-14 shows the Toys2 table without record 7.

ToyID	ToyName	Price	Description
1	ToyTrain1	$11.00	Red/blue battery powered train
2	ToyTrain2	$11.00	Green/red/blue battery powered train
3	ElectricTrain	$15.00	Red/white AC/DC powered train
4	LivingDoll1	$12.00	Asian American Doll
5	LivingDoll2	$12.00	African American Doll
6	DollHouse	$17.00	Grand Town House

Figure 3-14. Toys2 table

To delete all the records from the Toys2 table, type the following:

```
DELETE * FROM Toys2;
```

Summary

In this chapter, you learned how to create a table and how to populate a table with records. You learned about data types, field sizes, and constraints. You also learned how to update and delete records in a table.

Quiz 3

1. True or False. NOT NULL means no value.

2. True or False. A data type specifies the maximum number of characters that a cell in a column can hold.

3. What constraint is used to link the records of one table to the records of another table?

4. True or False. The WHERE keyword is used to insert a record into a table.

5. True or False. The UPDATE statement is used to update table names.

Project 3

Use the following values to insert a record into the Manufacturers table created earlier in the chapter:

Column Name	Value
ManufacturerID	1
ToyID	1
CompanyName	Matel
Address	2892 23rd Ave S
City	St. Petersburg
State	FL
PostalCode	33710
AreaCode	727
PhoneNumber	324-5421

Chapter 4

Retrieving Records

Introduction

A database is only useful if you can get records out of it. While there are many ways to get data from the database, the place to begin is the SELECT statement, which is the key to retrieving records. Then we will build on this statement to concatenate columns and create alternate names for columns. Finally, we will show how to get subsets of the database and sort the output.

Keywords

AS	ORDER BY
ASC	SELECT
DESC	TOP
DISTINCT	TOP PERCENT
DISTINCTROW	

Definitions

Alias — An alternate name for a table or column.

AS — Used to assign an alternate name to a column or table.

ASC — Used to sort column values in ascending order.

Clause — A segment of an SQL statement that assists in the selection and manipulation of data.

Concatenation — Merging values or columns together.

DESC — Used to sort column values in descending order.

DISTINCT — Used to display unique values in a column.

DISTINCTROW — Used to exclude records based on the entire duplicate records, not just duplicate fields.

ORDER BY — Used to sort retrieved records in descending or ascending order.

Query — A question or command posed to the database.

Query Design view — Enables you to create queries by selecting table and column names and specifying conditions on the data you want to retrieve.

Result set — Records retrieved from the database.

SELECT statement — Used to retrieve records from the database.

TOP — Used to display records that fall at the top or bottom of a range that is specified by an ORDER BY clause.

TOP PERCENT — Used to display a percentage of records that fall at the top or bottom of a range that is specified by an ORDER BY clause.

The SELECT Statement

The SELECT statement is used to retrieve records from the database. Records retrieved from the database are often referred to as a *result set*. Every SELECT statement contains the SELECT keyword and the FROM keyword. Let's begin by opening up the most basic query in the query grid.

In Access 2007, click Create from the menu running across the top of the screen. Next, click the Query Design button near the top-right side of the screen. This will cause the Show Table dialog box to appear. Select the table named **TableOne** and click the **Add** button, then click **Close** to close this dialog box.

⊃ **Note:**   TableOne was created in Example 1 of Chapter 3.

In the grid below, select the Field1 field from the drop-down menu in the Table category. Refer to Figure 4-1.

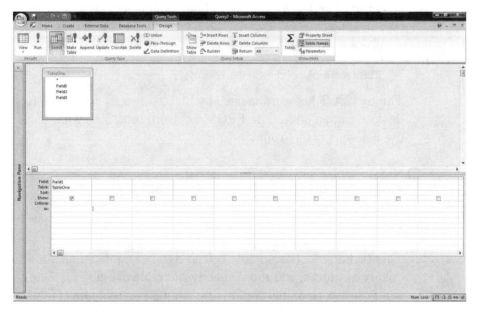

Figure 4-1. Query Design view

Now, switch to SQL view, as shown in Figure 4-2.

To switch to SQL view, use the View button and select SQL View. (Click the down arrow located on the View button to find the SQL View option.)

Figure 4-2. SQL view

Note that the derived SQL statement consists of two parts.
First there is the SELECT part followed by the field we
selected, then the FROM part showing which table was used
for the select.

Look at the following syntax for the SELECT statement:

```
SELECT Columnname(s) FROM TableName(s);
```

The SELECT keyword is used by SQL to specify what data is
desired from a table. The FROM keyword tells SQL what table
the columns come from.

➲ **Note:** When you view SQL script generated by Microsoft
**Access, the table name is shown with the column name. For
example, in Figure 4-2 you see the following:**

```
SELECT TableOne.Field1
```

This technique is commonly referred to as qualification. To
qualify a column, you must specify the table name (TableOne)
and type a period, followed by the name of the column (Field1).

➲ **Note:** TableOne was created in Example 1 of Chapter 3.

Qualification is normally used when you are querying more
than one table; therefore we will not use this technique unless
we are querying multiple tables.

In this chapter, we will keep it simple by having every
SELECT statement include one table after the FROM keyword. Later, in Chapter 8, we will expand on this concept and
show how to query multiple tables.

A few syntax rules are important to remember. When you
create a SELECT statement, every column name specified
after the SELECT keyword must be separated by a comma.
Additionally, when you specify more than one table after the
FROM keyword, all table names must also be separated by a
comma.

Take a look at Example 1.

Example 1

ToyID	ToyName	Price	Description
⊞ 1	ToyTrain1	$11.00	Red/blue battery powered train
⊞ 2	ToyTrain2	$11.00	Green/red/blue battery powered
⊞ 3	ElectricTrain	$15.00	Red/white AC/DC powered train
⊞ 4	LivingDoll1	$12.00	Asian American Doll
⊞ 5	LivingDoll2	$12.00	African American Doll
⊞ 6	DollHouse	$17.00	Grand Town House
⊞ 7	Doll/TownHouse	$15.00	Town House

Figure 4-3. Toys table

Say you want to display the values stored in the ToyName and Price columns from the original Toys table in Figure 4-3. Type the following script:

```
SELECT ToyName, Price
FROM Toys;
```

This script uses the SELECT keyword to specify the ToyName and Price columns from the Toys table. The FROM keyword is used to specify the name of the table (Toys) from which to retrieve records. The closing semicolon tells the DBMS where the query ends. Take a look at Figure 4-4, which shows the results from the query.

ToyName	Price
ToyTrain1	$11.00
ToyTrain2	$11.00
ElectricTrain	$15.00
LivingDoll1	$12.00
LivingDoll2	$12.00
DollHouse	$17.00
Doll/TownHouse	$15.00

Figure 4-4. Results (output)

Example 1 illustrates how to display two columns from a table. You can display single, multiple, or all columns from a table. The order in which you place the column names after the SELECT keyword determines the order in which they will be displayed in the output or result set. Take a look at Example 2, which shows how to display every column from a table.

Example 2

Say you want to display every column from the Toys table in Figure 4-3. In Access Query Design view, you open up a query and move the first field line, the "*" (or Toys.* line), down to the query grid. Refer to Figure 4-5.

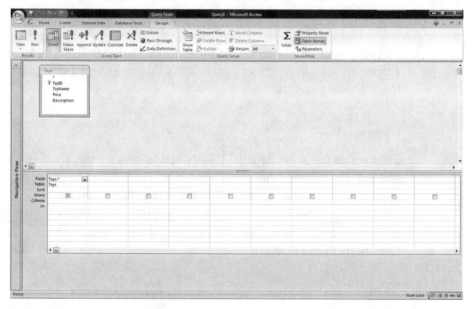

Figure 4-5. Query Design view

Shifting over to SQL view produces a corresponding SQL statement, as shown in Figure 4-6.

Figure 4-6. SQL view

Look at the following script:

```
SELECT *
FROM Toys;
```

This script combines an asterisk (*) with the SELECT key-word, which tells the DBMS to select every column from a table. The FROM keyword specifies the name of the table from which to retrieve records. Look at the results in Figure 4-7.

	ToyID	ToyName	Price	Description
⊞	1	ToyTrain1	$11.00	Red/blue battery powered train
⊞	2	ToyTrain2	$11.00	Green/red/blue battery powered
⊞	3	ElectricTrain	$15.00	Red/white AC/DC powered train
⊞	4	LivingDoll1	$12.00	Asian American Doll
⊞	5	LivingDoll2	$12.00	African American Doll
⊞	6	DollHouse	$17.00	Grand Town House
⊞	7	Doll/TownHouse	$15.00	Town House

Figure 4-7. Results (output)

➲ **Note:** Make sure you specify column names as they appear in the table. The space character is a delimiter character to SQL. Quite often an SQL statement will return an error because you have included a space in a column name. You think the two words are a single name, but SQL thinks other-wise. You can get around this ambiguity by surrounding the column name in brackets ([ ]).

➲ **Note:** Access does not perform any simplifying when it builds its SQL statements. Note in the example above that Access defines the field as table.field even though there is only one table and the table name is superfluous. Access SQL does a lot of this. For most of our examples we will be abbreviating the SQL statements. Both versions are processed the same way. (To try this, take out the table name from the SQL view, then con-vert it back to Design view. The same query will be presented. Unfortunately, if you now convert it back to SQL view you get the table name back.)

Another interesting point is that if you have the same field name in two tables that are used in a query (we will be getting to this soon) you *must* specify the table name. Otherwise Access gives you an error message.

The ORDER BY Clause

Clauses are segments of an SQL statement that assist in the selection and manipulation of data. The ORDER BY clause is often used in the SELECT statement to sort retrieved records in descending or ascending order. To demonstrate its use, open our first query in Query Design view, select the Sort row for our field, and select Ascending. Refer to Figure 4-7.

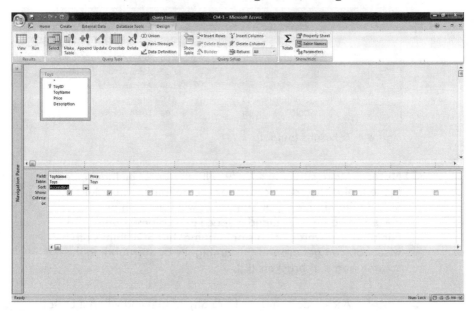

Figure 4-8. Query Design view

Then view the results in SQL view (Figure 4-9).

Figure 4-9. SQL view

Take a look at the following syntax for the ORDER BY clause:

```
ORDER BY ColumnName ASC | DESC
```

Note that the name of the column to sort is specified after the ORDER BY keywords. The sort order (either ASC or DESC) follows the column name. The *ASC* keyword means ascending order and the *DESC* keyword means descending order. Example 3 shows how to sort column values in descending order.

Sorting in Descending Order

Example 3

Say you want to sort the ToyName column in the Toys table in descending order. Look at the following script:

```
SELECT *
FROM Toys
ORDER BY ToyName DESC;
```

This script specifies the ToyName column after the ORDER BY keywords. The DESC keyword is specified after the column name and causes the DBMS to sort the values in the ToyName column in descending order. Look at the results in Figure 4-10.

ToyID	ToyName	Price	Description
2	ToyTrain2	$11.00	Green/red/blue battery powered
1	ToyTrain1	$11.00	Red/blue battery powered train
5	LivingDoll2	$12.00	African American Doll
4	LivingDoll1	$12.00	Asian American Doll
3	ElectricTrain	$15.00	Red/white AC/DC powered train
6	DollHouse	$17.00	Grand Town House
7	Doll/TownHouse	$15.00	Town House

Figure 4-10. Results (output)

Sorting in Ascending Order

Although the ASC keyword is used to sort values in ascending order, it is rarely implemented because the ORDER BY clause defaults to ascending order when no sort order is specified. The following example sorts the ToyName column in ascending order even though the ASC keyword is not specified.

Example 4

The following script sorts the ToyName column in ascending order.

```
SELECT *
FROM Toys
ORDER BY ToyName;
```

This script specifies the ToyName column after the ORDER BY keywords, causing the DBMS to sort the ToyName column in ascending order. Look at the results in Figure 4-11.

ToyID	ToyName	Price	Description
7	Doll/TownHouse	$15.00	Town House
6	DollHouse	$17.00	Grand Town House
3	ElectricTrain	$15.00	Red/white AC/DC powered train
4	LivingDoll1	$12.00	Asian American Doll
5	LivingDoll2	$12.00	African American Doll
1	ToyTrain1	$11.00	Red/blue battery powered train
2	ToyTrain2	$11.00	Green/red/blue battery powered

Figure 4-11. Results (output)

The following script is equivalent to Example 4:

```
SELECT *
FROM Toys
ORDER BY ToyName ASC;
```

Sorting Multiple Columns

The ORDER BY clause can also be used to sort multiple columns. Take a look at Example 5.

Example 5

SocialSecNum	Firstname	Lastname	Address	Zipcode	Areacode	PhoneNumber
111-10-1029	Tanya	Levin	2001 40th Ave S Honolulu, HI	96822	808	423-5671
165-35-4892	Willie	Coney	3900 35th Ave S. St. Pete, FL	33700	727	321-1111
444-57-3892	John	Allison	1400 22nd Ave N Atlanta, GA	98700	301	897-1600
452-72-0123	Yolanda	Cole	9021 Peachtree St N Tampa, FL	33622	813	827-4411
666-15-3392	Rosa	Coney	4399 Center Loop Tampa, FL	33677	813	898-0001

Figure 4-12. Employees table

Suppose you want to query the Employees table in Figure 4-12 to display each employee's last name sorted in ascending order. Additionally, you want to display first names sorted in ascending order within each duplicate last name. Take a look at the following script:

```
SELECT Lastname, Firstname
FROM Employees
ORDER BY Lastname, Firstname;
```

This script displays the Lastname and Firstname columns sorted in ascending order. The ORDER BY clause sorts the Lastname column in ascending order. Next, for all duplicate last names, the first names in the Firstname column are sorted in ascending order. Look at the results in Figure 4-13. The Lastname column shows one duplicate last name (Coney). The first names (Rosa, Willie) are sorted in ascending order within each duplicate last name.

Lastname	Firstname
Allison	John
Cole	Yolanda
Coney	Rosa
Coney	Willie
Levin	Tanya

Figure 4-13. Results (output)

In a nutshell, the ORDER BY clause is processed from left to right with parameters separated by commas. So, in Example 5 if you needed to sort by zip code in descending order, then by last name, then by first name, and finally by descending address, the ORDER BY clause would read as follows:

```
ORDER BY Zipcode DESC, Lastname, Firstname, Address DESC
```

Simple!

Example 6

This example sorts two columns in the Toys table in two different directions (ASC, DESC). Look at the following script:

```
SELECT *
FROM Toys

ORDER BY Price ASC,
Description DESC;
```

The preceding script sorts the Price column in ascending order and the Description column in descending order. The prices in the Price column are in ascending order and for every duplicate price the descriptions are sorted in descending order. Take a look at the results in Figure 4-14.

ToyID	ToyName	Price	Description
1	ToyTrain1	$11.00	Red/blue battery powered train
2	ToyTrain2	$11.00	Green/red/blue battery powered
4	LivingDoll1	$12.00	Asian American Doll
5	LivingDoll2	$12.00	African American Doll
7	Doll/TownHouse	$15.00	Town House
3	ElectricTrain	$15.00	Red/white AC/DC powered train
6	DollHouse	$17.00	Grand Town House

Figure 4-14. Results (output)

Sorting Using Numbers

Numbers are often used in the ORDER BY clause as a short-cut. Instead of typing the names of columns in the ORDER BY clause, you can use numbers to indicate either the placement of a column in a table or the placement of a column name after the SELECT keyword. Example 7 demonstrates this.

Example 7

Suppose you want to sort the third and second columns in the Employees table in Figure 4-12.
Take a look at the following script:

```
SELECT *
FROM Employees
ORDER BY 3, 2;
```

The preceding script uses numbers in the ORDER BY clause to sort the third and second columns in the Employees table. The number three (3) represents the Lastname column and the number two (2) represents the Firstname column in the Employees table. Note that the columns are numbered from left to right beginning with 1. Look at the results in Figure 4-15.

SocialSecNum ▾	Firstname ▾	Lastname ▾	Address ▾	Zipcode ▾	Areacode ▾	PhoneNumber ▾
111-10-1029	Tanya	Levin	2001 40th Ave S Honolulu, HI	96822	808	423-5671
165-35-4892	Willie	Coney	3900 35th Ave S. St. Pete, FL	33700	727	321-1111
444-57-3892	John	Allison	1400 22nd Ave N Atlanta, GA	98700	301	897-1600
452-72-0123	Yolanda	Cole	9021 Peachtree St N Tampa, FL	33622	813	827-4411
666-15-3392	Rosa	Coney	4399 Center Loop Tampa, FL	33677	813	898-0001

Figure 4-15. Results (output)

Although the Firstname column is displayed before the Lastname column, the Firstname column is sorted within each duplicate Lastname.

Numbers in the ORDER BY clause can also be used to indicate the placement of a column name after the SELECT keyword. The following example sorts columns based on the order in which they appear after the SELECT keyword.

Example 8

This example uses numbers to sort columns that are specified after the SELECT keyword. Look at the following script:

```
SELECT Lastname, Firstname, PhoneNumber
FROM Employees
ORDER BY 1, 2;
```

This script uses the ORDER BY clause to sort the Lastname and Firstname columns specified after the SELECT statement. Look at the results in Figure 4-16.

Lastname	Firstname	PhoneNumber
Allison	John	897-1600
Cole	Yolanda	827-4411
Coney	Rosa	898-0001
Coney	Willie	321-1111
Levin	Tanya	423-5671

Figure 4-16. Results (output)

Handling Duplicate Values

When tables contain duplicate column values, the DISTINCT and DISTINCTROW keywords are used to single out specific values among the duplicate values.

The DISTINCT Keyword

The DISTINCT keyword is used to display unique values in a column. In SQL, the DISTINCT keyword is used directly in the SELECT statement. Take a look at Example 9, which shows how to use the DISTINCT keyword.

Example 9

Suppose you want to display the unique prices stored in the Price column in the Toys table in Figure 4-3. Take a look at the following script:

```
SELECT DISTINCT Price
FROM Toys;
```

This script places the DISTINCT keyword before the Price column. This causes the DBMS to display only the unique values in the Price column. Figure 4-17 shows the unique values in the Price column.

Price
$11.00
$12.00
$15.00
$17.00

Figure 4-17. Results (output)

The DISTINCTROW Keyword

The DISTINCTROW keyword is used in queries that include more than one table in the FROM clause. It is used to exclude records based on the entire duplicate records, not just duplicate fields. Queries that contain more than one table in the FROM clause are referred to as joins. *Joins* enable you to use a single SELECT statement to query two or more tables simultaneously. You will learn more about joins and the DISTINCTROW keyword in Chapter 8.

➲ **Note:** Many people confuse the DISTINCT and DISTINCTROW keywords. Both result in unique records, but DISTINCT returns those records that are unique for just the fields referenced. DISTINCTROW returns all unique records for the underlying table and includes all fields for uniqueness even if they are not requested. So if there are two records that are identical except for a non-selected field, DISTINCT will return one record and DISTINCTROW will return two records.

Handling Duplicate Subsets of the Entire Result Collection

Often when you have large recordsets that take a long time to collect, you only want a sample of the records. Two keywords are used to reduce the number of records retrieved from a query: TOP and TOP PERCENT.

The TOP Keyword

The *TOP* keyword is used to display records that fall at the top or bottom of a range that is specified by an ORDER BY clause. Take a look at Example 10.

Example 10

ManufacturerID	ToyID	CompanyName	Address	City	State	PostalCode	AreaCode	PhoneNumber
1	1 Matel		2892 23rd Ave S	St. Petersburg	FL	33710	727	324-5421
2	2 Jurnes		1231 Lindsay Ave N	Tampa	FL	33618	813	234-3982
3	3 Radae		1872 3rd Ave N	Baltimore	MD	21210	240	713-0011
4	4 Winnies		6000 16th Ave N	San Diego	CA	92101	213	981-8745
5	5 Lenar		1230 9th Ave N	Baltimore	MD	21202	301	321-0987

Figure 4-18. Manufacturers table

Suppose you want to display the three company names with the highest postal code from the Manufacturers table in Figure 4-18. Look at the following script:

```
SELECT TOP 3 CompanyName, PostalCode
FROM Manufacturers
ORDER BY PostalCode DESC;
```

The preceding script uses the TOP keyword in combination with the number three (3) to display only the top three results from the range of values specified in the ORDER BY clause.

The SELECT statement instructs the DBMS to display the CompanyName and PostalCode columns from the Manufacturers table. The ORDER BY clause sorts the PostalCode column in descending order, and the TOP 3 specification in the SELECT statement displays only the top three records from the ORDER BY clause. Take a look at the results in Figure 4-19. Only three records are displayed.

CompanyName ▾	PostalCode ▾
Winnies	92101
Matel	33710
Jurnes	33618

Figure 4-19. Results (output)

The TOP keyword with a value can be added to a query in Design mode by placing a value in the Top Values property for the query.

As a side note, if you use the TOP keyword without the specification of an ORDER BY clause, the TOP keyword will base its selection of records on the order in which records appear in the table. Additionally, if there are fields with duplicate values, then Microsoft Access will display all duplicate values. For example, if duplicate values exist and you specify to receive TOP (*n*), you will receive the number of records you specified, plus any duplicates that exist. The TOP keyword is extremely useful when processing large sets of records. If you are interested in just getting the general idea of a query, it is far quicker to grab just a few records than it is to process all the records.

The following example demonstrates using the TOP keyword to display the bottom records.

Example 11

Suppose you want to display the three company names with the lowest postal code from the Manufacturers table in Figure 4-18. Look at the following script:

```
SELECT TOP 3 CompanyName, PostalCode
FROM Manufacturers
ORDER BY PostalCode;
```

In the preceding script, the ORDER BY clause sorts the PostalCode column in ascending order, and the TOP 3 specification displays only the top three records from the ORDER BY clause.

Look at Figure 4-20.

CompanyName	▾	PostalCode	▾
Lenar		21202	
Radae		21210	
Jurnes		33618	

Figure 4-20. Results (output)

➲ **Note:**   The TOP keyword is used to display records that fall at the top or bottom of a range that is specified by an ORDER BY clause. When you combine the TOP and ORDER BY keywords to return a specific number of items, duplicate items affect the total number of records that you return. In Examples 10 and 11, if the third and fourth postal codes were the same, the query would return four records. The TOP keyword doesn't choose between equal values.

The TOP PERCENT Keywords

The *TOP PERCENT* keywords are used to display a percentage of records that fall at the top or bottom of a range that is specified by an ORDER BY clause. Take a look at Example 12.

Example 12

Suppose you want to display the top 50 percent of company names from the Manufacturers table in Figure 4-18 based on the order of the total number of names. Look at the following script:

```
SELECT TOP 50 PERCENT CompanyName
FROM Manufacturers
ORDER BY CompanyName;
```

The preceding script uses the ORDER BY clause to sort the CompanyName column in ascending order. The TOP 50 PERCENT specification displays only the top 50 percent of records from the ORDER BY clause based on count. The results in Figure 4-21 display the top 50 percent of company names from the ORDER BY clause.

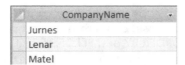

CompanyName
Jurnes
Lenar
Matel

Figure 4-21. Results (output)

Example 13

Suppose you want to display the bottom 50 percent of company names from the Manufacturers table in Figure 4-18 based on the order of the total number of names.

```
SELECT TOP 50 PERCENT CompanyName
FROM Manufacturers
ORDER BY CompanyName DESC;
```

The preceding script uses the ORDER BY clause to sort the CompanyName column in descending order. The TOP 50 PERCENT specification displays only the top 50 percent of records from the ORDER BY clause based on count. Take a look at the results in Figure 4-22.

CompanyName
Winnies
Radae
Matel

Figure 4-22. Results (output)

➲ **Note:** The TOP PERCENT keywords are used to display a percentage of records that fall at the top or bottom of a range that is specified by an ORDER BY clause. When you combine the TOP PERCENT and ORDER BY keywords to return a percentage of records, duplicate items affect the total number of records that you return.

⟳ **Note:** If your goal is to achieve an idea of the records wanted by quickly sampling a subset of the records, you defeat your goal if you request an ORDER BY or a PERCENT. The query will have to go through all the records before it can return the desired subset.

Creating an Alias

An *alias* is an alternate name for a table or column. Aliases are created using the AS keyword. Take a look at Example 14, which implements the creation of two aliases.

Example 14

CommitteeID	Firstname	Lastname	Address	Zipcode	Areacode	PhoneNumber
1	Leonard	Cole	1323 13th Ave N Atlanta, GA	98718	301	897-1241
2	Panzina	Coney	9033 Colfax Loop Tampa, FL	33612	813	223-6754
3	Kayla	Fields	2211 Peachtree St S Tampa, FL	33612	813	827-4532
4	Jerru	London	6711 40th Ave S Honolulu, HI	96820	808	611-2341
5	Debra	Brown	1900 12th Ave S Atlanta, GA	98718	301	897-0987

Figure 4-23. Committee2 table

Suppose you want to display the names, addresses, and phone numbers from the Committee2 table in Figure 4-23. Additionally, you want to create alternate column names for the Address and PhoneNumber columns. Look at the following script:

```
SELECT Firstname, Lastname, Address AS HomeAddress, PhoneNumber
     AS HomePhone
FROM Committee2;
```

The preceding script uses the AS keyword to create two alternate column names (HomeAddress and HomePhone). Look at the results in Figure 4-24.

Firstname	Lastname	HomeAddress	HomePhone
Leonard	Cole	1323 13th Ave N Atlanta, GA	897-1241
Panzina	Coney	9033 Colfax Loop Tampa, FL	223-6754
Kayla	Fields	2211 Peachtree St S Tampa, FL	827-4532
Jerru	London	6711 40th Ave S Honolulu, HI	611-2341
Debra	Brown	1900 12th Ave S Atlanta, GA	897-0987

Figure 4-24. Results (output)

Create an Alias that Contains a Space

Example 15

Suppose you want to recreate the query in Example 14, but this time you want to include a blank space in the aliases you created in the example. Look at the following script:

```
SELECT Firstname, Lastname, Address AS [Home Address],
       PhoneNumber AS [Home Phone]
FROM Committee2;
```

This script uses the AS keyword to create two alternate column names. This example is similar to Example 14, but each alias (Home Address, Home Phone) contains a blank space. The brackets are used to enclose an alias name that contains a blank space. Look at the results in Figure 4-25.

Firstname	Lastname	Home Address	Home Phone
Leonard	Cole	1323 13th Ave N Atlanta, GA	897-1241
Panzina	Coney	9033 Colfax Loop Tampa, FL	223-6754
Kayla	Fields	2211 Peachtree St S Tampa, FL	827-4532
Jerru	London	6711 40th Ave S Honolulu, HI	611-2341
Debra	Brown	1900 12th Ave S Atlanta, GA	897-0987

Figure 4-25. Results (output)

The most common reason for using aliases in queries is to avoid confusion between identical field names in two or more tables or to shorten the length of field names when the underlying table has very long, descriptive field names. When you have a field name like "Gross percentages for monthly commissions" that is used in numerous places in the query, it is tempting to just alias the field as "GC"!

⮑ **Note:** The AS keyword does not physically change column names in a table. It is specifically used to display results under an alternate column name. Additionally, if you do not create an alias for concatenated columns or values, Microsoft Access automatically generates a column name as an alias.

Concatenation

The SQL language also enables you to merge values or columns under alternate column names. Merging values or columns is commonly referred to as *concatenation*. Concatenation is performed in Microsoft Access using the ampersand (&) or the plus sign (+). Either symbol can be used to perform concatenation; the main difference between them is how they handle NULL fields. When you use the ampersand (&), if one of the fields is NULL it is replaced by an empty string. When using the plus sign (+), if one of the fields is NULL the result of the concatenation is NULL. This is very useful when you want to include values in the concatenation. Take a look at Example 16.

Concatenate Multiple Fields and Characters

Example 16

Say you want to concatenate the names and area codes in the Committee2 table in Figure 4-24. You want to insert a comma between the last name and first name and insert a space on either side of a slash character between the names and the area codes. You additionally want to display the concatenated columns under an alternate name. Look at the following script:

```
SELECT Lastname & ',' + ' ' + Firstname & ' / ' + Areacode AS
     NamesAndAreacodes
FROM Committee2;
```

This script uses the ampersand (&) to merge the Lastname column with a comma and the Firstname column with one space and a slash. The plus sign (+) is used to merge an empty string with the Lastname column and a comma, and to merge the slash and space with the Areacode column. The AS keyword is used to create an alias (NamesAndAreacodes). Look at the results in Figure 4-26.

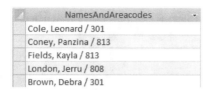

NamesAndAreacodes ▾
Cole, Leonard / 301
Coney, Panzina / 813
Fields, Kayla / 813
London, Jerru / 808
Brown, Debra / 301

Figure 4-26. Results (output)

Concatenate Multiple Fields from Multiple Tables

Example 17

Suppose you want to concatenate fields from the Manufacturers table (Figure 4-18) and the Toys table (Figure 4-3). Take a look at the following script:

```
SELECT Toys.ToyID& ', ' &Toys.ToyName& ' '
&Manufacturers.CompanyName AS Manufacturer

FROM Toys, Manufacturers

WHERE Toys.ToyID = Manufacturers.ToyID;
```

This query contains an advanced query called a join. Joins are used to query multiple tables in one SELECT statement. You will learn about joins further down the road in Chapter 8. We included this query to demonstrate how to concatenate fields from multiple tables.

Notice that the ampersand (&) is used to merge the ToyID and ToyName columns from the Toys table. The ampersand (&) is also used to merge the CompanyName column from the Manufacturers table with the ToyName column in the Toys table.

The FROM keyword specifies the tables (Toys, Manufacturers) from which to retrieve data.

There WHERE clause shows the relationship (ToyID) between the Toys and Manufacturers table. The Toys and Manufacturers tables are related through the ToyID column since the ToyID column is a primary key in the Toys table and a foreign key in the Manufacturers table. Look at the results in Figure 4-27.

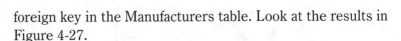
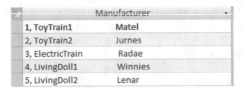

	Manufacturer
1, ToyTrain1	Matel
2, ToyTrain2	Jurnes
3, ElectricTrain	Radae
4, LivingDoll1	Winnies
5, LivingDoll2	Lenar

Figure 4-27. Results (output)

Summary

In this chapter, you learned how to retrieve records from a database. You learned how to create a SELECT statement, concatenate columns, and create alternate names for columns. You also learned how to use the TOP, TOP PERCENT, DISTINCT, DISTINCTROW, and ORDER BY keywords.

Quiz 4

1. What two keywords must be used in the SELECT statement?

2. Records retrieved from the database are often referred to as what?

3. True or False. The TOP keyword is used to display records that fall in the middle of a range specified by an ORDER BY clause.

4. True or False. The AS keyword is used to create an alias.

5. True or False. The DISTINCT keyword is used to display the duplicate values in a column.

Project 4

Use the Committee2 table in Figure 4-23 to create a query that displays the following output:

Name	FullAddress	TelephoneNumber
Brown, Debra	1900 12th Ave S Atlanta, GA 98718	301-897-0987
Cole, Leonard	1323 13th Ave N Atlanta, GA 98718	301-897-1241
Coney, Panzina	9033 Colfax Loop Tampa, FL 33612	813-223-6754
Fields, Kayla	2211 Peachtree St S Tampa, FL 33612	813-827-4532
London, Jerru	6711 40th Ave S Honolulu, HI 96820	808-611-2341

Figure 4-28

Chapter 5

Filtering Retrieved Records

Introduction

In this chapter, you will learn how to create conditionals via the WHERE clause. You will also learn how to use the comparison and logical operators to further refine the filtering of data within the recordsets.

Keywords

WHERE

Definitions

Comparison operators — Used to perform comparisons among expressions.

Expression — Any data type that returns a value.

Logical operators — Used to test for the truth of some condition.

WHERE clause — Used to filter retrieved records.

Wildcard characters — Special characters used to match parts of a value.

The WHERE Clause

Recall that a *clause* is a segment of an SQL statement that assists in the selection and manipulation of data. The WHERE clause is yet another clause commonly used in the SELECT statement. It is used to filter retrieved records.

Look at the following syntax for the WHERE clause:

```
WHERE [Search Condition];
```

The preceding syntax uses the WHERE keyword to specify a specific search condition. Field names and operators are used in the WHERE clause to create search conditions. The WHERE clause is an extension of one of the most basic Access query elements — the filter. To see an example of this, create a query in Design mode and set one of the fields in the query grid. Next set a criterion. Refer to Figure 5-1.

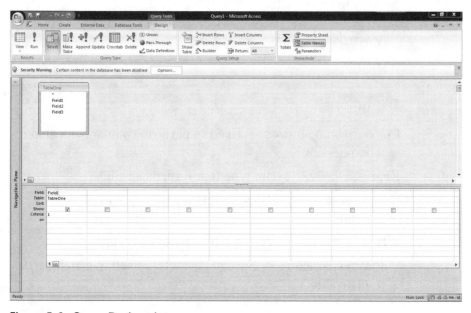

Figure 5-1. Query Design view

Now change the layout to SQL view to see the SQL representation of the query grid, as shown in Figure 5-2.

Figure 5-2. SQL view

As soon as the criterion was added, Access inserted the WHERE clause. One thing you will note about the SQL builder in Access is its extensive use of parentheses. They are optional and can be ignored when building SQL queries. In fact, if you were to delete all the parentheses in this query and rerun it, you will get exactly the same result as if you ran it directly from the query grid.

⊃ **Note:**   Access can be a bit frustrating at times. If you delete the parentheses, convert the query back to Design view, then reconvert it to SQL view, the parentheses reappear.

There are several different operators that can be used in the WHERE clause. In this chapter, we will discuss two categories of operators commonly used in the WHERE clause: comparison and logical.

Comparison Operators

The *comparison operators* are used to perform comparisons among expressions. An *expression* is any data type that returns a value. Table 5-1 shows the comparison operator symbols used in Microsoft Access.

Table 5-1. Comparison operator symbols

Name	Symbol
Greater Than	>
Greater Than or Equal To	>=
Equal	=
Less Than	<
Less Than or Equal To	<=
Not Equal	<>

Table 5-2 shows additional comparison operators that can be used in the WHERE clause.

Table 5-2. Additional comparison operators

Operator	Description
BETWEEN	Used to determine whether a value of an expression falls within a specified range of values.
IN	Used to match conditions in a list of expressions.
LIKE	Used to match patterns in data.
IS NULL	Used to determine if a field contains data.
IS NOT NULL	Used to determine if a field does not contain data.

Logical Operators

Logical operators are used to test for the truth of some condition. Table 5-3 describes each of the logical operators.

Table 5-3. Logical operators

Operator	Description
AND	Requires both expressions on either side of the AND operator to be true in order for data to be returned.
OR	Requires at least one expression on either side of the OR operator to be true in order for data to be returned.
NOT	Used to match any condition opposite of the one defined.

Operator Precedence

When multiple operators are used in the WHERE clause, operator precedence determines the order in which operations are performed. The following list shows the order of evaluation among operators from the highest level of binding (the operators that are performed first) to the lowest level of binding (those that are performed last).

- =, >, <, >=, <=, <>
- AND, OR
- NOT
- BETWEEN, IN, LIKE, IS NULL

If two operators in an expression have the same operator precedence level, they will be evaluated from left to right. Since parentheses have a higher precedence level than all operators, parentheses can be used to override defined precedence. Simply enclose specific expressions in parentheses and everything within the parentheses is evaluated first. Take a look at Example 1.

The AND, OR, =, and < Operators

Example 1

SerialNum ▾	Brand ▾	Department ▾	OfficeNumber ▾
G9277288282	Dell	HR	122
M6289288289	Dell	Accounting	134
R2871620091	Dell	Information Systems	132
W2121040244	Gateway	CustomerService	22
X8276538101	Dell	HR	311

Figure 5-3. Computers table

Suppose you want to query the Computers table in Figure 5-3. You want to display the SerialNum, Brand, and Department columns for computers located in office numbers less than 130 and with a brand name of either Dell or Gateway.

Using the query design grid in Figure 5-4, you would bring the SerialNum, Brand, and Department fields into the query grid, then select the filter operations in the Criteria row.

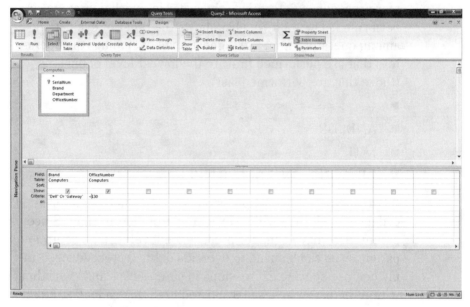

Figure 5-4. Query Design view

This produces the following script:

```
SELECT SerialNum, Brand, Department
FROM Computers
WHERE (Brand = 'Dell' OR Brand = 'Gateway')
AND OfficeNumber < 130;
```

The preceding script uses the equal (=) and less than (<) operators to perform comparisons among expressions. The AND and OR operators are used to separate two conditions. The AND operator requires that both expressions on either side of the AND operator be true in order for data to be returned. The OR operator requires that at least one expression on either side of the OR operator be true in order for data to be returned. Since the AND operator has precedence over the OR operator based on it occurring first, the conditions containing the OR operator are enclosed in parentheses to cause them to be evaluated before the AND condition. The query displays the SerialNum, Brand, and Department columns for all Gateway or Dell computers located in offices with an office number less than 130. Look at the results in Figure 5-5.

SerialNum ▾	Brand ▾	Department ▾
G9277288282	Dell	HR
W2121040244	Gateway	CustomerService

Figure 5-5. Results (output)

As a side note, whenever you use both the AND and the OR operators, always use parentheses to ensure that you retrieve the expected results.

The observant reader will note that we cheated a bit with this query grid. It would have been more correct to enter the criteria on two lines instead of combining the two values with the OR statement. Look at Figure 5-6.

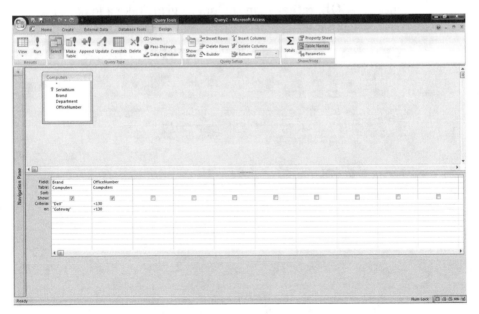

Figure 5-6. Query Design view

This produces a bit more involved SQL script, as shown in Figure 5-7.

Figure 5-7. SQL view

If you look a bit closer at the script, you will see that terms can be combined in the WHERE clause, producing the results shown earlier. This is one of the real strengths of SQL script. When you have a really complex WHERE conditional, it is often far easier to see what is really happening in the SQL text rather than in the query grid. It is also often easier to build the query in SQL, rather than the query grid. Take a look at Figures 5-8 and 5-9.

Figure 5-8. SQL view

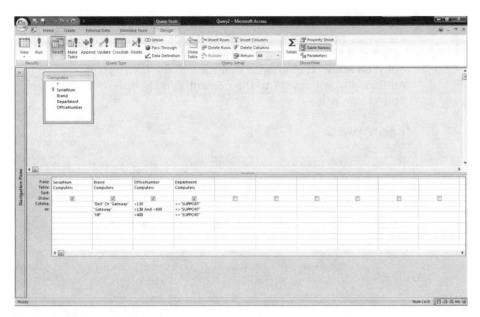

Figure 5-9. Query Design view

The LIKE Operator

The LIKE operator uses wildcard characters to match patterns in data. These are special characters used to match parts of a value. Table 5-4 shows the wildcard characters used with the LIKE operator.

Table 5-4. Wildcard characters used with the LIKE operator

Character	Description
?	Any single character.
*	Zero or more characters.
#	Any single digit (0-9).
[characters]	Any single character in a group of one or more characters.
[!characters]	Any single character not in a group of one or more characters.

⊃ Note: If your Access database is set to SQL Server compatible syntax (ANSI-92), you must use the percent sign (%) instead of the asterisk (*) and an exclamation mark (!) instead of the question mark (?) in queries that contain the LIKE operator. Additionally, you must use the percent sign (%) instead of the pound sign (#).

Example 2

ToolID ▾	ToolName ▾	Manufacturer ▾	Type ▾	Location ▾	Price ▾
1	Jigsaw	Dewalt	Power Tool	A	$60.00
2	Hand Drill	Dewalt	Power Tool	A	$30.00
3	Router	Dewalt	Power Tool	A	$40.00
4	Nail Gun	Bosch	Power Tool	A	$60.00
5	Sandpaper	Bosch	Sanding	B	$4.00
6	Scrapers	Bosch	Sanding	B	$8.00
7	Hammer	Makita	Hand Tool	C	$14.00
8	Pliers	Porter	Hand Tool	C	$9.00
9	Screwdriver	Makita	Hand Tool	C	$4.00
10	Tool Belt	Porter	Accessories	D	$15.00
11	Battery Charger	Dewalt	Accessories	D	$20.00

Figure 5-10. Tools table

Suppose you want to query the Tools table in Figure 5-10 to retrieve tools made by manufacturers that begin with the letter D and are located in warehouse sections A through C.

```
SELECT *
FROM Tools
WHERE Manufacturer LIKE 'D*' AND Location LIKE '[A-C]';
```

The preceding script uses the asterisk (*) wildcard character and the brackets ([ ]) with the LIKE operator in the WHERE clause. The letter D is placed in front of the asterisk to instruct the DBMS to retrieve manufacturers that begin with the letter D. The brackets ([ ]) are used to instruct the database to retrieve locations from A to C. Look at the results in Figure 5-11.

ToolID ▾	ToolName ▾	Manufacturer ▾	Type ▾	Location ▾	Price ▾
1	Jigsaw	Dewalt	Power Tool	A	$60.00
2	Hand Drill	Dewalt	Power Tool	A	$30.00
3	Router	Dewalt	Power Tool	A	$40.00

Figure 5-11. Results (output)

The following examples show implementations of other LIKE operator search patterns. Remember to use the percent sign (%) instead of the asterisk (*) if your Access database is set to SQL Server compatible syntax (ANSI-92).

Example 3

To retrieve manufacturers that end with the letter H, type the following:

```
SELECT *
FROM Tools
WHERE Manufacturer LIKE '*H';
```

Example 4

To retrieve any occurrence of the word Dewalt within the name of the manufacturer, type the following:

```
SELECT *
FROM Tools
WHERE Manufacturer LIKE '*Dewalt*';
```

Example 5

To retrieve data that matches a single character in the Manufacturer column, type the following:

```
SELECT *
FROM Tools
WHERE Manufacturer LIKE 'Bos?h';
```

The question mark (?) is used as a character placeholder.

➲ **Note:** If your Access database is set to SQL Server compatible syntax (ANSI-92), use an exclamation mark (!) instead of the question mark (?) in this type of query.

Example 6

To retrieve data that matches a single digit in the ToolID column, type the following:

```
SELECT *
FROM Tools
WHERE ToolID LIKE '1#';
```

The pound sign (#) is used as a digit placeholder.

⊃ **Note:** If your Access database is set to SQL Server compatible syntax (ANSI-92), use the percent sign (%) in place of the pound sign (#).

Example 7

To retrieve warehouse locations that are not A to C, type the following:

```
SELECT *
FROM Tools
WHERE Location LIKE '[!A-C]';
```

The ! symbol means NOT.

Example 8

To retrieve characters that are not digits from 1 to 5, type the following:

```
SELECT *
FROM Tools
WHERE ToolID LIKE '[!1-5]';
```

Example 9

To retrieve a combination of characters and digits, type the following:

```
SELECT *
FROM Computers
WHERE SerialNum LIKE 'm*[1-9]';
```

This script retrieves serial numbers from the Computers table that begin with the letter m and end with numbers 1 through 9.

> **Note:** If your Access database is set to SQL Server compatible syntax (ANSI-92), use the percent sign (%) in place of the asterisk (*).

The BETWEEN Operator

The BETWEEN operator is used to determine whether a value of an expression falls within a specified range of values. Take a look at Example 10.

Example 10

ToolID	ToolName	Manufacturer	Type	Location	Price
1	Jigsaw	Dewalt	Power Tool	A	$60.00
2	Hand Drill	Dewalt	Power Tool	A	$30.00
3	Router	Dewalt	Power Tool	A	$40.00
4	Nail Gun	Bosch	Power Tool	A	$60.00
5	Sandpaper	Bosch	Sanding	B	$4.00
6	Scrapers	Bosch	Sanding	B	$8.00
7	Hammer	Makita	Hand Tool	C	$14.00
8	Pliers	Porter	Hand Tool	C	$9.00
9	Screwdriver	Makita	Hand Tool	C	$4.00
10	Tool Belt	Porter	Accessories	D	$15.00
11	Battery Charger	Dewalt	Accessories	D	$20.00

Figure 5-12. Tools table

Suppose you want to query the Tools table in Figure 5-12 to retrieve tool IDs equal to or between 3 and 10. Look at the following script:

```
SELECT *
FROM Tools
WHERE ToolID BETWEEN 3 AND 10;
```

This script uses the BETWEEN operator in the WHERE clause to retrieve tool IDs equal to or between 3 and 10. The AND operator is used to specify values 3 and 10. Note that the BETWEEN operator always includes the expressions specified on either side of the AND operator. Look at the results in Figure 5-13.

ToolID ▾	ToolName ▾	Manufacturer ▾	Type ▾	Location ▾	Price ▾
3	Router	Dewalt	Power Tool	A	$40.00
4	Nail Gun	Bosch	Power Tool	A	$60.00
5	Sandpaper	Bosch	Sanding	B	$4.00
6	Scrapers	Bosch	Sanding	B	$8.00
7	Hammer	Makita	Hand Tool	C	$14.00
8	Pliers	Porter	Hand Tool	C	$9.00
9	Screwdriver	Makita	Hand Tool	C	$4.00
10	Tool Belt	Porter	Accessories	D	$15.00

Figure 5-13. Results (output)

This query is equivalent to the preceding query:

```
SELECT *
FROM Tools
WHERE ToolID >= 3 AND ToolID <=10;
```

What is the difference between the LIKE and the BETWEEN operators? At first glance one might expect that the expressions LIKE '[A-C]'* and BETWEEN 'A' and 'C' would produce the same results. While that would be true in some specific cases, generally the results will be different. Let's say you have the list A, Apple, B, Bear, C, Cat, D, and Dog. The LIKE '[A-C]*' example will collect the values A, Apple, B, Bear, C, and Cat. The BETWEEN 'A' and 'C' example will collect the values A, Apple, B, Bear, and C but not Cat because Cat comes after C, which is the maximum value of the sequence.

The IN and NOT Operators

The IN operator is used to match conditions in a list of expressions.

The NOT operator is used to match any condition opposite of the one defined. Take a look at Example 11.

Example 11

Say you want to query the Tools table to retrieve information on every tool except the ones manufactured by Bosch, Porter, or Makita. Look at the following script:

```
SELECT *
FROM Tools
WHERE Manufacturer NOT IN ('Bosch', 'Porter', 'Makita');
```

The preceding script uses the IN operator to specify three text values (Bosch, Porter, and Makita). The values are enclosed in parentheses and each individual value is enclosed in quotes. Remember that when you retrieve values from fields defined as a character data type, you must enclose the values in quotes. The NOT operator instructs the DBMS to match any condition opposite of the ones defined by the IN operator. Look at the results in Figure 5-14.

ToolID	ToolName	Manufacturer	Type	Location	Price
1	Jigsaw	Dewalt	Power Tool	A	$60.00
2	Hand Drill	Dewalt	Power Tool	A	$30.00
3	Router	Dewalt	Power Tool	A	$40.00
11	Battery Charger	Dewalt	Accessories	D	$20.00

Figure 5-14. Results (output)

The following query specifies the exact opposite of the preceding query. It retrieves records that contain the values (Bosch, Porter, and Makita) specified by the IN operator.

```
SELECT *
FROM Tools
WHERE Manufacturer IN ('Bosch', 'Porter', 'Makita');
```

Example 12

Suppose you want to retrieve tool IDs 2, 4, 6, and 8 from the Tools table. Look at the following script:

```
SELECT *
FROM Tools
WHERE ToolID IN (2, 4, 6, 8);
```

The preceding script uses the IN operator to specify four numbers (2, 4, 6, 8). The values are enclosed in parentheses. There are no quotes enclosing the numbers because the ToolID column in the Tools table contains a number data type as opposed to a text data type. Only values associated with a column containing text values must be enclosed in quotes. Look at the results in Figure 5-15.

ToolID ▾	ToolName ▾	Manufacturer ▾	Type ▾	Location ▾	Price ▾
2	Hand Drill	Dewalt	Power Tool	A	$30.00
4	Nail Gun	Bosch	Power Tool	A	$60.00
6	Scrapers	Bosch	Sanding	B	$8.00
8	Pliers	Porter	Hand Tool	C	$9.00

Figure 5-15. Results (output)

The IS NULL and IS NOT NULL Operators

The IS NULL operator is used to determine if a field contains data. The IS NOT NULL operator is used to determine if a field does not contain data. Take a look at Example 13.

Example 13

FriendsID ▾	Firstname ▾	Lastname ▾	Address ▾	Zipcode ▾	Areacode ▾	PhoneNumber ▾	Email ▾
1	John	Hill	2322 3rd Ave S Atlanta, GA	98753	301	822-1600	jhill@juno.com
2	Gina	Jones	7123 Kendle Rd Tampa, FL	33673	813	811-0001	
3	Timothy	Jones	1000 6th Ave N. St. Pete, FL	33700	727	366-1111	tjones@aol.com
4	Reginald	Coney	3210 7th Ave E Honolulu, HI	96111	808	423-0022	
5	Otis	Rivers	2400 Ferry Rd N Tampa, FL	33623	813	321-1432	orivers@hotmail.com

Figure 5-16. Friends table

Suppose you want to retrieve individuals who do not have an e-mail address but do have a phone number listed in the Friends table in Figure 5-16. Look at the following script:

```
SELECT Firstname, Lastname, Areacode, PhoneNumber, Email
FROM Friends
WHERE Email IS NULL AND PhoneNumber IS NOT NULL;
```

The preceding script implements the IS NULL and IS NOT NULL keywords in the WHERE clause. The IS NULL keywords are used to locate NULL values in the Email column. The IS NOT NULL keywords are used to locate values in the PhoneNumber column. Look at the results in Figure 5-17.

Firstname ▾	Lastname ▾	Areacode ▾	PhoneNumber ▾	Email ▾
Gina	Jones	813	811-0001	
Reginald	Coney	808	423-0022	

Figure 5-17. Results (output)

Summary

In this chapter, you learned how to create a WHERE clause. You also learned how to use the comparison and logical operators in the WHERE clause.

Quiz 5

1. True or False. An expression is a special character used to match parts of a value.

2. True or False. The following queries are equivalent:

    Query 1:

    ```
    SELECT *
    FROM Tools
    WHERE ToolID > 3 AND ToolID < 10;
    ```

    Query 2:

    ```
    SELECT *
    FROM Tools
    WHERE ToolID BETWEEN 3 AND 10;
    ```

3. Using the Friends table in Figure 5-16, what will the following query return?

    ```
    SELECT FriendsID
    FROM Friends
    WHERE Lastname = 'Jones' AND Email IS NULL;
    ```

4. True or False. The exclamation mark (!) in the following WHERE clause means NOT:

```
WHERE Location LIKE '[!A-C]';
```

5. True or False. The OR operator is processed before the AND operator in the order of evaluation.

Project 5

Use the Friends table in Figure 5-16 to write a query that returns records for individuals who live in Florida (FL).

Chapter 6

Creating Calculated Fields

Introduction

In this chapter, you will learn how to implement calculated fields in your queries. You will become familiar with the arithmetic operators, the aggregate functions, the string functions, and the date and time functions. You will also find a reference for additional functions used in Microsoft Access's SQL view.

Keywords

ABS ()
AVG ()
CCUR ()
COUNT (*)
COUNT (*ColumnName*)
DATE ()
DATEPART (*interval, date*
   [*firstweekday*]
   [, *firstweek*])
DAY ()
FIRST ()
FORMAT (*ColumnName,*
   DateFormat)

HOUR ()
INSTR (*Start, SourceString,*
   SearchString)
INT ()
LAST ()
LCASE ()
LEFT (*StringExpression, n*)
LEN ()
LTRIM ()
MAX ()
MID (*StringExpression, Start,*
   Length)
MIN ()

MINUTE ()   SUM ()
MONTH ()   TIME ()
NOW ()   TIMESERIAL (*hour, minute,*
Nz (*Variant* [, *ValueIfNull*])   *second*)
RIGHT (*StringExpression, n*)   TRIM ()
ROUND (*Fieldname,*   TRUNCATE (*Fieldname,*
   DecimalValue)   *DigitValue*)
RTRIM ()   UCASE ()
SECOND ()   VAR ()
SPACE ()   VARP ()
STDEV ()   WEEKDAY ()
STDEVP ()   YEAR ()

Definitions

Aggregate functions — Used to return a single value based on calculations on values stored in a column.

Arithmetic operators — Used to perform mathematical calculations.

Date and time functions — Used to manipulate values based on the time and date.

String functions — Used to manipulate strings of character(s).

Operators and Functions

In the previous chapter we described various operators that are used in the WHERE clause. There are other sets of operators that are used to modify the data in tables. This occurs commonly in the query grid, where you want to combine the result of two fields or format the data of a specific field. Take our Numbers table, for example.

ColumnOne ▾	ColumnTwo ▾	ColumnThree ▾
5	2	98
1	8	11
10	1	22
90	6	12
40	27	6
90	7	4
70	43	3
70	61	144

Figure 6-1. Numbers table

Assume that you want the sum of the first two columns and the difference of the first and third columns. This is easily done in the query grid as follows:

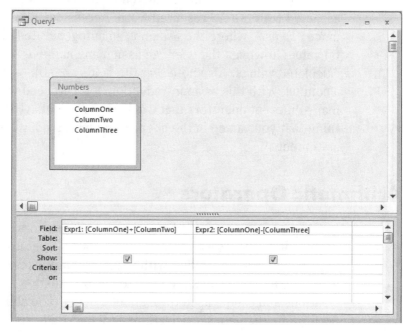

Figure 6-2. Query Design view

Changing this to SQL view gives the following SQL result:

Figure 6-3. SQL view

This is just like the SELECT statements you have seen previously with a few additions. Note that the fields are listed with the operator and that the calculated field has a new name assigned with the AS reserved word. Access defaults to the names Expr#, where the # sign is an autogenerated incremental value; however, the user can assign any name to these calculated values. Also note that the fields are still separated by a comma. With this as an introduction, let's proceed with the many different operators that can be used in SQL. (Hint: Anything that you can do in the query grid you can do in the SQL statement.)

Arithmetic Operators

In Chapter 5 you learned about an array of operators that can be used in the WHERE clause. Another set of operators that you should become familiar with is the arithmetic operators. The *arithmetic operators* are used to perform mathematical calculations and can be used throughout a query. The ability to perform mathematical calculations enables you to collect information beyond the data actually stored in the database. Take a look at Table 6-1, which shows the arithmetic operators used in Microsoft Access's SQL view.

Table 6-1. Arithmetic operators

Operator	Description
Negation (–)	Used to take the negative of a number.
Exponentiation (^)	Used to perform exponentiation.
Divide (/)	Used to perform division.
Multiply (*)	Used to perform multiplication.
Modulus (%)	Used to return the remainder in division.
Plus (+)	Used to perform addition.
Minus (–)	Used to perform subtraction.

Table 6-1 displays the arithmetic operators for Access SQL. These are the same basic operators used by most versions of SQL, except for the exponentiation operator, which is not present in Microsoft SQL. The order in which operators are executed when several operations occur in an expression is called *operator precedence*. The arithmetic operators in Table 6-1 are displayed in the order in which they are evaluated. First, negation is performed. This is followed by exponentiation. Next, division, multiplication, and modulo operations are performed. Finally, addition and subtraction operations are performed. When two or more operations of equal precedence occur together, the expression is evaluated from the left to the right.

Take a look at Example 1, which implements two of the arithmetic operators.

Use an Arithmetic Operator with SELECT

Example 1

ColumnOne ▾	ColumnTwo ▾	ColumnThree ▾
5	2	98
1	8	11
10	1	22
90	6	12
40	27	6
90	7	4
70	43	3
70	61	144

Figure 6-4. Numbers table

Figure 6-4 shows a table named Numbers. Suppose you want to add two values that are stored in two separate columns and multiply a value that is stored in a column by a specified value. Look at the following script:

```
SELECT (ColumnOne + ColumnTwo) AS AddColumns,
(ColumnThree * 2) AS MultiplyByTwo
FROM Numbers;
```

The preceding script uses the plus (+) operator to add the ColumnOne column to the ColumnTwo column. The result of the addition is displayed under an alternate name (AddColumns). Next, the multiply (*) operator is used to multiply the ColumnThree column by the value of 2. The result of the multiplication is also displayed under an alternate column name (MultiplyByTwo). Figure 6-5 shows the results from the query.

AddColumns ▾	MultiplyByTwo ▾
7	196
9	22
11	44
96	24
67	12
97	8
113	6
131	288

Figure 6-5. Results (output)

⊃ **Note:** In earlier chapters we used the asterisk (*) to display every column from a table. The asterisk can also be used to perform multiplication. Access determines which interpretation of the asterisk is to be used based on the content of the string. One of the most difficult factors in analyzing an incorrect SQL string is when Access gets confused. For example, if Access thinks that the asterisk is being used to designate all columns and not as a multiplication symbol, you might wonder where the error message came from. It has nothing to do with what you intended!

Use an Arithmetic Operator in the WHERE clause

Example 2

Suppose you want to retrieve records that are based on a WHERE clause that contains a comparison operator and an arithmetic operator. Look at the following:

```
SELECT ColumnOne, ColumnThree
FROM Numbers
WHERE ColumnOne < ColumnThree + 4;
```

The preceding query displays the ColumnOne and ColumnThree columns. The WHERE clause sets a criterion to only retrieve records where the first column (ColumnOne) is less than the result of Column Three added to the number four (ColumnThree + 4). Look at the results in Figure 6-6.

ColumnOne	ColumnThree
5	98
1	11
10	22
70	144

Figure 6-6. Results (output)

Aggregate Functions

Aggregate functions can also be used to perform mathematical calculations. They operate on several rows at one time and are used to return a single value based on values stored in a column. Unlike arithmetic operators, they cannot be used to calculate values stored in multiple columns.

Instead of retrieving actual information stored in the database, you can use aggregate functions to summarize data that is stored in the database. For example, aggregate functions can be used to average and sum values stored in a column.

Table 6-2 shows aggregate functions that are used most commonly in Microsoft Access's SQL view.

Table 6-2. Aggregate functions

Function	Description
AVG ()	Used to return the average of values stored in a column.
COUNT (*)	Used to count the rows in a table including NULL values.
COUNT (*ColumnName*)	Used to count the rows in a column excluding NULL values.
FIRST ()	Used to return the first value stored in a column.
LAST ()	Used to return the last value stored in a column.
MAX ()	Used to return the highest value stored in a column.
MIN ()	Used to return the lowest value stored in a column.
SUM ()	Used to return the sum of values stored in a column.

Take a look at Example 3, which implements many of the aggregate functions discussed in Table 6-2.

Using the AVG (), FIRST (), LAST (), SUM (), MAX (), and MIN () Functions

Example 3

Suppose you want to use the Numbers table in Figure 6-4 to average the values stored in the ColumnOne column, find the first and last values stored in the ColumnOne column, sum the values stored in the ColumnTwo column, and find the highest and lowest values stored in the ColumnTwo column. Take a look at the following script:

```
SELECT AVG (ColumnOne) AS Average, FIRST (ColumnOne) AS FirstValue,
LAST (ColumnOne) AS LastValue, SUM (ColumnTwo) AS Summed,
MAX (ColumnTwo) AS Highest, MIN (ColumnTwo) AS Lowest
FROM Numbers;
```

The preceding script uses the AVG (ColumnOne) function to average the values in the ColumnOne column. Notice that the name of the column is enclosed within the parentheses of the AVG () function. The FIRST (ColumnOne) and LAST (ColumnOne) functions are used to find the first and last values that are stored in the ColumnOne column.

The SUM (ColumnTwo) function is used to sum the values stored in the ColumnTwo column. The MAX (ColumnTwo) and MIN (ColumnTwo) functions are used to find the highest and lowest values stored in the ColumnTwo column. Figure 6-7 shows the results from the query.

Average	FirstValue	LastValue	Summed	Highest	Lowest
47	5	70	155	61	1

Figure 6-7. Results (output)

Using the COUNT () Function

Another popular aggregate function is the COUNT () function. The COUNT () function can be used in two ways. You can use it either to count the number of rows in a table or to count the rows in a specified column. To count the number of rows in a table, use the asterisk (*) within the function (COUNT (*)). To count the number of rows in a specified column, specify the name of a column in the function (COUNT (*ColumnName*)).

➲ **Note:** When you use COUNT (*ColumnName*), NULL values are excluded in the count. When you use COUNT (*), NULL values are included in the count. Example 4 demonstrates using both the COUNT (*) and COUNT (*ColumnName*) functions.

ColumnOne ▾	ColumnTwo ▾	ColumnThree ▾
5	2	98
1	8	11
10	1	22
90	6	
	27	6
90	7	4
70	43	3
70	61	144

Figure 6-8. Numbers table (altered)

Example 4

The Numbers table in Figure 6-8 has been altered slightly from the original Numbers table in Figure 6-4. The Numbers table in Figure 6-8 contains two NULL values. Notice that there is a value missing in the ColumnOne and ColumnThree columns.

Suppose you want to use the Numbers table in Figure 6-8 to count the rows in the table and the rows in the ColumnThree column. Look at the following script:

```
SELECT COUNT (*) AS TableCount,
COUNT (ColumnThree) AS ColumnCount
FROM Numbers;
```

The preceding script uses the COUNT (*) function to count the total number of rows in the Numbers table, including NULL values. The COUNT (ColumnThree) function is used to count the total number of rows in the ColumnThree column, excluding NULL values. Look at Figure 6-9 to see the results.

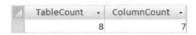

TableCount ▾	ColumnCount ▾
8	7

Figure 6-9. Results (output)

Sometimes you will see a column added to a query where the SELECT statement includes SUM (1) AS TableCount. This is the equivalent of COUNT (*)

String Functions and Operations

Arithmetic operators work on numbers. There is a corresponding set of operators that works on strings. In addition to these operators, there is a set of functions used to perform operations on strings. It should be noted that with a few exceptions, processing of strings as numbers or processing numbers as strings is not a good idea and in most cases simply cannot be done. Access will generate an error message if the wrong type of operator is used in an expression. Like arithmetic functions, string functions operate on one row at a time as opposed to aggregate functions, which operate on several rows at one time. Tables 6-3 and 6-4 show some of the string operators and functions used in Microsoft Access's SQL view.

Table 6-3. String operators

Operator	Description
&	Used to concatenate two strings together.
+	Used to concatenate two strings together with NULL suppression.

Table 6-4. String functions

Function	Description
LTRIM ()	Used to remove leading spaces from a string.
RTRIM ()	Used to remove trailing spaces from a string.
TRIM ()	Used to remove leading and trailing spaces from a string.
LEFT (*StringExpression*, *n*)	Used to return the leftmost *n* characters of a string. A *StringExpression* can be any string expression. The *n* represents the number of characters to return.
RIGHT (*StringExpression*, *n*)	Used to return the rightmost *n* characters of a string. A *StringExpression* can be any string expression. The *n* represents the number of characters to return.
UCASE (*StringExpression*)	Used to return a string in which all letters of an argument have been converted to uppercase.
LCASE (*StringExpression*)	Used to return a string in which all letters of an argument have been converted to lowercase.
LEN (*StringExpression*)	Used to return the number of characters in a string expression or the number of bytes required to store a variable.
MID (*StringExpression*, *Start*, *Length*)	Used to return a string that is part of another string. A *StringExpression* can be any string expression. *Start* represents the character position in the *StringExpression* at which the part to be returned begins. *Length* represents the number of characters to return.

Function	Description
INSTR (*Start, SourceString, SearchString*)	Used to return the position of the first occurrence of one string within another string. *Start* represents a numeric expression that sets the starting position for reading the *SourceString*. *SourceString* represents the string expression being searched. *SearchString* represents the string expression being sought.

Use of the + and &

The most common operation performed on strings is the joining of two or more strings to make a single string. This is commonly referred to as concatenation. Concatenation was discussed in Chapter 4.

Microsoft Access has two operators that perform this function: + and &. The difference between the two operators is how null strings are processed. The plus operator processes a null string as a blank, so "string1" + NULL = "string1". The ampersand processes the joining of any string with a null as null, so "string1" & NULL = NULL. This usefulness of having two functions is readily apparent when you consider that sometimes you want to see whatever is present and other times you want to see nothing if a field is blank. Consider the case of printing names with middle initials. Usually when you have a middle initial, you want to display it as the initial followed by a period. If you use the + operator, the result will be perfect unless there is no middle initial. In these cases you would get a lone period. Using the & operator gives you the preferred result of nothing.

Take a look at Example 5, which uses an example we discussed in Chapter 4.

Example 5

The following script uses the ampersand (&) to merge the Lastname column with a comma and the Firstname column with one space and a slash. The plus sign (+) is used to merge an empty string with the Lastname column and a comma, and to merge the slash and space with the Areacode column. The AS keyword is used to create an alias (NamesAndAreacodes).

```
SELECT Lastname & ',' + ' ' + Firstname & ' / ' + Areacode AS
       NamesAndAreacodes
FROM Committee2;
```

Look at the results in Figure 6-10.

NamesAndAreacodes
Cole, Leonard / 301
Coney, Panzina / 813
Fields, Kayla / 813
London, Jerru / 808
Brown, Debra / 301

Figure 6-10. Results (output)

Using the LEFT (), UCASE (), LEN (), and TRIM () Functions

Example 6

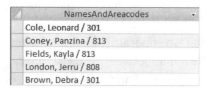

SerialNum	Brand	Department	OfficeNumber
G9277288282	Dell	HR	122
M6289288289	Dell	Accounting	134
R2871620091	Dell	Information Systems	132
W2121040244	Gateway	CustomerService	22
X8276538101	Dell	HR	311

Figure 6-11. Computers table

Suppose you want to query the Computers table in Figure 6-11. You want to retrieve the first two characters/numbers from each value stored in the SerialNum column. Additionally, you want to display all the values in the Brand column in all uppercase letters, display the total number of characters for each value in the Department column, and trim any existing and trailing spaces from the values stored in the OfficeNumber column. Look at the following script:

```
SELECT LEFT (SerialNum, 2) AS FirstTwoChars,
UCASE (Brand) AS Uppercase, LEN (Department) AS TotalChars,
TRIM (OfficeNumber) AS TrimSpaces
FROM Computers;
```

The preceding script uses the LEFT (SerialNum, 2) function to return the first two leftmost characters from the values stored in the SerialNum column. The column name (SerialNum) specifies which column to return data from and the number two (2) specifies how many characters to return. The UCASE (Brand) function is used to return all the values in the Brand column converted to uppercase. The LEN (Department) function is used to return the total number of characters for each value stored in the Department column. Finally, the TRIM (OfficeNumber) function is used to remove leading and trailing spaces from the values stored in the OfficeNumber column. Figure 6-12 shows the results from the query.

FirstTwoChars	▾	Uppercase	▾	TotalChars	▾	TrimSpaces	▾
G9		DELL		2		122	
M6		DELL		10		134	
R2		DELL		19		132	
W2		GATEWAY		15		22	
X8		DELL		2		311	

Figure 6-12. Results (output)

Using the MID () and INSTR () Functions

Example 7

SerialNum	Brand	Department	OfficeNumber
G9277288282	Dell	HR	122
M6289288289	Dell	Accounting	134
R2871620091	Dell	Information Systems	132
W2121040244	Gateway	CustomerService	22
X8276538101	Dell	HR	311

Figure 6-13. Computers table

Suppose you want to query the Computers table in Figure 6-13 to retrieve the first five characters/numbers from each value stored in the SerialNum column. You also want to display the numeric position of the first occurrence of the number 2 in each value stored in the SerialNum column. Look at the following script:

```
SELECT MID (SerialNum, 1, 5) AS FirstFiveChars,
INSTR (1, SerialNum, 2) AS PositionOfTwos
FROM Computers;
```

The preceding script uses the MID (SerialNum, 1, 5) function to retrieve the first five characters/numbers from each value stored in the SerialNum column. The column name (SerialNum) represents the column from which to retrieve characters/numbers. The 1 represents the character position in the SerialNum column at which the part to be returned begins. The 5 represents the number of characters to return.

The INSTR (1, SerialNum, 2) function is used to display the numeric position of the first occurrence of the number 2 in each value stored in the SerialNum column. The 1 represents the numeric expression that sets the starting position for reading the values stored in the SourceString (SerialNum column). The column name (SerialNum) represents the column to search, and the 2 represents the string expression being sought. Look at the results in Figure 6-14.

FirstFiveChars	PositionOfTwos
G9277	3
M6289	3
R2871	2
W2121	2
X8276	3

Figure 6-14. Results (output)

One of the more important features of the INSTR function is that the function returns specific values depending upon whether or not the searched for string is in the source string. Refer to Table 6-5.

Table 6-5. INSTR function

If	InStr returns
Searched in string is zero-length	0
Searched in string is Null	Null
Searched for string is zero-length	*start*
Searched for string is Null	Null
Searched for string is not found	0
Searched for string is found within *Searched in string*	Position at which match is found
start > *Searched in string*	0

➲ **Note:**   The MID (*StringExpression, Start, Length*) function is very similar to the LEFT (*StringExpression, n*) and RIGHT (*StringExpression, n*) functions. However, the MID (*String-Expression, Start, Length*) function enables you to better pinpoint where you want to begin your extraction of characters rather than limit you to the beginning or end of the string.

Date and Time Functions

Another collection of functions that can be very useful in your queries is the set of *date and time functions,* which are used to manipulate values based on the date and time.

Before we begin using the date and time functions it is important to note that Microsoft Access stores all dates and times as numbers.

The numeric representation of dates is called a Julian (or serial) date. Microsoft Access designates day 0 as 12/30/1899 and increments all other dates starting from this date. For example, 7/7/93 is stored as 34157, which represents 34,157 days since 12/30/1899. Negative numbers represent dates prior to 12/30/1899.

Times in Microsoft Access are stored as a fraction of a day. An hour is equivalent to 1/24 of a day (or 0.0416666), each minute is equivalent to 1/1440 of a day (or 0.0006944), and each second is equivalent to 1/86400 (or 0.0000115). For example, 3:00 a.m. is stored as 1/8 of a day (or .125). Table 6-6 shows some of the most commonly used date and time functions in Microsoft Access's SQL view.

Table 6-6. Date and time functions

Function	Description
DATE ()	Used to return the current date.
DATEPART (*interval, date* [*firstweekday*] [, *firstweek*])	Used to return a value from a date. *Interval* represents a string expression that is the interval of time you use to return. *Date* represents the name of a Date/Time field. *Firstweekday* represents an integer that specifies the first day of the week. *Firstweek* is a constant that specifies the first week of the year.

Function	Description
DATEPART (Cont.)	Specific values for *interval* are: **Setting Description** yyyy Year q Quarter m Month y Day of year d Day w Weekday ww Week h Hour n Minute s Second
DAY ()	Used to return the day of the month from a date.
FORMAT (*ColumnName, DateFormat*)	Formats a number, date, time, or string according to instructions contained in a format expression. *ColumnName* stores the values that need formatting. *DateFormat* represents the format in which you want to display values.
HOUR ()	Used to return an integer from 0 to 23, which represents the hour of the day matching the time provided as an argument.
MINUTE ()	Used to return an integer from 0 to 59, which represents the minute of the hour matching the time provided as an argument.
MONTH ()	Used to return the month from a date.
NOW ()	Used to return the current date and time.
SECOND ()	Used to return an integer from 0 to 59, which represents the second of the minute matching the time provided as an argument.
TIME ()	Used to return the current time.
TIMESERIAL (*hour, minute, second*)	Used to return the time for a specific hour, minute, and second. Hour represents an hour from 0 (12:00 a.m.) to 23 (11:00 p.m), or a numeric expression. Minute represents a minute from 0 to 59, or a numeric expression. Second represents a second from 0 to 59, or a numeric expression.
WEEKDAY ()	Used to return the day of the week from a date.
YEAR ()	Used to return the year from a date.

Inserting Dates into a Table

Example 8

ActivityID ▾	ActivityName ▾	StartDate ▾	EndDate ▾
1	Aerobics	1/1/2008	1/9/2008
2	Games	1/2/2008	1/10/2008
3	Outdoor activities	1/3/2008	1/10/2008
4	Trips and tours	1/1/2008	1/17/2008
5	Arts and crafts	1/17/2008	1/27/2008
6	Resident discussion groups	1/9/2008	1/17/2008
7	Coffee or cocktail hours	1/1/2008	

Figure 6-15. Activities table

Suppose you want to insert a new record containing dates into the Activities table in Figure 6-15. Look at the following script:

```
INSERT INTO Activities (ActivityID, ActivityName, StartDate,
    EndDate)
VALUES (8, ' Remotivation therapy', #01/01/08#, #01/31/08#);
```

The above script inserts four values into the Activities table. Two of the values are dates. Although Microsoft Access stores dates as numbers, dates must be enclosed in pound signs. Figure 6-16 shows the addition of the new record. The dates are all aligned to the right because, like numeric fields, all date values are aligned to the right by default.

⮑ **Note:**   To see the addition of the new record you must open the Activities table. Type the following to open the Activities table: SELECT * FROM Activities.

⮑ **Note:**   If you specify a time part when entering a date, that value will be included in the date; otherwise, Access assumes that you are using midnight as the time.

ActivityID ▾	ActivityName ▾	StartDate ▾	EndDate ▾
1	Aerobics	1/1/2008	1/9/2008
2	Games	1/2/2008	1/10/2008
3	Outdoor activities	1/3/2008	1/10/2008
4	Trips and tours	1/1/2008	1/17/2008
5	Arts and crafts	1/17/2008	1/27/2008
6	Resident discussion groups	1/9/2008	1/17/2008
7	Coffee or cocktail hours	1/1/2008	
8	Remotivation therapy	1/1/2008	1/31/2008

Figure 6-16. Results (output)

Using the FORMAT () Function

Example 9

Suppose you want to retrieve the start dates in a different
format than they appear in the Activities table in Figure 6-15.
Look at the following script:

```
SELECT ActivityName, FORMAT (StartDate, 'mmmm-dd-yyyy') AS BeginDate
FROM Activities;
```

The above script uses a date format (mmmm-dd-yyyy) in the
FORMAT () function that enables you to spell out the full name
of the month, the two-digit day, and the full four-digit year.
Table 6-7 displays the date formats available in Microsoft
Access's SQL view. As you can see, there are an almost unlim-
ited number of ways to format date and time.

Table 6-7. Microsoft Access date formats

Date Formats	Description
/	Date separator.
c	Same as the General Date predefined format.
d	Day of the month in one or two numeric digits, as needed (1 to 31).
dd	Day of the month in two numeric digits (01 to 31).
ddd	First three letters of the weekday (Sun to Sat).
dddd	Full name of the weekday (Sunday to Saturday).

Date Formats	Description
ddddd	Same as the Short Date predefined format.
dddddd	Same as the Long Date predefined format.
w	Day of the week (1 to 7).
ww	Week of the year (1 to 53).
m	Month of the year in one or two numeric digits, as needed (1 to 12).
mm	Month of the year in two numeric digits (01 to 12).
mmm	First three letters of the month (Jan to Dec).
mmmm	Full name of the month (January to December).
q	Date displayed as the quarter of the year (1 to 4).
y	Number of the day of the year (1 to 366).
yy	Last two digits of the year (01 to 99).
yyyy	Full year (0100 to 9999).
h	Hour in one or two digits, as needed (0 to 23).
hh	Hour in two digits (00 to 23).
n	Minute in one or two digits, as needed (0 to 59).
nn	Minute in two digits (00 to 59).
s	Second in one or two digits, as needed (0 to 59).
ss	Second in two digits (00 to 59).
ttttt	Same as the Long Time predefined format.
AM/PM	Twelve-hour clock with the uppercase letters "AM" or "PM", as appropriate.
am/pm	Twelve-hour clock with the lowercase letters "am" or "pm", as appropriate.
A/P	Twelve-hour clock with the uppercase letter "A" or "P", as appropriate.
a/p	Twelve-hour clock with the lowercase letter "a" or "p", as appropriate.
AMPM	Twelve-hour clock with the appropriate morning/afternoon designator as defined in the Regional Settings Properties dialog box in the Windows Control Panel.

Figure 6-17 displays the results from the query in Example 9.

ActivityName	BeginDate
Aerobics	January-01-2008
Games	January-02-2008
Outdoor activities	January-03-2008
Trips and tours	January-01-2008
Arts and crafts	January-17-2008
Resident discussion groups	January-09-2008
Coffee or cocktail hours	January-01-2008
Remotivation therapy	January-01-2008

Figure 6-17. Results (output)

Using the DATE (), TIME (), MONTH (), DAY (), and YEAR () Functions

Example 10

Say you want to display the current date and time. Additionally, you want to display the ending dates of all activities in the Activities table with the month, day, and year displayed in separate columns. Take a look at the following script:

```
SELECT DATE () AS TodaysDate, TIME () AS CurrentTime, MONTH
(EndDate) AS EndDateMonth, DAY (EndDate) AS EndDateDay, YEAR
(EndDate) AS EndDateYear
FROM Activities;
```

The above script uses the DATE () and TIME () functions to display the current system date and time. The MONTH (EndDate) function is used to display the numeric representation of the month from the date stored in the EndDate field. The DAY (EndDate) function is used to display the numeric representation of the day from the date stored in the EndDate field. The YEAR (EndDate) function displays the numeric representation of the year from the date stored in the EndDate field. Figure 6-18 displays the results.

TodaysDate	CurrentTime	EndDateMonth	EndDateDay	EndDateYear
3/22/2008	10:15:58 PM	1	9	2008
3/22/2008	10:15:58 PM	1	10	2008
3/22/2008	10:15:58 PM	1	10	2008
3/22/2008	10:15:58 PM	1	17	2008
3/22/2008	10:15:58 PM	1	27	2008
3/22/2008	10:15:58 PM	1	17	2008
3/22/2008	10:15:58 PM			
3/22/2008	10:15:58 PM	1	31	2008

Figure 6-18. Results (output)

Miscellaneous Functions

Table 6-8 shows additional functions that can be used in Microsoft Access's SQL view.

Table 6-8. Miscellaneous functions

Function	Description
ABS ()	Returns the absolute value of a number.
CCUR (*expression*)	Used to convert a value to currency.
INT ()	Returns the integer part of a numeric field.
Nz (*Variant* [, *ValueIfNull*])	Returns a zero, a zero-length string (" "), or another specified value when a table value (or variant) is NULL. *Variant* represents a variable of data type variant. *ValueIfNull* represents a variant that supplies a value to be returned if the variant argument is NULL.
ROUND (*Fieldname, DecimalValue*)	Rounds a number off to the specified number of decimal places. *Fieldname* represents the column that stores the values for rounding. *DecimalValue* represents the decimal value to round by.
SPACE ()	Used to add spaces to fields.
STDEV ()	Used to calculate the standard deviation by using a portion, called a sample, of the total number of values in a field for a specified numeric field in a query.

Function	Description
STDEVP ()	Used to calculate the standard deviation by using all of the values in a field for a specified numeric field in a query.
TRUNCATE (*Fieldname, DigitValue*)	Truncates numeric fields to the specified number of digits.
VAR ()	Used to calculate the variance by using a portion, called a sample, of the total number of values in a field for a specified numeric field in a query.
VARP ()	Used to calculate the variance by using all of the values in a field for a specified numeric field in a query.

Using the CCUR () Function

Example 11

ColumnOne ▾	ColumnTwo ▾	ColumnThree ▾
5	2	98
1	8	11
10	1	22
90	6	12
40	27	6
90	7	4
70	43	3
70	61	144

Figure 6-19. Numbers table

For our last example, let's take a look at one of the functions (CCUR ()) listed in the miscellaneous functions table above.

The CCUR () function is used to convert a value to currency. Take a look at the following query, which demonstrates the use of the CCUR () function:

```
SELECT ColumnOne, CCUR (ColumnOne + 2.00) AS
TwoDollarIncrease
FROM Numbers
WHERE ColumnOne IN (10, 70, 90);
```

The preceding SQL script queries the Numbers table in Figure 6-19. The WHERE clause specifies a condition for three records (10, 70, 90). The query retrieves the ColumnOne column and the ColumnOne column added to two dollars. The CCUR () function is used to display the two dollar increase as currency. Notice the dollar sign in the TwoDollarIncrease column in Figure 6-20.

ColumnOne ▾	TwoDollarIncrease ▾
10	$12.00
90	$92.00
90	$92.00
70	$72.00
70	$72.00

Figure 6-20. Results (output)

Summary

In this chapter, you learned how to implement calculated fields in your queries. You learned how to use arithmetic operators, aggregate functions, string functions, and the date and time functions. You were also introduced to some additional functions used in Microsoft Access's SQL view.

Quiz 6

1. True or False. The divide (/) operator is used to return the remainder in division.

2. True or False. Aggregate functions operate on only one row at a time.

3. True or False. The ddd date format displays the full names of days.

4. True or False. The CURRENTTIME () function is used to return the current time.

5. True or False. The numeric representation of dates is called a Julian (or serial) date.

Project 6

Use the Computers table in Figure 6-13 to display today's date and time, the SerialNum column, and the last five numbers from each serial number in the SerialNum column.

Chapter 7

Grouping Data

Introduction

In this chapter you will learn how to use the GROUP BY and HAVING clauses to group and filter data.

Keywords

GROUP BY
HAVING
ORDER BY
WHERE

Definitions

GROUP BY clause — Used with aggregate functions to combine groups of records into a single functional record.

HAVING clause — Used with the GROUP BY clause to set conditions on groups of data calculated from aggregate functions.

The GROUP BY Clause

In Chapter 4 we covered the ORDER BY clause, which affects the results of a query by returning records in either descending or ascending order. In this chapter we will be covering the GROUP BY clause, which is used with aggregate functions to combine groups of records into a single record. We briefly mentioned a method of grouping records in Chapter 6 with the discussion of aggregate functions. Recall that they are used to return a single value based on values stored in a column. Examples of aggregate functions include the following: AVG (), COUNT (), MAX (), MIN (), and SUM (). The GROUP BY clause is far more powerful since it provides a means for grouping specific subsets of records and presenting calculations on each of the subsets.

Before we get started using the GROUP BY clause, let's take a moment to discuss the rules for using the GROUP BY clause. To use the GROUP BY clause the following must apply:

- The GROUP BY clause can only be used in queries that contain at least one aggregate function. (Otherwise there is no need for the GROUP BY!)

- All column names retrieved from the database (specified after the SELECT keyword) must be present in the GROUP BY clause. Note that this does not include column names that are specified within functions or alternate column names (aliases).

You have probably used the GROUP BY clause without realizing it since every time you run a query in the query grid with Totals turned on, you are in effect running an aggregate query (see Figure 7-1).

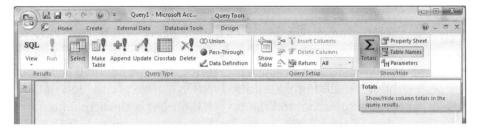

Figure 7-1

Enabling Totals modifies the query grid by adding the Total row to the grid. Using the Totals option (located under the Design menu) for each field presents the user with several functions, including Group By (the default that is used when totals are not desired).

Example 1

TransactionID ▼	ProductID ▼	CustomerID ▼	DateSold ▼
1	VR300	2	2/3/2008
2	CT200	2	2/5/2008
3	ET100	5	2/6/2008
4	PO200	1	2/8/2008
5	TH100	3	2/8/2008
6	RX300	4	2/10/2008
7	CE300	2	2/22/2008
8	OT100	6	2/20/2008
9	LF300	6	2/18/2008
10	BN200	1	2/17/2008

Figure 7-2. Transactions table

Figure 7-2 shows a table named Transactions. The Transactions table represents sales at a company. The TransactionID column is the primary key column. The ProductID column represents a unique ID for products, and each product ID contains a corresponding customer ID that represents a customer. Customer IDs that appear more than once represent customers who purchased multiple products. The DateSold column represents the date a product was sold.

Suppose you want to count the total number of products each customer purchased. Using the query grid (Figure 7-3) you would start with the basic select query with two columns: CustomerID and ProductID. (Notice that the full field name is TotalProductsPurchased:ProductID. The text to the left of the colon is the alias, and the text to the right is the actual field name.) Select Totals from the Design menu, and select Count in the Total row for the TotalProductsPurchased column.

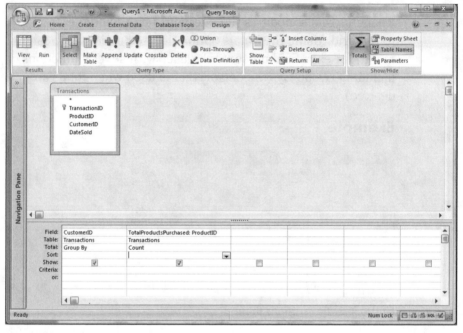

Figure 7-3. Query Design view

Changing the view to SQL (Figure 7-4) produces the following result:

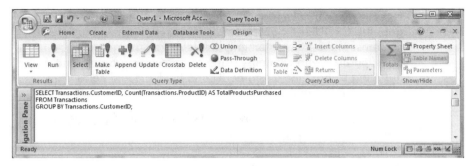

Figure 7-4. SQL view

With a bit of cleanup and changing the name of the result of the count to the more descriptive TotalProductsPurchased, we produce the following script:

```
SELECT CustomerID, COUNT (ProductID) AS TotalProductsPurchased
FROM Transactions
GROUP BY CustomerID;
```

The preceding script displays two columns (CustomerID and TotalProductsPurchased). The COUNT (ProductID) function is used to count each product ID. The GROUP BY clause groups the results from the aggregate function COUNT (ProductID) per each customer ID. Take a look at Figure 7-5, which shows each customer ID and the total number of products purchased.

CustomerID ▾	TotalProductsPurchased ▾
1	2
2	3
3	1
4	1
5	1
6	2

Figure 7-5. Results (output)

➲ **Note:** As you have probably discovered from using the query grid, the GROUP BY clause can also be used to group multiple columns. In the SQL statement, the fields you are grouping by are separated with commas. Using our previous example and grouping by both the CustomerID and the DateSold fields produces the following:

```
SELECT Sales.CustomerID, Count(Sales.ProductID) AS CountOfProductID,
        Sales.DateSold
FROM Sales
GROUP BY Sales.CustomerID, Sales.DateSold
```

Using the GROUP BY Clause with the ORDER BY Clause

The GROUP BY clause can also be used in conjunction with the ORDER BY clause to sort the query results. Take a look at the following rules for using the GROUP BY clause with the ORDER BY clause.

■ The ORDER BY clause cannot be used in a query containing an aggregate function and no GROUP BY clause.

■ The GROUP BY clause must appear before the ORDER BY clause.

Example 2 implements a query using the GROUP BY and ORDER BY clauses.

Example 2

Suppose you want to duplicate the query in Example 1, but this time you want to sort the output by the total amount of purchases per customer. In Design view, add the Sort option on the ProductID column to the previous query.

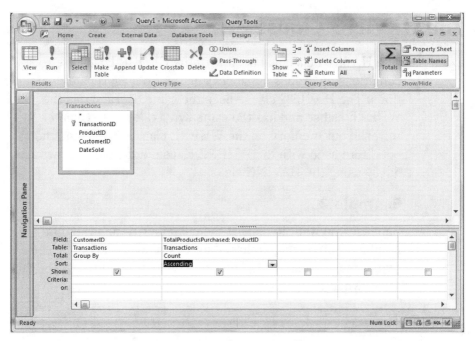

Figure 7-6. Query Design view

Changing to SQL view and simplifying produces the following:

```
SELECT CustomerID, COUNT (ProductID) AS TotalProductsPurchased
FROM Transactions
GROUP BY CustomerID
ORDER BY COUNT (ProductID);
```

The preceding script uses the ORDER BY clause to sort the output by the total amount of purchases per customer COUNT (ProductID). Take a look at the results in Figure 7-7.

CustomerID	TotalProductsPurchased
5	1
4	1
3	1
6	2
1	2
2	3

Figure 7-7. Results (output)

The HAVING Clause

The HAVING clause is used with the GROUP BY clause to set conditions on groups of data calculated from aggregate functions. The HAVING clause uses the same operators as the WHERE clause and has the same syntax. Refer to Chapter 5 to refresh your memory on the WHERE clause syntax and the operators used with the WHERE clause. Example 3 shows a query using the HAVING clause.

Example 3

Suppose you want to display the customer ID and the total number of products purchased for customers who purchased two or more products. In Design view you would represent this as shown in Figure 7-8:

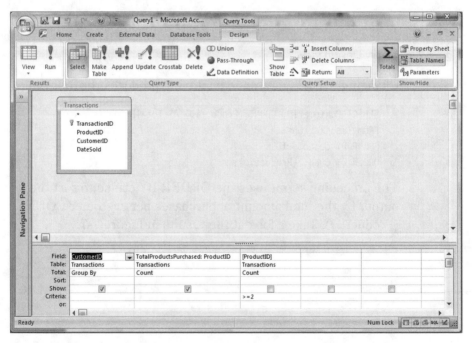

Figure 7-8. Query Design view

In SQL view (Figure 7-9) this produces the following result:

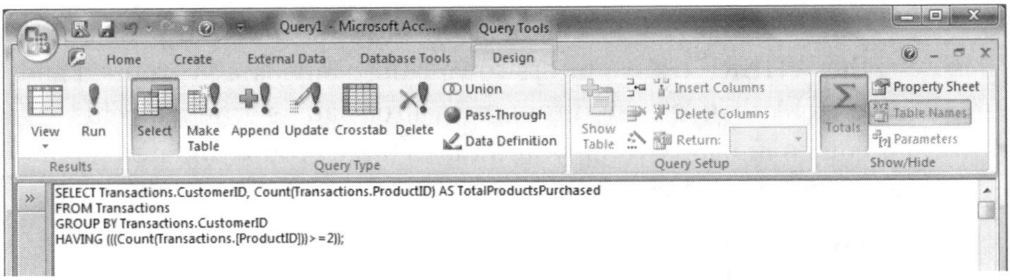

Figure 7-9. SQL view

When simplified it looks like this:

```
SELECT CustomerID, COUNT (ProductID) AS TotalProductsPurchased
FROM Transactions
GROUP BY CustomerID
HAVING COUNT (ProductID) >= 2;
```

The preceding script uses the COUNT (ProductID) function to count the product IDs. The GROUP BY clause groups the results of the aggregate function (COUNT (ProductID)) per each customer ID. The HAVING clause specifies the display of only the total counts that are greater than or equal to 2. Notice that the HAVING clause follows the GROUP BY clause. If you try to place the HAVING clause before the GROUP BY clause, you will receive an error. Refer to Figure 7-10 to see the results.

CustomerID ▾	TotalProductsPurchased ▾
1	2
2	3
6	2

Figure 7-10. Results (output)

Using the HAVING Clause with the WHERE Clause

The WHERE clause can be used with the HAVING clause since the WHERE clause filters rows before any data is grouped and the HAVING clause filters rows after data is grouped. This comes in handy when you want to filter groups and items that are not in the same query.

➲ **Note:**   Whenever you use the GROUP BY clause with a WHERE clause, the GROUP BY clause must appear after the WHERE clause.

Take a look at Example 4, which shows a query using both the HAVING and the WHERE clauses.

Example 4

Suppose you want to count the total number of products purchased for customer IDs less than or equal to 6 with a total count of products purchased that is greater than or equal to 2. Take a look at the following script:

```
SELECT CustomerID, COUNT (ProductID) AS TotalProductsPurchased
FROM Transactions
WHERE CustomerID <= 6
GROUP BY CustomerID
HAVING COUNT (ProductID) >= 2;
```

This script uses the WHERE clause to instruct Microsoft Access to only include customer IDs less than or equal to 6, while the HAVING clause is used to instruct Microsoft Access to include only the total products purchased greater than or equal to 2. Figure 7-11 shows the results from the query.

CustomerID	▾	TotalProductsPurchased	▾
1		2	
2		3	
6		2	

Figure 7-11. Results (output)

Notice that for this example we started with the SQL statement and have not shown the query in Design view. This is to stress a point. The query grid for this query is as follows (Figure 7-12):

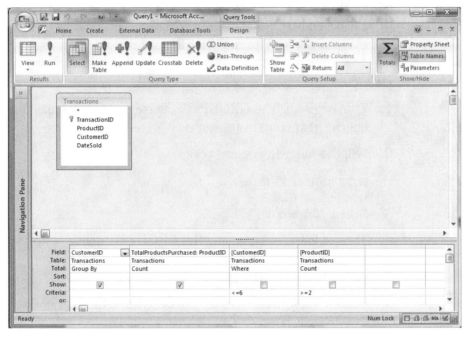

Figure 7-12. Query Design view

As the query gets more complex, you will rapidly discover that the SQL statement is far more descriptive and easier to interpret than the query grid. While one of the authors spends most of his time in Design view with only occasional initial query writing in SQL view, he often has to change over to SQL view to see how Access is really interpreting the query. Sometimes what you think you have written in Design view is not what actually is occurring. SQL view removes possible ambiguity and shows what is really going to happen!

Summary

In this chapter, you have learned how to use the GROUP BY clause in queries that contain aggregate functions. You have additionally learned how to use the GROUP BY clause with the ORDER BY and HAVING clauses. You also learned how to use the HAVING clause with the WHERE clause.

Quiz 7

1. True or False. The GROUP BY clause can only be used in queries that contain at least two aggregate functions.

2. Will the following query work?

   ```
   SELECT DATE () AS TodaysDate
   FROM Transactions
   GROUP BY CustomerID;
   ```

3. True or False. When using the GROUP BY clause with a WHERE clause, the GROUP BY clause must appear before the WHERE clause.

4. True or False. The GROUP BY clause must appear before the ORDER BY clause.

5. True or False. The HAVING clause filters rows before any data is grouped.

Project 7

Use the Transactions table in Figure 7-2 to display the customer IDs and the total number of products purchased by customers who only purchased one product.

Chapter 8

Creating Table Joins and Unions

Introduction

In this chapter, you will learn how to retrieve records from multiple tables using table joins and unions. You will also learn how to create table aliases, perform qualification, create a Cartesian product, and implement the DISTINCTROW keyword.

Keywords

DISTINCTROW	RIGHT JOIN
INNER JOIN	UNION
LEFT JOIN	UNION ALL
ON	

Definitions

Cartesian product — Result produced when each row in one table is multiplied by the total number of rows in another table.

INNER JOIN — Used to instruct the DBMS to combine matching values from two tables.

LEFT JOIN — Selects every record from the table specified to the left of the LEFT JOIN keywords.

ON — Used to specify a condition.

Qualification — Used to match a column with a specific table.

RIGHT JOIN — Selects every record from the table specified to the right of the RIGHT JOIN keywords.

Self join — Used to join a table to itself.

UNION — Used to combine records from two queries while excluding duplicate records.

UNION ALL — Used to combine records from two queries while including duplicate records.

Table Joins — An Overview

Table joins provide one of the most powerful features in the SQL query language. A *join* enables you to use a single SELECT statement to query two or more tables simultaneously. There are three main types of joins used in Access SQL: inner join, self join, and outer join.

Qualification

In our previous examples, when we have changed from Design view to SQL view, Access has placed the table name into the SQL statement. We have taken the liberty of removing the table qualification since with only one table it is not required, but when a query contains more than one table, it is no longer optional. While it is the practice in some cases for each column in a database to have a unique name (often by adding an abbreviation of the name of the table to each field name), it is not unusual to have fields in multiple tables with the same name. Commonly, the primary key of the first table shares the same name as the foreign key of the secondary table. This is almost to be expected if you think about it, since the fields of the two tables contain the same type of information. For this reason you must specify which table a column refers to so that Microsoft Access knows exactly which table a column belongs to. To accomplish this you must use a technique called *qualification*. As might be expected based on what we have removed from our previous Access converted SQL queries, to qualify a table you must enter the name of the table followed by a period and the name of the column. The rules for qualification are as follows:

- In the actual join, the field names must be fully qualified.

- Where there is no possible ambiguity on the source of a field name, that field does not need to be qualified elsewhere in the SQL statement, although it can be.

- If there is a possibility of ambiguity (i.e., if the field name occurs in multiple tables even if it is not used in the query), the field *must* be qualified.

Take a look at the following syntax for qualification:

```
Tablename.Columnname
```

Qualification is demonstrated in all of the examples throughout this chapter.

Inner Join

Inner joins, also referred to as equi-joins, are the most basic type of join and match column values that are common between tables. In other words, you are matching every instance of a value in one field of the first table to every instance of that value in the second table. To create an inner join in Access Design mode you add both tables to the query grid, then connect the field of the first table to the matching field in the second table. In SQL you create an inner join using the INNER JOIN and ON keywords. The INNER JOIN keywords are used to instruct the DBMS to combine matching values from two tables. The ON keyword is used to specify a condition. Additionally you must specify the column names to retrieve, the tables to retrieve records from, and the relationships between tables (specifying primary keys and foreign keys).

Example 1

CustomerID	Firstname	Lastname	Address	City	State	Zipcode	Areacode	PhoneNumber
1	Kayla	Allison	6725 3rd Ave N	Atlanta	GA	98700	301	897-3412
2	Devin	Fields	1001 30th St S	Tampa	FL	33677	813	828-8754
3	Gene	Spencer	3910 35th Ave S.	St. Pete	FL	33700	727	321-1111
4	Spencer	Madewell	32101 60th Ave E	Honolulu	HI	96822	808	423-4444
5	Reggie	Collins	1526 1st St N	Tampa	FL	33622	813	847-9002
6	Penny	Penn	2875 Treetop St N	Tampa	FL	33621	813	821-7812

Figure 8-1. Customers table

TransactionID	ProductID	CustomerID	DateSold
1	VR300	2	2/3/2008
2	CT200	2	2/5/2008
3	ET100	5	2/6/2008
4	PO200	1	2/8/2008
5	TH100	3	2/8/2008
6	RX300	4	2/10/2008
7	CE300	2	2/22/2008
8	OT100	6	2/20/2008
9	LF300	6	2/18/2008
10	BN200	1	2/17/2008

Figure 8-2. Transactions table

Suppose you want to query the Customers table in Figure 8-1 and the Transactions table in Figure 8-2 to retrieve the customer's ID, last name, each product the customer purchased, and the dates the purchases were made. Using our usual Design view, we would build the query as follows in Figure 8-3:

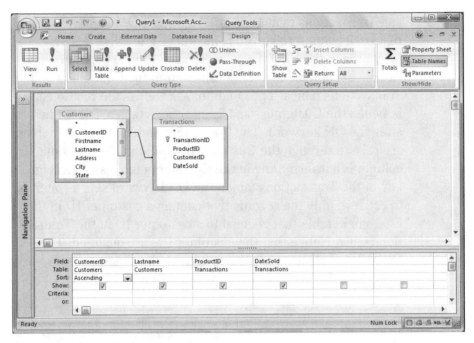

Figure 8-3. Query Design view

Changing to SQL view (Figure 8-4) produces the following SQL statement. Note the INNER JOIN keywords combining the two tables, Customers and Transactions, and the ON keyword showing which fields of the two tables are to be linked.

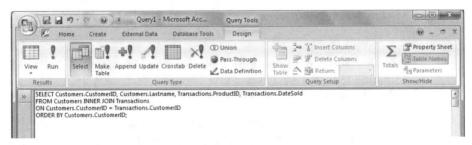

Figure 8-4. SQL view

The preceding script specifies four columns (Customers.CustomerID, Customers.Lastname, Transactions.ProductID, and Transactions.DateSold) to retrieve data from the Customers and Transactions tables specified in the FROM clause. Notice that each column retrieved is qualified. The INNER JOIN keywords in the FROM clause are used to instruct Microsoft Access to combine matching values from the Customers and Transactions tables. The condition, as well as the relationship between the Customers and Transactions tables, is specified after the ON keyword. The Customers and Transactions tables are related through the CustomerID column. The CustomerID column is a primary key in the Customers table and a foreign key in the Transactions table. The ON keyword sets a condition to retrieve only the records that contain a customer ID in the Customers table that is equal to a customer ID in the Transactions table. Notice that the customer IDs are qualified. The ORDER BY clause sorts the results by the Customers.CustomerID column. Look at the results in Figure 8-5.

CustomerID	Lastname	ProductID	DateSold
1	Allison	BN200	2/17/2008
1	Allison	PO200	2/8/2008
2	Fields	CE300	2/22/2008
2	Fields	CT200	2/5/2008
2	Fields	VR300	2/3/2008
3	Spencer	TH100	2/8/2008
4	Madewell	RX300	2/10/2008
5	Collins	ET100	2/6/2008
6	Penn	LF300	2/18/2008
6	Penn	OT100	2/20/2008

Figure 8-5. Results (output)

➲ **Note:** You can also perform the preceding inner join by omitting the INNER JOIN and ON keywords and using a WHERE clause, as shown in the following query:

```
SELECT Customers.Lastname, Customers.Firstname,
Transactions.ProductID, Transactions.DateSold
FROM Customers, Transactions
WHERE Customers.CustomerID = Transactions.CustomerID
ORDER BY Lastname;
```

The preceding query is similar to the query shown in Figure 8-4. It retrieves the customer's first and last name, each product the customer purchased, and the dates purchases were made. It uses a WHERE clause instead of the INNER JOIN and ON keywords. If you choose to use the INNER JOIN keywords, you must use the ON keyword. You cannot use the INNER JOIN keywords with the WHERE clause.

➔ **Note:** Most Access programmers would not think about representing the query in this fashion since it goes against every method of teaching how to build Access queries. Converting the above SQL back to Design view produces the following query:

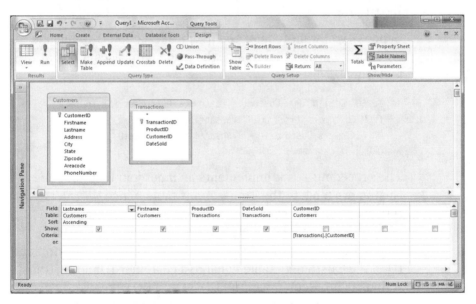

Figure 8-6. Query Design view

There are very few Access programmers who think of queries like this but as we will show, it is an extremely useful tool!

Using the DISTINCTROW Keyword

The DISTINCTROW keyword is used to exclude records based on the entire duplicate records, not just duplicate fields. It is very similar to the DISTINCT keyword discussed in Chapter 4, but DISTINCTROW is based on entire rows, not just individual fields.

The DISTINCTROW keyword is used in queries that include more than one table in the FROM clause, as do joins. It only retrieves unique values when you retrieve columns from some but not all of the tables specified in the FROM clause. Take a look at Example 2.

Example 2

Suppose you want to alter the query in Example 1 to include only the names of customers who made purchases. Look at the following script:

```
SELECT DISTINCTROW Customers.Lastname, Customers.Firstname
FROM Customers INNER JOIN Transactions
ON Customers.CustomerID = Transactions.CustomerID
ORDER BY Lastname;
```

The preceding script implements an inner join that joins the Customers table to the Transactions table. Since the query retrieves columns from one table and not both tables in the FROM clause, the DISTINCTROW keyword displays the unique first and last names of customers who have a customer ID in the Customers table equal to a customer ID in the Transactions table. Remember, the DISTINCTROW keyword only retrieves unique values when you retrieve columns from some but not all of the tables specified in the FROM clause.

Self Join

The second type of join is the self join. *Self joins* enable you to join a table to itself. They are useful when you want to find records that have values in common with other rows in the same table. In Figure 8-7, we have modified the Employees table to represent an instance when self joins might be used. Each employee has a supervisor who is in turn an employee of the company. Rather than have a separate table of supervisors, it is easier to normalize the information and just provide a field in each employee's record that points to that employee's supervisor.

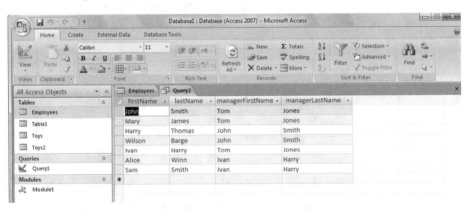

Figure 8-7. Modified Employees table

In the query grid this would be represented by dragging the Employees table to the query grid twice, then linking the two tables together and mentally tracking which instance of the table is used for the main employee information and which instance is used for the supervisor information (Figure 8-8).

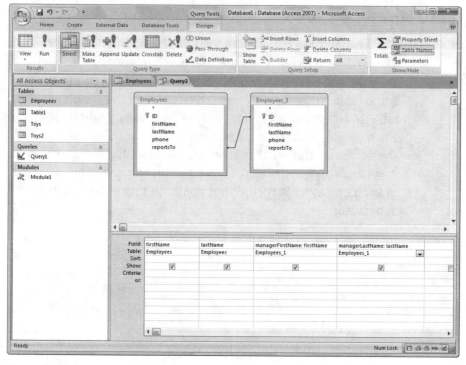

Figure 8-8

In SQL, in order to join a table to itself you must use table aliases. Table aliases are created just like column aliases. By creating table aliases, Microsoft Access perceives the table being joined to itself as an additional separate table. This can be seen in the following script:

```
SELECT Employees.firstName, Employees.lastName,
       Employees_1.firstName AS managerFirstName,
       Employees_1.lastName AS managerLastName
FROM Employees INNER JOIN Employees AS Employees_1
ON Employees.reportsTo = Employees_1.ID;
```

When run, the result is that the person an individual reports to can be viewed as a name (Figure 8-9).

| Employees |||||||
ID ▾	firstName ▾	lastName ▾	phone ▾	reportsTo ▾	Add New Field
4	John	Smith	3434	5	
5	Tom	Jones	4544	0	
6	Mary	James	4566	5	
7	Harry	Thomas	4564	4	
8	Wilson	Barge	4343	4	
9	Ivan	Harry	4534	5	
10	Alice	Winn	4344	9	
11	Sam	Smith	4432	9	
* (New)					

Figure 8-9

Table aliases are also used as a shortcut for typing entire table names. Example 3 shows a self join containing table aliases.

Example 3

CustomerID ▾	Firstname ▾	Lastname ▾	Address ▾	City ▾	State ▾	Zipcode ▾	Areacode ▾	PhoneNumber ▾
1	Kayla	Allison	6725 3rd Ave N	Atlanta	GA	98700	301	897-3412
2	Devin	Fields	1001 30th St S	Tampa	FL	33677	813	828-8754
3	Gene	Spencer	3910 35th Ave S.	St. Pete	FL	33700	727	321-1111
4	Spencer	Madewell	32101 60th Ave E	Honolulu	HI	96822	808	423-4444
5	Reggie	Collins	1526 1st St N	Tampa	FL	33622	813	847-9002
6	Penny	Penn	2875 Treetop St N	Tampa	FL	33621	813	821-7812

Figure 8-10. Customers table

Suppose you want to query the Customers table in Figure 8-10 to retrieve the names and IDs of customers who live in the same state as the state for customer ID 2. Look at the following script:

```
SELECT C1.Lastname, C1.Firstname, C1.CustomerID, C1.State
FROM Customers AS C1, Customers AS C2
WHERE C1.State = C2.State
AND C2.CustomerID = 2;
```

This script creates two table aliases (C1, C2) for the Customers table in the FROM clause. The table aliases are used throughout the query to represent two separate Customers tables. Every instance of a table alias represents a table. The WHERE clause is used to set a condition to retrieve only the records that contain a state in the C1 table that is equal to the state in the C2 table, and each state must be equal to the state for customer ID 2 in the C2 table. Figure 8-9 shows the results of the query.

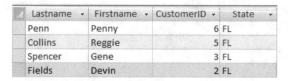

Lastname	Firstname	CustomerID	State
Penn	Penny	6	FL
Collins	Reggie	5	FL
Spencer	Gene	3	FL
Fields	Devin	2	FL

Figure 8-11. Results (output)

Nested Join

SQL also enables you to create nested joins. Look at the following example, which joins three tables.

Example 4

ProductID	ProductName	Price	SalePrice	InStock	OnOrder
AN200	Animated Picture	$20.00	$18.00	10	20
BN200	Animated Rainbow	$20.00	$18.00	10	20
CE300	Miniature Train Set	$60.00	$54.00	1	30
CT200	China Puppy	$15.00	$13.50	20	40
ET100	Wooden Clock	$11.00	$9.90	100	0
LF300	Friendly Lion	$14.00	$12.60	0	30
OT100	Dancing Bird	$10.00	$9.00	10	20
PO200	Glass Rabbit	$50.00	$45.00	50	20
RX300	Praying Statue	$25.00	$22.50	3	40
TH100	Crystal Cat	$75.00	$67.50	60	20
VR300	China Doll	$20.00	$13.00	100	0

Figure 8-12. Products table

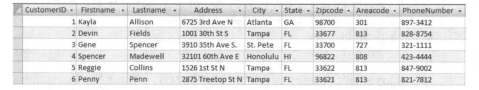

CustomerID	Firstname	Lastname	Address	City	State	Zipcode	Areacode	PhoneNumber
1	Kayla	Allison	6725 3rd Ave N	Atlanta	GA	98700	301	897-3412
2	Devin	Fields	1001 30th St S	Tampa	FL	33677	813	828-8754
3	Gene	Spencer	3910 35th Ave S.	St. Pete	FL	33700	727	321-1111
4	Spencer	Madewell	32101 60th Ave E	Honolulu	HI	96822	808	423-4444
5	Reggie	Collins	1526 1st St N	Tampa	FL	33622	813	847-9002
6	Penny	Penn	2875 Treetop St N	Tampa	FL	33621	813	821-7812

Figure 8-13. Customers table

TransactionID ▼	ProductID ▼	CustomerID ▼	DateSold ▼
1	VR300	2	2/3/2008
2	CT200	2	2/5/2008
3	ET100	5	2/6/2008
4	PO200	1	2/8/2008
5	TH100	3	2/8/2008
6	RX300	4	2/10/2008
7	CE300	2	2/22/2008
8	OT100	6	2/20/2008
9	LF300	6	2/18/2008
10	BN200	1	2/17/2008

Figure 8-14. Transactions table

Suppose you want to query the tables in Figures 8-12, 8-13, and 8-14 to retrieve each customer's first and last name along with the products purchased and complete sales information from the Transactions table. Using the query grid in Figure 8-15, this is a simple operation.

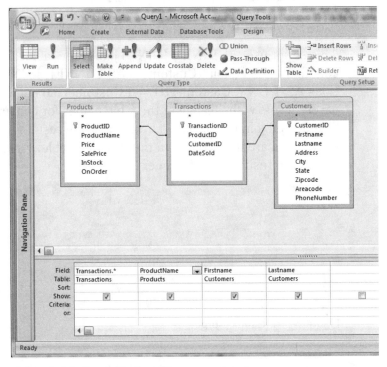

Figure 8-15. Query Design view

Converting to SQL view (Figure 8-16) produces the SQL equivalent:

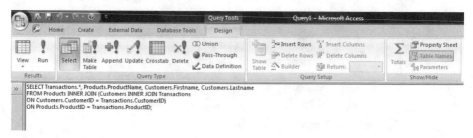

```
SELECT Transactions.*, Products.ProductName, Customers.Firstname, Customers.Lastname
FROM Products INNER JOIN (Customers INNER JOIN Transactions
ON Customers.CustomerID = Transactions.CustomerID)
ON Products.ProductID = Transactions.ProductID;
```

Figure 8-16. SQL view

Look at the following script:

```
SELECT T.*, P.ProductName, C.Firstname, C.Lastname
FROM Products AS P INNER JOIN
(Customers AS C INNER JOIN Transactions AS T
ON C.CustomerID = T.CustomerID)
ON P.ProductID = T.ProductID;
```

This script uses an INNER JOIN to join three tables. The script contains a nested join (Customers AS C INNER JOIN Transactions AS T ON C.CustomerID = T.CustomerID) enclosed in parentheses, with aliasing of the table names for convenience. The nested join is performed first. Next, the results of the nested join are used to join to the Products table. Figure 8-17 shows the results from the query.

TransactionID	ProductID	CustomerID	DateSold	ProductName	Firstname	Lastname
1	VR300	2	2/3/2008	China Doll	Devin	Fields
2	CT200	2	2/5/2008	China Puppy	Devin	Fields
3	ET100	5	2/6/2008	Wooden Clock	Reggie	Collins
4	PO200	1	2/8/2008	Glass Rabbit	Kayla	Allison
5	TH100	3	2/8/2008	Crystal Cat	Gene	Spencer
6	RX300	4	2/10/2008	Praying Statue	Spencer	Madewell
7	CE300	2	2/22/2008	Miniature Train Set	Devin	Fields
8	OT100	6	2/20/2008	Dancing Bird	Penny	Penn
9	LF300	6	2/18/2008	Friendly Lion	Penny	Penn
10	BN200	1	2/17/2008	Animated Rainbow	Kayla	Allison

Figure 8-17. Results (output)

➔ **Note:** You may have produced a slightly different SQL query like the following (Figure 8-18) if you tried to duplicate the example:

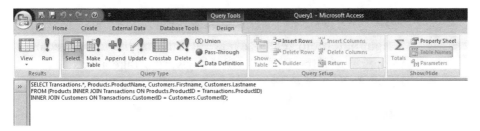

Figure 8-18. SQL view

This is a result of the order in which the tables were added to the query grid. Equi-join query operations are associative in nature (recall your first year of algebra; it doesn't matter if you add A+(B+C) or (A+B)+C, the result will be the same). So it doesn't matter which tables you operate on first — the results will be identical.

The following script shows another method for writing the query:

```
SELECT T.*, P.ProductName, C.Firstname, C.Lastname
FROM Products AS P, Customers AS C, Transactions AS T
WHERE C.CustomerID = T.CustomerID AND
P.ProductID = T.ProductID;
```

This script simply lists all the tables in the FROM clause and then shows the relationship and condition in a WHERE clause. I prefer this method since it is simpler to compose.

Outer Joins

Outer joins are used to retrieve all records from multiple tables even if there is no matching record in the joined table. In other words, the results of an outer join will be the resulting recordset of an inner join plus those records that do not have a corresponding record in the second table. There are two types of outer joins used in Access SQL: the right outer join and the left outer join. The keywords are abbreviated as RIGHT JOIN and LEFT JOIN respectively.

Right Outer Join

A right outer join selects every record from the table specified to the right of the RIGHT JOIN keywords. Take a look at Example 5.

Example 5

CustomerID	Firstname	Lastname	Address	City	State	Zipcode	Areacode	PhoneNumber
1	Tom	Evans	3000 2nd Ave S	Atlanta	GA	98718	301	232-9000
2	Larry	Genes	1100 23rd Ave S	Tampa	FL	33618	813	982-3455
3	Sherry	Jones	100 Free St S	Tampa	FL	33618	813	890-4231
4	April	Jones	2110 10th St S	Santa Fe	NM	88330	505	434-1111
5	Jerry	Jones	798 22nd Ave S	St. Pete	FL	33711	727	327-3323
6	John	Little	1500 Upside Loop N	St. Pete	FL	33711	727	346-1234
7	Gerry	Lexington	5642 5th Ave S	Atlanta	GA	98718	301	832-8912
8	Henry	Denver	8790 8th St N	Holloman	NM	88330	505	423-8900
9	Nancy	Kinn	4000 22nd St S	Atlanta	GA	98718	301	879-2345

Figure 8-19. Customers2 table

TransactionID	ProductID	CustomerID	DateSold
1	VR300	2	2/3/2008
2	CT200	2	2/5/2008
3	ET100	5	2/6/2008
4	PO200	1	2/8/2008
5	TH100	3	2/8/2008
6	RX300	4	2/10/2008
7	CE300	2	2/22/2008
8	OT100	6	2/20/2008
9	LF300	6	2/18/2008
10	BN200	1	2/17/2008

Figure 8-20. Transactions table

Suppose you want to query the Customers2 table shown in Figure 8-19 and the Transactions table shown in Figure 8-20 to display customers and information about their purchases. Additionally, you want to display customers on the mailing list who have not yet made any purchases.

Using Access Design view, this would be represented by the query shown in Figure 8-22.

➲ **Note:** You modify the type of join by highlighting the join, clicking on the join line, right-clicking, selecting Join Properties, then specifying the join type in the Join Properties dialog (Figure 8-21).

Figure 8-21. Join Properties dialog

After clicking on the OK button, the outer join is represented by the arrow joining the two tables, as shown in Figure 8-22.

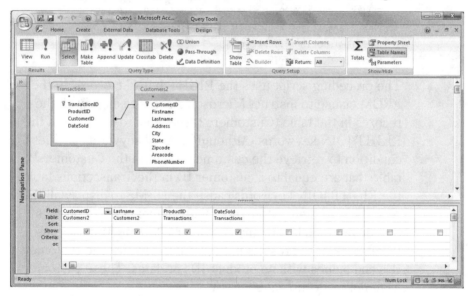

Figure 8-22. Query Design view

Converting to SQL view (Figure 8-23) shows the SQL query:

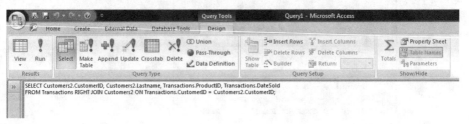

SELECT Customers2.CustomerID, Customers2.Lastname, Transactions.ProductID, Transactions.DateSold
FROM Transactions RIGHT JOIN Customers2 ON Transactions.CustomerID = Customers2.CustomerID;

Figure 8-23. SQL view

Putting in our usual aliases and ordering by the customer ID produces the following script:

```
SELECT C.CustomerID, C.Lastname, T.ProductID, T.DateSold
FROM Transactions AS T RIGHT JOIN Customers2 AS C
ON C.CustomerID = T.CustomerID
ORDER BY C.CustomerID;
```

The preceding script uses the RIGHT JOIN keywords in the FROM clause to instruct Microsoft Access to display all the records in the table (Customers2) specified to the right of the RIGHT JOIN keywords. Although the ON keyword specifies a condition to retrieve the customer IDs from the Customers2 table that are equal to a customer ID in the Transactions table, the RIGHT JOIN keywords cause the DBMS to display all the records from the Customers2 table, including those records that do not match with any customer ID in the Transactions table. Look at the results in Figure 8-24. Notice the customer IDs and names with no product IDs or dates. These customers have not made any purchases yet.

CustomerID ▾	Lastname ▾	ProductID ▾	DateSold ▾
1	Evans	PO200	2/8/2008
1	Evans	BN200	2/17/2008
2	Genes	VR300	2/3/2008
2	Genes	CT200	2/5/2008
2	Genes	CE300	2/22/2008
3	Jones	TH100	2/8/2008
4	Jones	RX300	2/10/2008
5	Jones	ET100	2/6/2008
6	Little	OT100	2/20/2008
6	Little	LF300	2/18/2008
7	Lexington		
8	Denver		
9	Kinn		

Figure 8-24. Results (output)

⮑ **Note:** A term commonly used when dealing with joins is Cartesian product. A *Cartesian product* exists when you create a join without the specification of a relationship between tables. A Cartesian product causes each row in one table to be multiplied by the total number of rows in another table. This is rarely the result sought after when creating a join. Be careful to always specify the relationship between joined tables.

Left Outer Join

A left outer join works much like a right outer join except it selects every record from the table specified to the left of the LEFT JOIN keywords. Take a look at Example 6.

Example 6

Suppose you want to query the Customers2 table shown in Figure 8-19 and the Transactions table shown in Figure 8-20 to display customers and information about their purchases. Additionally, you want to display customers on the mailing list who have not yet made any purchases. This is exactly what we did in Example 5, but this time we'll use LEFT JOIN instead of RIGHT JOIN. Look at the following script:

```
SELECT C.CustomerID, C.Lastname, T.ProductID, T.DateSold
FROM Customers2 AS C LEFT JOIN Transactions AS T
ON C.CustomerID = T.CustomerID
ORDER BY C.CustomerID;
```

The preceding script is equivalent to the script in Example 5. The LEFT JOIN keywords in the FROM clause are used to instruct Microsoft Access to display all the records in the table (Customers2) specified to the left of the LEFT JOIN keywords. Look at the results in Figure 8-25. As you can see, the results are the same as the results for Example 5.

CustomerID	Lastname	ProductID	DateSold
1	Evans	PO200	2/8/2008
1	Evans	BN200	2/17/2008
2	Genes	VR300	2/3/2008
2	Genes	CT200	2/5/2008
2	Genes	CE300	2/22/2008
3	Jones	TH100	2/8/2008
4	Jones	RX300	2/10/2008
5	Jones	ET100	2/6/2008
6	Little	OT100	2/20/2008
6	Little	LF300	2/18/2008
7	Lexington		
8	Denver		
9	Kinn		

Figure 8-25. Results (output)

What does this look like in the Access query grid? Using the simplified version of the SQL query, we type the text into the SQL view as shown in Figure 8-26:

SELECT Customers2.CustomerID, Customers2.Lastname, Transactions.ProductID, Transactions.DateSold
FROM Customers2 LEFT JOIN Transactions ON Customers2.CustomerID = Transactions.CustomerID;

Figure 8-26. SQL view

Then we convert this to Design view (Figure 8-27) and, surprise, we get the same query that we started with in the section on right joins. Access is somewhat arbitrary in that no matter how the tables are entered into the query grid, it will try to interpret the operation as a right join. In this respect, if you want more control of your joins, you will find that it is easier to do them in SQL view. Several times I have wondered what exactly was being done by my Access queries. The answers became apparent when the query was converted to SQL.

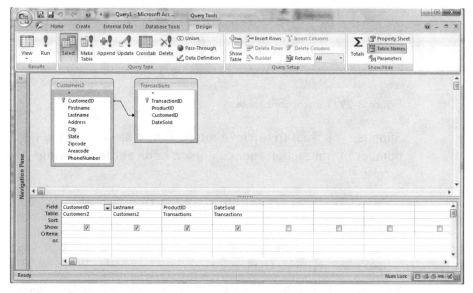

Figure 8-27. Query Design view

Create a Join that Contains an Aggregate Function

In Chapter 7, you learned how to create queries that contain aggregate functions. Now let's use an aggregate function while joining two tables. Take a look at Example 7.

Example 7

CustomerID	Firstname	Lastname	Address	City	State	Zipcode	Areacode	PhoneNumber
1	Kayla	Allison	6725 3rd Ave N	Atlanta	GA	98700	301	897-3412
2	Devin	Fields	1001 30th St S	Tampa	FL	33677	813	828-8754
3	Gene	Spencer	3910 35th Ave S.	St. Pete	FL	33700	727	321-1111
4	Spencer	Madewell	32101 60th Ave E	Honolulu	HI	96822	808	423-4444
5	Reggie	Collins	1526 1st St N	Tampa	FL	33622	813	847-9002
6	Penny	Penn	2875 Treetop St N	Tampa	FL	33621	813	821-7812

Figure 8-28. Customers table

TransactionID ▾	ProductID ▾	CustomerID ▾	DateSold ▾
1	VR300	2	2/3/2008
2	CT200	2	2/5/2008
3	ET100	5	2/6/2008
4	PO200	1	2/8/2008
5	TH100	3	2/8/2008
6	RX300	4	2/10/2008
7	CE300	2	2/22/2008
8	OT100	6	2/20/2008
9	LF300	6	2/18/2008
10	BN200	1	2/17/2008

Figure 8-29. Transactions table

Suppose you want to retrieve the customer names and the total number of transactions per customer. Look at the following script:

```
SELECT FirstName, LastName, COUNT (Transactions.CustomerID) AS
TotalTransactions
FROM Customers, Transactions
WHERE Transactions.CustomerID = Customers.CustomerID
GROUP BY FirstName, LastName;
```

The preceding script uses an aggregate (COUNT ()) function after the SELECT keyword. The FROM clause specifies two tables (Customers, Transactions). The WHERE clause shows the relationship between the Customers and the Transactions tables.

Whenever you use an aggregate function in a query, you also must use the GROUP BY clause. Recall from Chapter 7, all column names retrieved from the database (specified after the SELECT keyword) must be present in the GROUP BY clause. Take a look at the results in Figure 8-30.

FirstName ▾	LastName ▾	TotalTransactions ▾
Devin	Fields	3
Gene	Spencer	1
Kayla	Allison	2
Penny	Penn	2
Reggie	Collins	1
Spencer	Madewell	1

Figure 8-30. Results (output)

UNION and UNION ALL Keywords

Access has three types of queries that cannot be performed with the standard query grid: pass-through, data definition, and union. The most common of these is the union query, which has two variations: standard UNION and UNION ALL.

UNION

The UNION keyword is used to combine records from two queries while excluding duplicate records. Take a look at Example 8.

Example 8

CommitteeID	Firstname	Lastname	Address	Zipcode	Areacode	PhoneNumber
1	Yolanda	Cole	3466 42nd Ave E. St. Pete, FL	33711	727	321-1111
2	John	Allison	2345 40th Ave N Honolulu, HI	96820	808	423-4222
3	Kayla	Fields	2211 Peachtree St S Tampa, FL	33612	813	827-4532
4	Debra	Brown	1900 12th Ave S Atlanta, GA	98718	301	897-0987
5	Leonard	Miles	400 22nd Ave N Atlanta, GA	98718	301	897-1723

Figure 8-31. Committee1 table

CommitteeID	Firstname	Lastname	Address	Zipcode	Areacode	PhoneNumber
1	Leonard	Cole	1323 13th Ave N Atlanta, GA	98718	301	897-1241
2	Panzina	Coney	9033 Colfax Loop Tampa, FL	33612	813	223-6754
3	Kayla	Fields	2211 Peachtree St S Tampa, FL	33612	813	827-4532
4	Jerru	London	6711 40th Ave S Honolulu, HI	96820	808	611-2341
5	Debra	Brown	1900 12th Ave S Atlanta, GA	98718	301	897-0987

Figure 8-32. Committee2 table

Figures 8-31 and 8-32 show two committees that the employees of a company belong to. Some employees belong to one committee and some belong to both committees. Suppose you want to display the last name and first name of employees who belong to at least one committee without displaying duplicate names of the employees who belong to both committees. In older versions of Access you had to do this through a two-step process. First you would create a blank query. Next, while focus was on the query you would select from the Query menu **SQL Specific** and **Union**. This process is simplified a bit in

Access 2007. Now you just select the Design tab, then select Union to create a union query template (Figure 8-33).

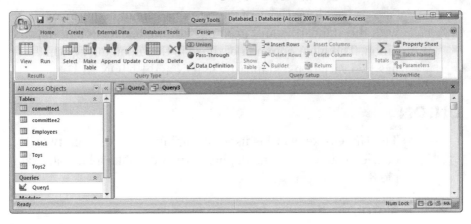

Figure 8-33

Look at the following script:

```
SELECT Lastname, Firstname
FROM Committee1
UNION
SELECT Lastname, Firstname
FROM Committee2;
```

Visually you can see that the union query is a combination of two queries. The first selects records from the first table and the second selects records from the second table. We have found it convenient to create the two component queries individually in temporary queries in Design view, convert the Design views to SQL views, highlight and copy the entire blocks of text, then paste them into the union query. The union query is then completed by adding the word UNION between the two copied queries and deleting the ";" terminator in the first query.

This procedure is shown in the following three figures.

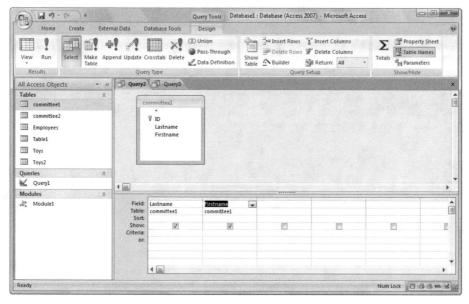

Figure 8-34

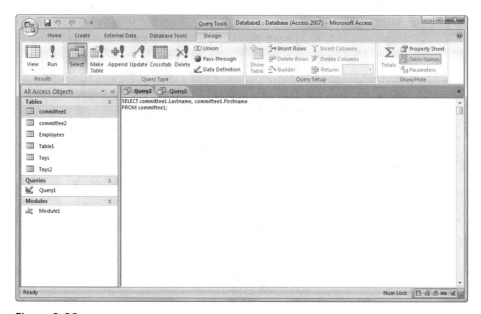

Figure 8-35

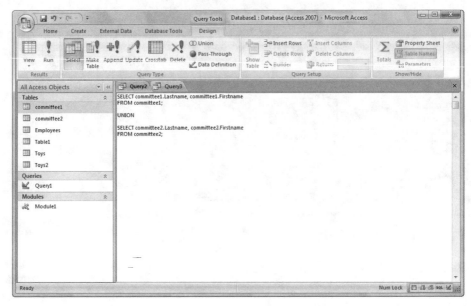

Figure 8-36

While this case is quite simple and can be typed in directly, using the cut and paste method is often easier (and less likely to produce errors) if you have complicated component queries.

The preceding script uses the UNION keyword to exclude duplicate records from the results of two queries. The first query retrieves the Lastname and Firstname columns from the Committee1 table. The second query retrieves the Lastname and Firstname columns from the Committee2 table. The placement of the UNION keyword between the two queries causes only unique records to be displayed. Look at the results in Figure 8-37.

Lastname	Firstname
Allison	John
Brown	Debra
Cole	Leonard
Cole	Yolanda
Coney	Panzina
Fields	Kayla
London	Jerru
Miles	Leonard

Figure 8-37. Results (output)

➲ **Note:** When you compare two tables, both tables must have the same number of fields, but the fields do not have to be the same data type.

UNION ALL

The UNION ALL keywords are used to combine records from two queries while including duplicate records. Take a look at Example 9.

Example 9

Suppose you want to display the last names and first names of the employees who belong to a committee, including duplicate names of people belonging to two committees. Look at the following script:

```
SELECT Lastname, Firstname
FROM Committee1
UNION ALL
SELECT Lastname, Firstname
FROM Committee2
ORDER BY Lastname, Firstname;
```

The preceding script uses the UNION ALL keywords to include duplicate records from the results of two queries. The first query retrieves the Lastname and Firstname columns from the Committee1 table. The second query retrieves the Lastname and Firstname columns from the Committee2 table. The placement of the UNION ALL keywords between the two queries causes all records from both queries to be displayed, including duplicate records. The ORDER BY clause sorts the Lastname and Firstname columns in ascending order. As you can see in Figure 8-38, Debra Brown and Kayla Fields belong to both Committee1 and Committee2.

171

Lastname	Firstname
Allison	John
Brown	Debra
Brown	Debra
Cole	Leonard
Cole	Yolanda
Coney	Panzina
Fields	Kayla
Fields	Kayla
London	Jerru
Miles	Leonard

Figure 8-38. Results (output)

Union all queries are processed the same way as union queries by Access. The only difference is that you use the UNION ALL keyword instead of the UNION keyword.

Note: It is possible to create a union query by beginning with a standard select query, going into SQL view, and adding the UNION keyword and the second select query information. Access is smart enough to know that the query is no longer a select query but a union query. If the query is saved and reloaded or run, it will be marked as a union query from that point on and will not support Design view.

Summary

In this chapter, you learned how to retrieve records from multiple tables using table joins and unions. You also learned how to create table aliases, perform qualification, create a Cartesian product, and use the DISTINCTROW keyword.

Quiz 8

1. True or False. A join enables you to use a single SELECT statement to query two or more tables simultaneously.

2. True or False. The following shows the correct syntax to qualify a table and column name: Tablename,Columnname.

3. True or False. Table aliases are created just like column aliases.

4. True or False. The UNION ALL keyword is used to combine records from two queries while excluding duplicate records.

5. True or False. A left outer join is used to select every record from the table specified to the left of the LEFT JOIN keywords.

Project 8

Use the Products table in Figure 8-12 and the Transactions table in Figure 8-14 to create an outer join that will display product IDs with customer IDs and purchase dates for customers who purchased a product (product ID). Additionally, display product IDs of products that have not been purchased yet.

Chapter 9

Creating Subqueries

Introduction

In this chapter you will learn how to retrieve records from multiple tables using correlated and non-correlated subqueries. You will also learn how to create nested subqueries and how to use the IN, EXISTS, ANY, SOME, NOT, and ALL keywords.

Keywords

ALL	IN
ANY	NOT
EXISTS	SOME

Definitions

ALL — Used to retrieve records from the main query that match all of the records in the subquery.

ANY — Used to retrieve records from the main query that match any of the records in the subquery.

Correlated subquery — Executes once for each record a referenced query returns.

EXISTS — Used to check for the existence of a value in the subquery.

IN — Used to compare values in a column against column values in another table or query.

Non-correlated subquery — Executes once since it contains no reference to an outside query.

NOT — Used to match any condition opposite of the one defined.

SOME — Used to retrieve records from the main query that match any of the records in the subquery.

Subquery — A query linked to another query enabling values to be passed among queries.

Subqueries

Since *subqueries* enable values to be passed among queries, they are commonly used to query multiple tables and can often be used as an alternative to a JOIN statement. Subqueries are linked to other queries using predicates (IN, EXISTS, ANY, SOME, NOT, and ALL) and/or comparison operators (=, <>, <, >, <=, and >=).

Correlated and Non-Correlated Subqueries

There are two types of subqueries: correlated and non-correlated. A *correlated subquery* references another query or queries outside the subquery. Due to this reference, correlated subqueries execute once for each record a referenced query returns. *Non-correlated subqueries* contain no reference to outside queries and only execute once.

All subqueries must be enclosed in parentheses and all tables must contain a corresponding key relationship.

The IN Subquery

The IN predicate is used to compare values in a column against column values in another table or query. Recall in Chapter 5 that we used the IN keyword to match conditions in a list of expressions. It can also be very effective for linking subqueries. Keep in mind though that a subquery linked by the IN predicate can only return one column. Subqueries linked using the IN predicate process the last subquery first, working

upward. Take a look at Example 1, which shows a non-correlated IN subquery.

Example 1

CustomerID ▾	Firstname ▾	Lastname ▾	Address ▾	City ▾	State ▾	Zipcode ▾	Areacode ▾	PhoneNumber ▾
1	Kayla	Allison	6725 3rd Ave N	Atlanta	GA	98700	301	897-3412
2	Devin	Fields	1001 30th St S	Tampa	FL	33677	813	828-8754
3	Gene	Spencer	3910 35th Ave S.	St. Pete	FL	33700	727	321-1111
4	Spencer	Madewell	32101 60th Ave E	Honolulu	HI	96822	808	423-4444
5	Reggie	Collins	1526 1st St N	Tampa	FL	33622	813	847-9002
6	Penny	Penn	2875 Treetop St N	Tampa	FL	33621	813	821-7812

Figure 9-1. Customers table

SalesID ▾	ProductID ▾	CustomerID ▾	DateSold ▾
1	BN200	2	3/3/2008
2	CT200	3	2/5/2008
3	ET100	5	2/6/2007
4	PO200	1	7/8/2008
5	TH100	3	2/8/2008
6	RX300	4	2/10/2007
7	CT200	2	2/22/2008
8	ET100	6	2/20/2008
9	LF300	6	2/18/2008
10	BN200	1	2/17/2008

Figure 9-2. Sales table

Suppose you want to query the Customers table in Figure 9-1
and the Sales table in Figure 9-2 to retrieve customers who
purchased product ID CT200 or product ID PO200. Look at the
following script:

```
SELECT CustomerID, Lastname, Firstname
FROM Customers
WHERE CustomerID
IN
(SELECT CustomerID
FROM Sales
WHERE ProductID = 'CT200' OR ProductID = 'PO200');
```

This script uses the IN predicate to compare the customer IDs
in the Customers table to the customer IDs in the Sales table.
The non-correlated subquery is enclosed in parentheses and is
processed first. It instructs Microsoft Access to retrieve the
customer IDs from the Sales table that have a product ID equal

to CT200 or PO200. Moving upward, the next query uses the customer IDs retrieved from the subquery to find a matching customer ID in the Customers table. The CustomerID, Lastname, and Firstname columns from the Customers table are displayed for each matching customer ID value. The Customers and Sales tables are related through the CustomerID column (WHERE CustomerID IN SELECT CustomerID). Figure 9-3 shows the results from the query.

CustomerID ▾	Lastname ▾	Firstname ▾
1	Allison	Kayla
2	Fields	Devin
3	Spencer	Gene

Figure 9-3. Results (output)

Just as this is a bit more complex using SQL, it is also a bit more complex using the Access query grid. The key is to consider the subquery as a second query that is called by the first. So, the inner query becomes the embedded part of the SQL query and is a separate query called by the main query. In other words, we have the following two queries (Figures 9-4 and 9-5)…

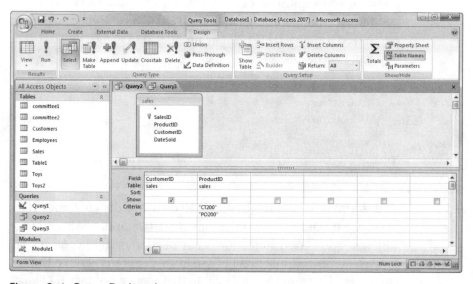

Figure 9-4. Query Design view

...as the embedded query that is called by the main query.

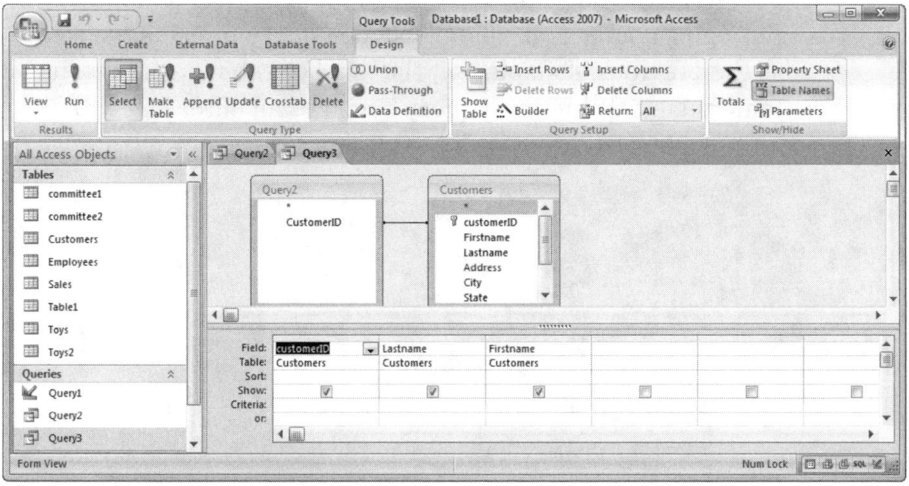

Figure 9-5. Query Design view

➲ **Note:** You can retrieve all the customers who did not purchase product ID CT200 or product ID PO200 by including the NOT operator. Take a look at the following script:

```
SELECT CustomerID, Lastname, Firstname
FROM Customers
WHERE CustomerID
NOT IN
(SELECT CustomerID
FROM Sales
WHERE ProductID = 'CT200' OR ProductID = 'PO200');
```

In the preceding script the NOT operator is used to instruct Microsoft Access to match any condition opposite of the one defined. Look at the results in Figure 9-6.

CustomerID	Lastname	Firstname
4	Madewell	Spencer
5	Collins	Reggie
6	Penn	Penny

Figure 9-6. Results (output)

This operation is a bit more complex using the Access query grid since the only way to perform the NOT IN operation is through an outer join. The embedded query remains the same as the previous example, but the join between it and the Customers table in the main query becomes an outer join with a filter applied to the recordset as follows (Figure 9-7):

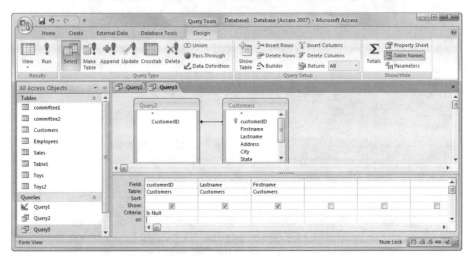

Figure 9-7. Query Design view

The EXISTS Subquery

The EXISTS predicate is used to check for the existence of a value in the subquery. Example 2 shows a correlated subquery linked to another query.

Example 2

Suppose you want to query the Customers table in Figure 9-1 and the Sales table in Figure 9-2 to retrieve product IDs and dates for products purchased by customers who live in Florida. Look at the following script:

```
SELECT ProductID, DateSold
FROM Sales
WHERE EXISTS
(SELECT CustomerID
```

```
FROM Customers
WHERE Customers.CustomerID = Sales.CustomerID
AND State = 'FL');
```

The preceding script uses the EXISTS predicate to check for the existence of a value in the correlated subquery. Remember, correlated queries reference queries outside the subquery and they execute once for each record a referenced query returns. The correlated subquery makes a reference to the above query in the WHERE clause of the subquery (WHERE Customers.CustomerID = Sales.CustomerID). The EXISTS predicate instructs Microsoft Access to retrieve the ProductID and DateSold columns that satisfy the condition in the subquery WHERE clause. Look at the results in Figure 9-8.

ProductID	DateSold
BN200	3/3/2008
CT200	2/5/2008
ET100	2/6/2007
TH100	2/8/2008
CT200	2/22/2008
ET100	2/20/2008
LF300	2/18/2008

Figure 9-8. Results (output)

The following query retrieves product IDs and dates for products not purchased by customers who live in Florida.

```
SELECT ProductID, DateSold
FROM Sales
WHERE NOT EXISTS
(SELECT CustomerID
FROM Customers
WHERE Customers.CustomerID = Sales.CustomerID
AND State = 'FL');
```

Once again, this SQL query can be represented by two Access queries, one of which calls the second.

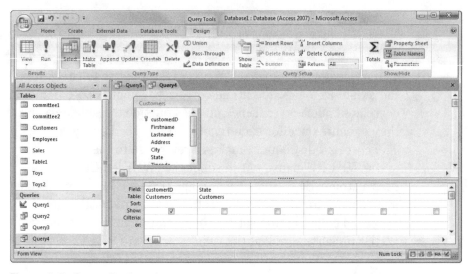

Figure 9-9. Query Design view

The first query filters all customers not in Florida; the second query takes these customers and determines their orders.

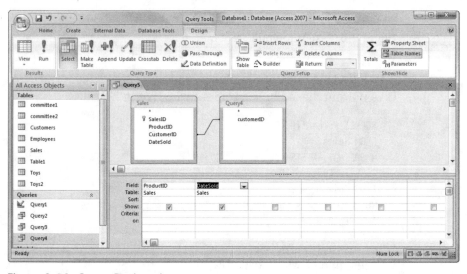

Figure 9-10. Query Design view

○ **Note:** If you import the SQL query directly into an Access query and change to Design view, an interesting thing happens: Access builds a query grid but uses the full subquery in the SELECT statement as one of the fields! It seems as if the Microsoft programmers decided to only do half of the grid conversion work in SQL.

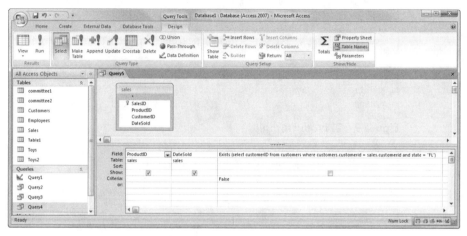

Figure 9-11. Query Design view

The ANY and SOME Subqueries

The ANY and SOME predicates are used to retrieve records from the main query that match any of the records in the subquery. The ANY and SOME predicates can be used interchangeably. They are used much like the IN predicate, yet the IN predicate cannot be used with comparison operators (=, <>, <, >, <=, and >=). Take a look at Example 3, which shows a query using the ANY predicate.

Example 3

ProductID ▾	ProductName ▾	Price ▾	SalePrice ▾	InStock ▾	OnOrder ▾
AN200	Animated Picture	$20.00	$18.00	10	20
BN200	Animated Rainbow	$20.00	$18.00	10	20
CE300	Miniature Train Set	$60.00	$54.00	1	30
CT200	China Puppy	$15.00	$13.50	20	40
ET100	Wooden Clock	$11.00	$9.90	100	0
LF300	Friendly Lion	$14.00	$12.60	0	30
OT100	Dancing Bird	$10.00	$9.00	10	20
PO200	Glass Rabbit	$50.00	$45.00	50	20
RX300	Praying Statue	$25.00	$22.50	3	40
TH100	Crystal Cat	$75.00	$67.50	60	20
VR300	China Doll	$20.00	$13.00	100	0

Figure 9-12. Products table

SalesID ▾	ProductID ▾	CustomerID ▾	DateSold ▾
1	BN200	2	3/3/2008
2	CT200	3	2/5/2008
3	ET100	5	2/6/2007
4	PO200	1	7/8/2008
5	TH100	3	2/8/2008
6	RX300	4	2/10/2007
7	CT200	2	2/22/2008
8	ET100	6	2/20/2008
9	LF300	6	2/18/2008
10	BN200	1	2/17/2008

Figure 9-13. Sales table

Suppose you want to query the Products table in Figure 9-12 and the Sales table in Figure 9-13 to display product information on products that have a product ID greater than any product ID sold on February 6, 2007. Look at the following script:

```
SELECT *
FROM Products
WHERE ProductID > ANY
(SELECT ProductID
FROM Sales
WHERE DateSold = #2/6/07#);
```

This script combines a comparison operator (>) with the ANY predicate to retrieve records from the main query that are greater than any of the records in the non-correlated subquery. The Products and Sales tables are related through the Product ID column (WHERE ProductID > ANY (SELECT ProductID)). Look at the results in Figure 9-14.

ProductID ▾	ProductName ▾	Price ▾	SalePrice ▾	InStock ▾	OnOrder ▾
LF300	Friendly Lion	$14.00	$12.60	0	30
OT100	Dancing Bird	$10.00	$9.00	10	20
PO200	Glass Rabbit	$50.00	$45.00	50	20
RX300	Praying Statue	$25.00	$22.50	3	40
TH100	Crystal Cat	$75.00	$67.50	60	20
VR300	China Doll	$20.00	$13.00	100	0

Figure 9-14. Results (output)

The ALL Subquery

The ALL predicate is used to retrieve records from the main query that match all of the records in the subquery. Take a look at Example 4.

Example 4

ProductID ▾	ProductName ▾	Price ▾	SalePrice ▾	InStock ▾	OnOrder ▾
AN200	Animated Picture	$20.00	$18.00	10	20
BN200	Animated Rainbow	$20.00	$18.00	10	20
CE300	Miniature Train Set	$60.00	$54.00	1	30
CT200	China Puppy	$15.00	$13.50	20	40
ET100	Wooden Clock	$11.00	$9.90	100	0
LF300	Friendly Lion	$14.00	$12.60	0	30
OT100	Dancing Bird	$10.00	$9.00	10	20
PO200	Glass Rabbit	$50.00	$45.00	50	20
RX300	Praying Statue	$25.00	$22.50	3	40
TH100	Crystal Cat	$75.00	$67.50	60	20
VR300	China Doll	$20.00	$13.00	100	0

Figure 9-15. Products table

185

Suppose you want to query the Products table in Figure 9-15 to retrieve product information on products that have less than 20 items in stock. Look at the following script:

```
SELECT ProductID, ProductName, InStock, OnOrder
FROM Products
WHERE InStock < ALL
(SELECT InStock
FROM Products
WHERE InStock = 20);
```

The preceding script combines a comparison operator (<) with the ALL predicate to retrieve records from the main query that are less than all of the records in the non-correlated subquery. Look at the results in Figure 9-16.

ProductID	ProductName	InStock	OnOrder
AN200	Animated Picture	10	20
BN200	Animated Rainbow	10	20
CE300	Miniature Train Set	1	30
LF300	Friendly Lion	0	30
OT100	Dancing Bird	10	20
RX300	Praying Statue	3	40

Figure 9-16. Results (output)

Nested Subqueries

Subqueries can also be nested inside other queries. Subqueries that are nested within other queries are processed first, working outward. Example 5 shows a query nested within another query.

Example 5

CustomerID	Firstname	Lastname	Address	City	State	Zipcode	Areacode	PhoneNumber
1	Kayla	Allison	6725 3rd Ave N	Atlanta	GA	98700	301	897-3412
2	Devin	Fields	1001 30th St S	Tampa	FL	33677	813	828-8754
3	Gene	Spencer	3910 35th Ave S.	St. Pete	FL	33700	727	321-1111
4	Spencer	Madewell	32101 60th Ave E	Honolulu	HI	96822	808	423-4444
5	Reggie	Collins	1526 1st St N	Tampa	FL	33622	813	847-9002
6	Penny	Penn	2875 Treetop St N	Tampa	FL	33621	813	821-7812

Figure 9-17. Customers table

SalesID	ProductID	CustomerID	DateSold
1	BN200	2	3/3/2008
2	CT200	3	2/5/2008
3	ET100	5	2/6/2007
4	PO200	1	7/8/2008
5	TH100	3	2/8/2008
6	RX300	4	2/10/2007
7	CT200	2	2/22/2008
8	ET100	6	2/20/2008
9	LF300	6	2/18/2008
10	BN200	1	2/17/2008

Figure 9-18. Sales table

Suppose you want to query the Customers table in Figure 9-17 and the Sales table in Figure 9-18 to retrieve the customer ID and date of each customer's first purchase. Look at the following script:

```
SELECT CustomerID,
(SELECT MIN (DateSold)
FROM Sales
WHERE Sales.CustomerID = Customers.CustomerID) AS
DateOfFirstPurchase
FROM Customers
ORDER BY CustomerID;
```

This script nests a correlated subquery within another query. The correlated subquery contains an aggregate function (MIN ()) that retrieves the lowest date in the DateSold column. The correlated subquery makes a reference to the outer query in the WHERE clause of the subquery (WHERE Sales.CustomerID = Customers.CustomerID) and is executed once for every customer retrieved from the Customers table. The comma after the CustomerID column (SELECT CustomerID,) in the outer query instructs Microsoft Access to expect an additional alias column (DateOfFirstPurchase). The alias column is specified after the AS keyword in the script. Look at the result in Figure 9-19.

CustomerID ▾	DateOfFirstPurchase ▾
1	2/17/2008
2	2/22/2008
3	2/5/2008
4	2/10/2007
5	2/6/2007
6	2/18/2008

Figure 9-19. Results (output)

This is one case where it is much easier to use the query grid since we can use the built-in MIN () function with an aggregate query to get the same information.

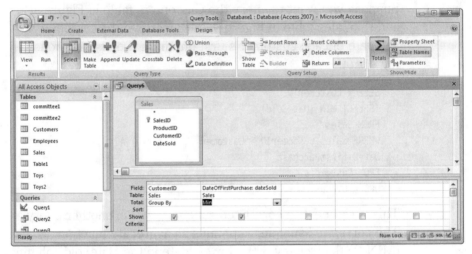

Figure 9-20. Query Design view

One point that we have made repeatedly in this book is that there are often many ways to achieve the same result. This is a perfect example of that point. On the other hand, it also highlights one of the major differences between looking at queries from the SQL perspective and from the Access perspective. In the SQL realm, things are done one at a time in a logical and concise order. Commands can be nested and combined to produce very specific results. It might not be the easiest or most straightforward approach, but there is a great deal of power in SQL. Access provides a simple, direct method to obtain a specific result. It is easy to use and provides considerable power in a simple grid. But its simplicity also is often its major failing. The limitations of the grid to perform some actions and the inability to know what really is happening in the grid without resorting to the SQL view shows how important it is to understand SQL.

Using a Subquery to Find the Second Highest Value

Example 6

ProductID	ProductName	Price	SalePrice	InStock	OnOrder
AN200	Animated Picture	$20.00	$18.00	10	20
BN200	Animated Rainbow	$20.00	$18.00	10	20
CE300	Miniature Train Set	$60.00	$54.00	1	30
CT200	China Puppy	$15.00	$13.50	20	40
ET100	Wooden Clock	$11.00	$9.90	100	0
LF300	Friendly Lion	$14.00	$12.60	0	30
OT100	Dancing Bird	$10.00	$9.00	10	20
PO200	Glass Rabbit	$50.00	$45.00	50	20
RX300	Praying Statue	$25.00	$22.50	3	40
TH100	Crystal Cat	$75.00	$67.50	60	20
VR300	China Doll	$20.00	$13.00	100	0

Figure 9-21. Products table

Suppose you want to retrieve the second highest price in the Products table in Figure 9-21. Look at the following script:

```
SELECT MAX (Price) AS SecondHighestPrice
FROM Products
WHERE Price NOT IN
(SELECT MAX (Price) FROM Products);
```

This script uses the NOT IN predicates to compare the results of the main query to the results of the subquery.

The subquery is processed first. It finds the highest price in the Products table. Moving upward the next query works with the NOT IN keywords to retrieve the highest price not in the result set of the subquery.

Since the subquery can only retrieve one record, the main query is used to retrieve a value NOT IN the result set of the subquery. In turn, the main query retrieves the next highest price in the price column of the Products table. Take a look at the results in Figure 9-22.

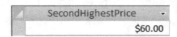

Figure 9-22. Results (output)

Summary

In this chapter, you learned how to retrieve records from multiple tables using correlated and non-correlated subqueries. You also learned how to create nested subqueries and use the IN, EXISTS, ANY, SOME, NOT, and ALL keywords.

Quiz 9

1. True or False. A correlated subquery executes once for each record a referenced query returns.

2. True or False. The NOT operator is used to instruct Microsoft Access to match any condition opposite of the one defined.

3. True or False. The IN predicate is often used with the following comparison operators: =, <>, <, >, <=, and >=.

4. True or False. A subquery linked by the IN predicate can return two columns.

5. True or False. Subqueries nested within other queries are processed first, working outward.

Project 9

Use the Products table in Figure 9-21 to create a subquery that retrieves the ProductID and ProductName columns for products that have 30 or more items on order.

Chapter 10

Creating Views

Introduction

In this chapter, you will learn the definition of a view and how views are used in Microsoft Access's SQL view. You will learn how to create a view, filter a view, update data in tables through a view, and delete a view.

Keywords

CREATE VIEW
DROP VIEW

Definitions

CREATE VIEW — Used to instruct the DBMS to create a new view.

DROP VIEW — Used to delete a view.

A *view* is a saved query that queries one or more tables. Views are commonly used to restrict data from users for security purposes, shorten complex queries, and combine data from multiple tables. A view is also commonly referred to as a *virtual table* because a view can be referenced in much the same way as a table. Keep in mind, though, that views are not tables at all. The main distinction between a view and a table is that a view does not store data. Views store SQL statements but they do not store any data stored in the database. They are used to return and update data stored in actual tables. From an Access standpoint, a view can be considered a query. The only time the two can be considered as different entities is when you are using a true SQL back end. Queries kept and maintained on the SQL side would be views; if calculated on the Access side, queries.

Creating a View

To create a view in Microsoft Access's SQL view, create a query on one or more tables and save the query under a specified name. Look at Example 1, which shows the steps to follow to create and save a view.

Example 1

SerialNum	Brand	Department	OfficeNumber
G9277288282	Dell	HR	122
M6289288289	Dell	Accounting	134
R2871620091	Dell	Information Systems	132
W2121040244	Gateway	CustomerService	22
X8276538101	Dell	HR	311

Figure 10-1. Computers table

Suppose you want to create a view that stores information from the Computers table in Figure 10-1. You want the view to include the following columns from the Computers table: SerialNum, Brand, and OfficeNumber. The following script creates a view:

```
SELECT SerialNum, Brand, OfficeNumber
FROM Computers;
```

This script displays three columns (SerialNum, Brand, and OfficeNumber) from the Computers table. To save the view, follow these steps:

1. Open the File menu and select **Save**.

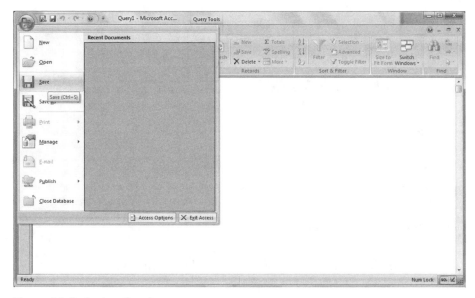

Figure 10-2. Saving the view

2. When the Save As dialog box appears, type **ComputerBrandLoc** and click **OK**.

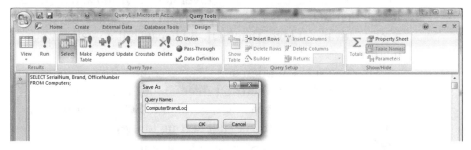

Figure 10-3. Naming the view

3. Next, close SQL view and return to the main Access window. Click **Queries** from the drop-down menu on the left to display your new view named ComputerBrandLoc (see Figure 10-4).

Figure 10-4. Naming the view

You have now successfully created your first view.

Creating a View Using the **CREATE VIEW** Keywords in **SQL-92**

In Chapter 2, we discussed SQL versions SQL-89 and SQL-92. Recall that SQL-92 is the latest version of SQL and functions at a more advanced level than SQL-89 because it contains more features.

Most versions of Microsoft Access come with version SQL-89 installed. In Microsoft Access 2002 and higher you have the option to set the SQL version to SQL-92 for the current database and as the default setting for new databases. (Refer to Chapter 2 for specific instructions.)

In version SQL-92, the CREATE VIEW keywords can be used to create a view. When you use the CREATE VIEW keywords you do not name and save your view using the method described in Example 1. Look at the following script, which implements the CREATE VIEW keywords in the creation of a view in version SQL-92.

```
CREATE VIEW ComputerBrandLoc (SerialNum, Brand, OfficeNumber)
AS SELECT SerialNum, Brand, OfficeNumber
FROM Computers;
```

This script creates a query that is equivalent to the query in Example 1. It implements the CREATE VIEW keywords to create a new view named ComputerBrandLoc. Notice that the name (ComputerBrandLoc) of the view follows the CREATE VIEW keywords. When you create a view using this method, the view name cannot have the same name as an existing table, just as a query cannot duplicate a table name.

After the name of the view, the names of the columns that are used in the SELECT statement are defined. The columns are enclosed in parentheses. Note that the definition of column names after the name of the view is optional. The AS keyword is used to define the SELECT statement.

Create a View that Contains a Complex Join

Example 2

CustomerID ▾	Firstname ▾	Lastname ▾	Address ▾	City ▾	State ▾	Zipcode ▾	Areacode ▾	PhoneNumber ▾
1	Kayla	Allison	6725 3rd Ave N	Atlanta	GA	98700	301	897-3412
2	Devin	Fields	1001 30th St S	Tampa	FL	33677	813	828-8754
3	Gene	Spencer	3910 35th Ave S.	St. Pete	FL	33700	727	321-1111
4	Spencer	Madewell	32101 60th Ave E	Honolulu	HI	96822	808	423-4444
5	Reggie	Collins	1526 1st St N	Tampa	FL	33622	813	847-9002
6	Penny	Penn	2875 Treetop St N	Tampa	FL	33621	813	821-7812

Figure 10-5. Customers table

TransactionID ▾	ProductID ▾	CustomerID ▾	DateSold ▾
1	VR300	2	2/3/2008
2	CT200	2	2/5/2008
3	ET100	5	2/6/2008
4	PO200	1	2/8/2008
5	TH100	3	2/8/2008
6	RX300	4	2/10/2008
7	CE300	2	2/22/2008
8	OT100	6	2/20/2008
9	LF300	6	2/18/2008
10	BN200	1	2/17/2008

Figure 10-6. Transactions table

Suppose you want to create a view (version SQL-92) containing one of the complex joins created in Chapter 8. Take a look at the following query:

```
CREATE VIEW CustomersTotalTransactions AS
SELECT FirstName, LastName, COUNT (Transactions.CustomerID) AS
TotalTransactions
FROM Customers, Transactions
WHERE Transactions.CustomerID = Customers.CustomerID
GROUP BY FirstName, LastName;
```

This script uses the CREATE VIEW keywords to create a view named CustomersTotalTransactions. The AS keyword is used to define a SELECT statement that contains an inner join. The SELECT statement retrieves customer names and the total number of transactions per customer.

Be sure to save your CREATE VIEW query.

Query the CustomersTotalTransactions View

Example 3

Now that the CustomersTotalTransactions view (Example 2) is created, you can query the view much like a table. Look at the following script:

```
SELECT FirstName, LastName, TotalTransactions
FROM CustomersTotalTransactions
WHERE Lastname IN ('Allison', 'Penn', 'Spencer');
```

This script retrieves the first name, last name, and total transactions of the following customers: Allison, Penn, Spencer.

Take a look at Figure 10-7.

FirstName	LastName	TotalTransactions
Gene	Spencer	1
Kayla	Allison	2
Penny	Penn	2

Figure 10-7. Results (output)

⟳ **Note:** So, the big question is, "what is the difference between a view and a query?" The answer is "in Access, very little." In most implementations of SQL, however, there is a big difference. A query is generally not used as a source itself to get data; rather it is the result. So every time you build a query to pull data from another query, just think of it as a view.

Filtering a Record through a View

Once you create a view you can query it like a table. Don't forget that when you query a view, the data is retrieved from the tables specified in the view. The view itself does not contain data. Look at Example 4, which creates a query that queries the ComputerBrandLoc view.

Example 4

Suppose you want to create a query that displays every record from the ComputerBrandLoc view.

Look at the following script:

```
SELECT *
FROM ComputerBrandLoc;
```

The preceding script implements a simple SELECT statement that displays every record from the ComputerBrandLoc view. Figure 10-8 shows the results from this query.

SerialNum	Brand	OfficeNumber
G9277288282	Dell	122
M6289288289	Dell	134
R2871620091	Dell	132
W2121040244	Gateway	22
X8276538101	Dell	311

Figure 10-8. Results (output)

Example 5 shows another query on the ComputerBrandLoc view.

Example 5

Suppose you want to query the ComputerBrandLoc view to return serial numbers, brand names, and an alias column named OfficeLocation. Additionally, you want to add WHERE and ORDER BY clauses to your query. Take a look at the following script:

```
SELECT SerialNum, Brand, OfficeNumber AS OfficeLocation
FROM ComputerBrandLoc
WHERE Brand = 'Dell'
ORDER BY SerialNum;
```

As you can see, the preceding script implements the AS, WHERE, and ORDER BY keywords. The AS keyword specifies an alias (OfficeLocation), the WHERE clause specifies to only retrieve the Dell brand, and the ORDER BY clause sorts the results by the SerialNum column. Look at the results in Figure 10-9.

SerialNum	Brand	OfficeLocation
G9277288282	Dell	122
M6289288289	Dell	134
R2871620091	Dell	132
X8276538101	Dell	311

Figure 10-9. Results (output)

Updating a Record through a View

Views can also be used to update data stored in tables. When you update a view it automatically updates the tables where the data is actually stored. Take a look at Example 6, which demonstrates this.

Example 6

SerialNum	Brand	OfficeNumber
G9277288282	Dell	122
M6289288289	Dell	134
R2871620091	Dell	132
W2121040244	Gateway	22
X8276538101	Dell	311

Figure 10-10. ComputerBrandLoc view

Suppose you want to update data in the Computers table through the ComputerBrandLoc view. You want to update the serial number for the computer located in office 122. The update will change the serial number from G9277288282 to D8828292772. Look at the following script:

```
UPDATE ComputerBrandLoc
SET SerialNum = 'D8828292772'
WHERE SerialNum = 'G9277288282'
AND OfficeNumber = 122;
```

This script implements an UPDATE statement to update the Computers table through the ComputerBrandLoc view. Figure 10-11 shows the updated serial number in the Computers table.

SerialNum	Brand	Department	OfficeNumber
D8828292772	Dell	HR	122
M6289288289	Dell	Accounting	134
R2871620091	Dell	Information Systems	132
W2121040244	Gateway	CustomerService	22
X8276538101	Dell	HR	311

Figure 10-11. Computers table

Deleting a View

To delete a view you must use the DROP VIEW keywords. Take a look at Example 7.

Example 7

Suppose you want to delete the ComputerBrandLoc view. Look at the following script:

```
DROP VIEW ComputerBrandLoc;
```

This script uses the DROP VIEW keywords to delete the view named ComputerBrandLoc.

> **Note:** When you delete a view, the tables in the view are not affected. On the other hand, if you delete a table on which a view is dependent, the view becomes invalid.

Summary

In this chapter you learned how to create and filter views and how to update table data through a view. You also learned how to delete a view and query a view.

Quiz 10

1. True or False. Updating data in views does not affect data stored in tables.

2. Views are commonly referred to as what?

3. True or False. Views are deleted using the DELETE keyword.

4. True or False. Views are created in SQL-92 using the CREATE VIEW keywords.

5. True or False. Deleting a table on which a view is dependent does not affect the view.

Project 10

Use the ComputerBrandLoc view in Figure 10-7 to update the Computers table in Figure 10-1. Update the office number for serial number X8276538101 from 311 to 136.

Chapter 11

Table Management and Indexes

Introduction

In this chapter, you will learn how to modify a column in an existing table, delete a table, and improve data retrieval time using indexes.

Keywords

ADD	DROP INDEX
ALTER COLUMN	IGNORE NULL
ALTER TABLE	PRIMARY
CREATE INDEX	UNIQUE
DEFAULT	WITH
DISALLOW NULL	

Definitions

ALTER TABLE — Used to modify table definitions in an existing table.

DISALLOW NULL — Used to prevent null data from being inserted into a column.

IGNORE NULL — Used to cause null data in a table to be ignored for an index.

INDEX — Sorts and saves the values of a column in a different location on the computer with a pointer to the presorted records.

PRIMARY — Used to designate a column as a primary key.

UNIQUE — Used to ensure that only unique, non-repeating values are inserted in an indexed column.

After a table is created it is often necessary to modify the columns defined in it. The ALTER TABLE statement is used to modify table definitions in an existing table. The ALTER TABLE statement can be used to add a column to a table, change a column, or remove a column from a table. It can also be used to modify (add/remove) constraints and to set a default value for a column. In Chapter 3, you learned how to use the ALTER TABLE statement to modify constraints in existing tables.

➲ **Note:** You can only modify one column at a time. It is not recommended that you modify a table once it contains data.

Adding a Column to an Existing Table

To add a column to an existing table use the ADD keyword in the ALTER TABLE statement and specify a table name, column name, data type, and a field size if necessary.

Look at the following syntax for adding a column to an existing table:

```
ALTER TABLE Tablename
ADD ColumnName Datatype (Field size);
```

➲ **Note:** In version SQL-92 or higher you can use the following alternate syntax:

```
ALTER TABLE Tablename
ADD COLUMN ColumnName Datatype (Field size);
```

This syntax implements the additional COLUMN keyword in the ALTER TABLE statement.

Take a look at Example 1, which adds an additional column to an existing table.

Example 1

ColumnOne	ColumnTwo	ColumnThree
5	2	98
1	8	11
10	1	22
90	6	12
40	27	6
90	7	4
70	43	3
70	61	144

Figure 11-1. Numbers table

Suppose you want to add a column named ColumnFour to the existing Numbers table in Figure 11-1. Look at the following script:

```
ALTER TABLE Numbers
ADD ColumnFour INTEGER;
```

This script uses the ALTER TABLE keywords to instruct Microsoft Access to modify the Numbers table. The ADD keyword is used to add a new column named ColumnFour with an INTEGER data type. Look at the results in Figure 11-2.

ColumnOne	ColumnTwo	ColumnThree	ColumnFour
5	2	98	
1	8	11	
10	1	22	
90	6	12	
40	27	6	
90	7	4	
70	43	3	
70	61	144	

Figure 11-2. Results (output)

Changing a Column

The ALTER TABLE statement can also be used to change a column's name, data type, or field size. Keep in mind that you cannot change the name of a column unless you first remove the column and then add the new column. You'll learn how to remove (delete) a column later in this chapter. Additionally, it is important to note that changes to columns that contain data may cause a loss of data. Use caution when modifying data types and field sizes in columns that contain data.

To change a column's data type or field size, use the ALTER COLUMN keywords in the ALTER TABLE statement and specify a table name, column name, data type, and a field size if necessary. Look at the following syntax for changing a column's data type and field size:

```
ALTER TABLE Tablename
ALTER COLUMN ColumnName Datatype (Field size);
```

Now take a look at Example 2, which modifies the data type of an existing table.

Example 2

Suppose you want to change the data type for the newly created column (ColumnFour) in the Numbers table in Example 1. You want to change the data type from an INTEGER data type to a CHAR data type and you want to add a field size of 3. Look at the following script:

```
ALTER TABLE Numbers
ALTER COLUMN ColumnFour CHAR (3);
```

This script uses the ALTER TABLE statement to modify the Numbers table. The ALTER COLUMN keywords are used to specify a new data type (CHAR) and field size (3) for the ColumnFour column.

To view the results from the ALTER TABLE statement in Microsoft Access 2007, select **Tables** from the View drop-down window on the left. Right-click on the **Numbers** table and select **Design View**.

Look under the Field Name column to view a column and under the Datatype column to view a data type for a column. The General tab near the bottom of the screen shows information pertaining to an individual column.

➲ **Note:** The CHAR data type is a TEXT data type.

Setting a Default Value for a Column

SQL-92 enables you to additionally use the ALTER TABLE statement to set a default value for a column each time a new record is entered in a table and no value is specified for that column.

To set a default value for a column, use the DEFAULT keyword in the ALTER TABLE statement. Additionally, you can specify a table name, column name, data type, field size if necessary, and a value to default to. Look at the following syntax for setting a default value:

```
ALTER TABLE Tablename
ALTER COLUMN ColumnName Datatype (Field size) DEFAULT Defaultvalue
```

Refer to Example 3 to see an example of setting a default value.

Example 3

Suppose you want to set a default value of 10 for the Column-Four column in the Numbers table each time a new record is entered and no value is specified for the ColumnFour column. Look at the following script:

```
ALTER TABLE Numbers
ALTER COLUMN ColumnFour CHAR (3) DEFAULT 10
```

The preceding script uses the DEFAULT keyword to set the ColumnFour column in the Numbers table to 10 each time a new record is entered and no value is specified for the ColumnFour column. Look at the results in Figure 11-3. After a new record was entered into the Numbers table with no value for the fourth column, the ColumnFour column defaulted to 10. Note that this does not affect existing columns, just new ones.

ColumnOne ▾	ColumnTwo ▾	ColumnThree ▾	ColumnFour ▾
5	2	98	
1	8	11	
10	1	22	
90	6	12	
40	27	6	
90	7	4	
70	43	3	
70	61	144	
3	8	8	10

Figure 11-3. Results (output)

Removing a Column from a Table

To remove a column from a table, use the DROP keyword in the ALTER TABLE statement and specify a table name and column name. Look at the following syntax for removing a column:

```
ALTER TABLE Tablename
DROP ColumnName;
```

Look at Example 4, which removes a column from an existing table.

Example 4

Suppose you want to remove the column created in Example 1 (ColumnFour). Look at the following script:

```
ALTER TABLE Numbers
DROP ColumnFour;
```

The preceding script removes the ColumnFour column from the Numbers table. Look at the results in Figure 11-4.

ColumnOne ▾	ColumnTwo ▾	ColumnThree ▾
5	2	98
1	8	11
10	1	22
90	6	12
40	27	6
90	7	4
70	43	3
70	61	144
3	8	8

Figure 11-4. Results (output)

Removing a Table

To remove an entire table, you do not use the ALTER TABLE keywords but rather DROP TABLE. Look at the following syntax for removing a table:

```
DROP TABLE Tablename;
```

In the syntax, the DROP TABLE keywords are used with the name of the table to delete.

Improving Data Retrieval Time Using Indexes

Indexes enable you to reduce your data retrieval time during the execution of a query by presorting and ordering the data in a field using external pointers to optimally group the records. Indexes help to retrieve records much faster because the DBMS must only search through the presorted grouped records rather than search through every record in a table until a match is found. For example, when you pick up a dictionary, you narrow your selection by looking through pages that are alphabetized and have tabs separating the letters as opposed to flipping through every page for unalphabetized entries. Be aware that although indexes reduce your data retrieval time, they can reduce speed on updates on columns that are indexed because the index may possibly have to be rebuilt. Additionally, if you have too many indexes, retrieval time can increase due to the operations associated with maintaining an index. Indexed data can use up a lot of memory, so make sure you decide which columns would benefit from an index and which would not. For example, columns that contain non-unique data will not benefit as much as columns that contain unique data.

In most databases indexes are stored as separate files or tables. Access is a bit unique since the indexes are stored along with the table in a single file.

○ **Note:** The primary key column of a table is a type of index because it is always physically sorted in ascending order.

Take a look at the following syntax for creating an index:

```
CREATE INDEX Indexname
ON Tablename (ColumnName [ASC | DESC]);
```

As you can see in the above syntax, to create an index you must use the CREATE INDEX keywords. Following these keywords you must specify a unique name for your index. Additionally, you must use the ON keyword to specify the table name, column name, and sort order (ascending or descending).

○ **Note:** If you do not specify a sort order in your index, it will automatically default to ascending order.

Index Options

There are four options available to you when creating an index. These options are available in an additional clause called the WITH clause: UNIQUE, PRIMARY, DISALLOW NULL, and IGNORE NULL. The WITH clause is used to enforce validation rules. Table 11-1 explains the four options used in the WITH clause.

Table 11-1. WITH clause options

Options	Description
UNIQUE	Used to ensure that only unique, non-repeating values are inserted in an indexed column.
PRIMARY	Used to designate a column as a primary key.
DISALLOW NULL	Used to prevent null data from being inserted into a column.
IGNORE NULL	Used to cause null data in a table to be ignored for an index. (Records with a null value in the declared field will not be counted in the index.)

Take a look at Example 5, which shows how to create an index.

Creating an Index

Example 5

ProductID ▾	ProductName ▾	Price ▾	SalePrice ▾	InStock ▾	OnOrder ▾
AN200	Animated Picture	$20.00	$18.00	10	20
BN200	Animated Rainbow	$20.00	$18.00	10	20
CE300	Miniature Train Set	$60.00	$54.00	1	30
CT200	China Puppy	$15.00	$13.50	20	40
ET100	Wooden Clock	$11.00	$9.90	100	0
LF300	Friendly Lion	$14.00	$12.60	0	30
OT100	Dancing Bird	$10.00	$9.00	10	20
PO200	Glass Rabbit	$50.00	$45.00	50	20
RX300	Praying Statue	$25.00	$22.50	3	40
TH100	Crystal Cat	$75.00	$67.50	60	20
VR300	China Doll	$20.00	$13.00	100	0

Figure 11-5. Products table

Suppose you want to create a unique index that will not allow nulls in the ProductName column in the Products table in Figure 11-5. Look at the following script:

```
CREATE UNIQUE INDEX ProductNameIdx
ON Products (ProductName)
WITH DISALLOW NULL;
```

This script creates an index named ProductNameIdx. The index is defined on the ProductName column in the Products table. The UNIQUE keyword is used to ensure that only unique, non-repeating values are inserted into the Product-Name column, while the DISALLOW NULL keywords are used to prevent null data from being inserted into the ProductName column. The DISALLOW NULL keywords are similar to the NOT NULL keywords used in the CREATE TABLE statement.

Indexing in Descending Order

Indexes default to ascending order but you can also sort a column in descending order. To sort by descending order, you simply need to add the DESC keyword to your SQL script. Take a look at Example 6.

Example 6

Suppose you want to create an index that sorts the ProductName column in descending order. Take a look at the following script:

```
CREATE UNIQUE INDEX ProductNameIdx2
ON Products (ProductName DESC)
WITH DISALLOW NULL;
```

This script creates an index named ProductNameIdx2. The index is defined on the ProductName column in the Products table. The DESC keyword is defined immediately following the ProductName column. The DESC keyword ensures that the data in the ProductName column is stored in descending order.

The UNIQUE keyword is used to ensure there are no repeating values. The DISALLOW NULL keywords are used to prevent null values in the ProductName column.

Viewing and Editing Indexes

To view or edit an index for a particular table, open a table in Design view. To open a table in Design view, choose **Tables** from the View drop-down in Access 2007. Right-click on the name of the table you want to open and choose **Design View**. Finally, click the **Index** button to view all the indexes for a table. Take a look at Figure 11-6.

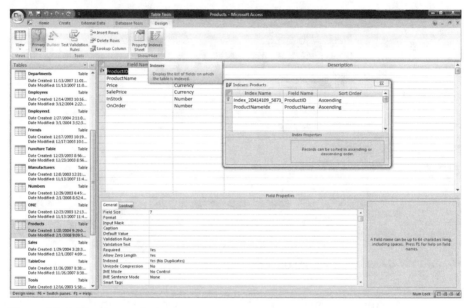

Figure 11-6. Viewing an index

The Indexes dialog box shows the name of the index, the field name the index is associated with, and the sort order of the index. Additionally, when you click on the name of an index, the index properties are displayed. You can edit an index by modifying values in the dialog box.

You can also create a new index based on multiple fields in a table. This is a common process when you want a unique index but only the values in multiple fields might constitute a unique value.

Alternately, you can create an index while in Design view for a table. When a field is selected, go to the field properties and select the Indexed property. You can select No, the field is not indexed; Yes (Duplicates OK), where the index is not a unique value; or Yes (No Duplicates), where the values in the indexed field have to be unique.

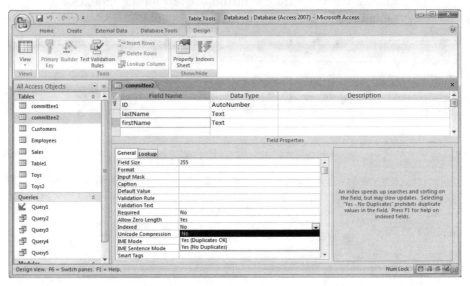

Figure 11-7. Manually creating an index

If you try to make a field that already has data an indexed field with no duplicates and the data does not consist of unique values, the system will not let you save the new index.

Deleting an Index

To delete an index from a table, you must use the DROP INDEX keywords. Look at the following syntax for deleting an index:

```
DROP INDEX Indexname
ON Tablename;
```

Example 7

To delete the index named ProductNameIdx created in Example 5, type the following script:

```
DROP INDEX ProductNameIdx
ON Products;
```

This script deletes the index named ProductNameIdx from the Products table.

➲ **Note:** When you delete a table, all indexes pertaining to that table are deleted as well.

Summary

In this chapter, you learned how to modify columns in an existing table, delete a table, and improve data retrieval time by the use of indexes.

Quiz 11

1. True or False. The DISALLOW NULL option is used in the WITH clause.

2. Which option is used in the WITH clause to cause null data in a table to be ignored for an index?

3. True or False. The DELETE TABLE keywords are used to delete or remove an index.

4. True or False. The ALTER TABLE keywords are used to modify columns in an existing table.

5. What keywords are used in the ALTER TABLE statement to change a column's data type or field size?

Project 11

1. Add a column named NewColumn to the Numbers table in Figure 11-1. Additionally, add a CHAR data type with a field size of 3.

2. Create a unique index named NewColumnIdx for the NewColumn column you created in the Numbers table.

Chapter 12

Temporary Tables vs. Views

Introduction

In this chapter, you will learn about temporary tables and how they are created, accessed, queried, indexed, and deleted. You will also learn the differences between temporary tables and views.

Definitions

Temporary table — A table that encompasses the result of a saved SELECT statement.

View — A saved query that queries one or more tables.

As discussed earlier in this book, a *view* is a saved query that queries one or more tables. They are commonly used to restrict data from users for security purposes, shorten complex queries, and combine data from multiple tables. Views are very useful in Microsoft Access since they enable you to query data in the database in much the same way as you would a table.

Temporary tables are created for many of the same reasons you would create views. If you do not necessarily need to access up-to-date information stored in the database, temporary tables can be a great alternative to views.

In many DBMSs a temporary table is referred to as a table that exists temporarily in a database and is automatically dropped once you log out of the database. However, in

Microsoft Access this is not the case since a temporary table in Access is not deleted unless you manually delete it.

In Microsoft Access a *temporary table* is a table that encompasses the result of a saved SELECT statement.

Even though temporary tables can be a nice alternative to views, keep in mind that there are some major differences between the two. First, a view is not a table and does not store data, whereas a temporary table is a table and actually contains data. Second, when you change data in a view, the data stored in the underlying tables is also changed. However, when you change data in a temporary table, it only affects the data stored in the temporary table and does not affect data stored in the actual tables. Let's take another look at the view we created earlier in the book.

Creating a View

The following script creates a view that stores information from the Computers table in Figure 12-1. The view includes the following columns from the Computers table: SerialNum, Brand, and OfficeNumber.

Example 1

SerialNum	Brand	Department	OfficeNumber
G9277288282	Dell	HR	122
M6289288289	Dell	Accounting	134
R2871620091	Dell	Information Systems	132
W2121040244	Gateway	CustomerService	22
X8276538101	Dell	HR	311

Figure 12-1. Computers table

The following script creates a view:

```
SELECT SerialNum, Brand, OfficeNumber
FROM Computers;
```

To save the view, follow these steps:

1. Click the **Microsoft Office** button and select **Save** from the drop-down menu.

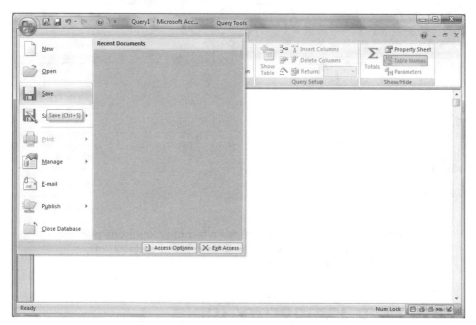

Figure 12-2. Saving the view

2. When the Save As dialog box appears, type **ComputerBrandLoc** and click **OK**.

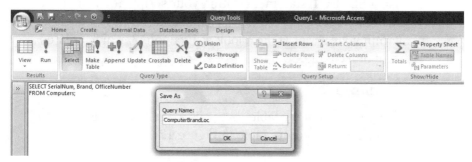

Figure 12-3. Naming the view

3. Next, click **Queries** from the View drop-down in Access 2007 to view your new view named ComputerBrandLoc.

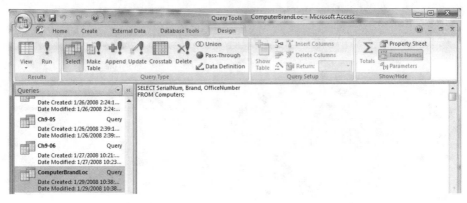

Figure 12-4. Viewing the view

⟶ **Note:** Refer to Chapter 10 for alternative methods of creating views in different versions (SQL-89 and SQL-92) of Microsoft Access.

Creating a Temporary Table

Creating temporary tables in Access is slightly different from creating views in Access. Since temporary tables encompass the result of a saved SELECT statement, you must create or use a SELECT statement within your script. You also must create a name for your temporary table and use the INTO keyword within your script. Take a look at Example 2, which creates a temporary table.

Example 2

Create a temporary table that uses a SELECT statement to query the Computers table in Figure 12-1.

After you type and execute the following script, click Yes to paste the rows into the new table called Temp1.

```
SELECT SerialNum, Brand, OfficeNumber INTO Temp1
FROM Computers;
```

This script displays three columns (SerialNum, Brand, OfficeNumber) from the Computers table. Typing INTO Temp1 after the columns specified in the SELECT statement causes Microsoft Access to create a temporary table called Temp1.

To view the temporary table, type the following script:

```
SELECT *
FROM Temp1;
```

Take a look at the results in Figure 12-5.

SerialNum	▾	Brand	▾	OfficeNumber	▾
G9277288282		Dell		122	
M6289288289		Dell		134	
R2871620091		Dell		132	
W2121040244		Gateway		22	
X8276538101		Dell		311	

Figure 12-5. Results (output)

Accessing the Temporary Table

Temporary tables are located in the Tables group in the Navigation pane on the left side of the Microsoft Access 2007 window. To access the Temp1 table, choose **Tables** from the View drop-down and then double-click the **Temp1** table in the list of tables.

Take a look at Figure 12-6.

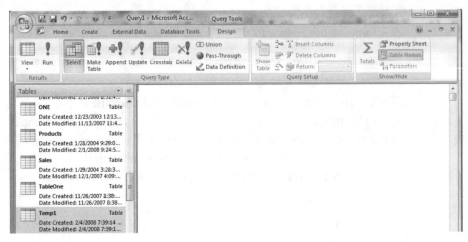

Figure 12-6. Locating the Temp1 table

Querying a Temporary Table

Once you create a temporary table you can query it just like you would a normal table. The following example creates a query that queries the Temp1 table.

Example 3

Suppose you want to create a query that displays information on Dell computers in the Temp1 table. Look at the following script:

```
SELECT *
FROM Temp1
WHERE Brand = 'Dell'
ORDER BY SerialNum;
```

This script implements a simple SELECT statement that retrieves every column from the Temp1 table where the Brand is Dell. The ORDER BY clause sorts the output by the SerialNum column. Figure 12-7 shows the results from the query.

SerialNum	Brand	OfficeNumber
G9277288282	Dell	122
M6289288289	Dell	134
R2871620091	Dell	132
X8276538101	Dell	311

Figure 12-7. Results (output)

Indexing a Temporary Table

Temporary tables can be indexed just like you would an ordi-nary table. Remember, indexes help to retrieve records much faster because the DBMS must only search through presorted records rather than through every record in a table until a match is found. An index sorts and saves the values of a column in a different location on the computer with a pointer to the presorted records. Refer to Chapter 11 for more on indexes. Example 4 creates an index on the Temp1 table.

Example 4

Suppose you want to create a unique index that will not allow nulls in the SerialNum column in the Temp1 temporary table. Look at the following script:

```
CREATE UNIQUE INDEX SerialNumIdx
ON Temp1 (SerialNum)
WITH DISALLOW NULL;
```

This script creates an index named SerialNumIdx. The index is defined on the SerialNum column in the Temp1 temporary table. The UNIQUE keyword is used to ensure that only unique, non-repeating values are inserted into the SerialNum column. The DISALLOW NULL keywords are used to prevent null data from being inserted into the SerialNum column.

Updating a Temporary Table

As we stated earlier, a temporary table can be updated without affecting the data stored in the main tables of the database. When you update a view it automatically updates the tables where the data is actually stored. Take a look at Example 5.

Example 5

SerialNum	Brand	OfficeNumber
G9277288282	Dell	122
M6289288289	Dell	134
R2871620091	Dell	132
W2121040244	Gateway	22
X8276538101	Dell	311

Figure 12-8. Temp1 table

Suppose you want to update the office number from 22 to 123 for serial number W2121040244 in the Temp1 temporary table in Figure 12-8. Look at the following script:

```
UPDATE Temp1
SET OfficeNumber = 123
WHERE OfficeNumber = 22
AND SerialNum = 'W2121040244';
```

This script implements an UPDATE statement that updates the Temp1 table. Figure 12-9 shows the updated office number in the Temp1 temporary table.

SerialNum	Brand	OfficeNumber
G9277288282	Dell	122
M6289288289	Dell	134
R2871620091	Dell	132
W2121040244	Gateway	123
X8276538101	Dell	311

Figure 12-9. Temp1 table

Copying Records from One Temporary Table to a New Temporary Table Simultaneously

Example 6

Suppose you want to create a new temporary table and copy records from another temporary table into your new table at the same time. Look at the following script:

```
SELECT *
INTO Temp2
FROM Temp1;
```

This script creates a new temporary table named Temp2 and copies the records from the Temp1 table into the new Temp2 table. It uses the SELECT and FROM keywords to specify the table name (Temp1) and column names (* specifies all columns) from which to retrieve the records to insert. The INTO keyword is used to create a table named Temp2 and to insert the records retrieved from the table (Temp1) specified after the FROM keyword. Figure 12-10 shows the populated Temp2 table.

SerialNum	Brand	OfficeNumber
G9277288282	Dell	122
M6289288289	Dell	134
R2871620091	Dell	132
W2121040244	Gateway	123
X8276538101	Dell	311

Figure 12-10. Temp2 table

223

Deleting a Temporary Table

Temporary tables are deleted just like regular tables in a database. Unlike temporary tables in most other DBMSs, they are not automatically dropped when you close down or log out of the database. Example 7 shows an example of how to delete a temporary table.

Example 7

Suppose you want to delete the Temp1 temporary table. Look at the following script:

```
DROP TABLE Temp1;
```

This script uses the DROP TABLE keywords to delete the temporary table named Temp1.

Why Do We Need Temporary Tables?

After reading this chapter, you may still wonder "Why do I need temporary tables?" There are two major reasons: convenience and necessity. The first reason should be obvious. When you have a complex query that takes a long time to run and returns a small set of records as a result, you might want to keep this resulting set available, especially if you refer to it in several subsequent steps of your process. Remember, every time a query is run, you have to rebuild the result. If it takes 10 minutes to run a particular query, it means that each time that query is used, you spend another 10 minutes getting the answer. When you are only talking about a few records, it becomes worthwhile to spend the second necessary to save the query as a temporary table, then reference the temporary table.

The other time you need temporary tables is when you want to update records in a dataset that would not otherwise be updateable. An example of this is when you want to remove duplicate records from a table. Access is smart enough to know that the group by query produces a result set that is not unique. In other words, more than one record could have been used to produce a resulting record. So, since the records can refer to more than one record, the recordset is uneditable.

Examine the following records.

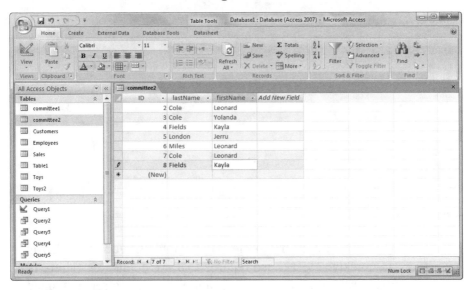

Figure 12-11

In this simple case, you have some names that are duplicated. The easy way to identify the duplicates is by creating a query (Figure 12-12) that groups the records by first and last name, determines which names have more than one record, and lists the ID of those records that are duplicates.

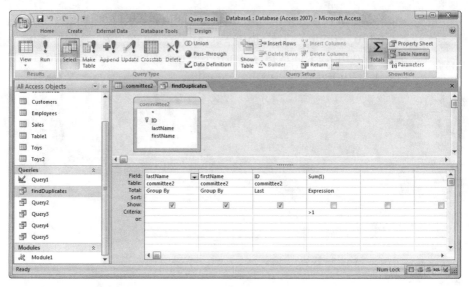

Figure 12-12

By joining this query to the original table (Figure 12-13), you can quickly select those records that are duplicates. There is a small problem, however; you cannot delete the records since the underlying query contains non-unique records.

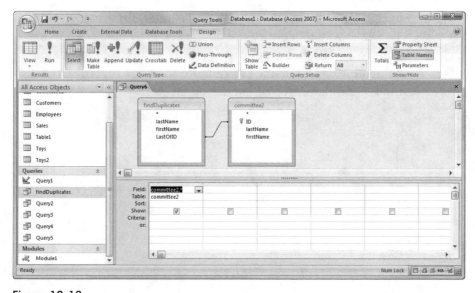

Figure 12-13

A temporary table lets you get around the problem since Access does not care where it got its values from, just that it follows all the rules and therefore is updateable. So, to go back to our example, we turn the findDuplicates query into a make-table query (Figure 12-14) and have it build a temporary table that duplicates the results from the original query. We then can build our join and the records can then be deleted.

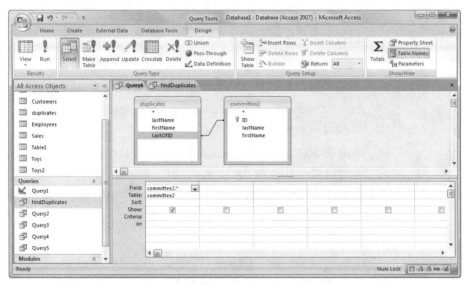

Figure 12-14

Summary

In this chapter, you learned the difference between a view and a temporary table. You also learned how to create, access, query, update, create an index for, and delete a temporary table.

Quiz 12

1. True or False. Updating data in temporary tables does not affect data stored in tables.

2. True or False. Temporary tables are automatically dropped when you log off or close Access.

3. True or False. Temporary tables are deleted using the DELETE keyword.

4. True or False. You must use the INTO keyword to create a temporary table in Access.

5. True or False. Temporary tables store the most current, up-to-date data.

Project 12

Create a temporary table named Temp2 that selects all the information from a table named Flowers with the following column names: FlowerID, Type, Color, Size.

Chapter 13

Parameter Queries

Introduction

In this chapter you will learn how to create queries that prompt the user for information. You will learn how to create a parameter query, customize a dialog box, create multiple prompts to the user, use the LIKE keyword to prompt the user, prompt the user for dates, and create a button on a form that will prompt a user.

Definitions

Parameter query — A query that enables the user to set the criteria for selecting records at run time by filling in a dialog box.

Parameter Queries

Up to this point you have learned how to create queries that display results based on the design of the query. You can also create queries that display results that are based on criteria set by a user. This type of query prompts the user for information when the query is executed. It is referred to as a *parameter query*. Parameter queries enable the user to set the criteria for selecting records at run time by filling in a dialog box. They are very useful because they enable the user to change the outcome of a query. Parameter queries can be created in either Design view or SQL view. In this chapter we will use SQL view to create simple queries and then use Design view to create a criterion that will prompt the user for information. You will also learn how to create queries to prompt the user in SQL view.

Creating a Simple Query

Let's begin by creating a simple query in SQL view. Take a look at Example 1.

Example 1

ToolID ▾	ToolName ▾	Manufacturer ▾	Type ▾	Location ▾	Price ▾
1	Jigsaw	Dewalt	Power Tool	A	$60.00
2	Hand Drill	Dewalt	Power Tool	A	$30.00
3	Router	Dewalt	Power Tool	A	$40.00
4	Nail Gun	Bosch	Power Tool	A	$60.00
5	Sandpaper	Bosch	Sanding	B	$4.00
6	Scrapers	Bosch	Sanding	B	$8.00
7	Hammer	Makita	Hand Tool	C	$14.00
8	Pliers	Porter	Hand Tool	C	$9.00
9	Screwdriver	Makita	Hand Tool	C	$4.00
10	Tool Belt	Porter	Accessories	D	$15.00
11	Battery Charger	Dewalt	Accessories	D	$20.00

Figure 13-1. Tools table

Use the Tools table in Figure 13-1 to retrieve tools that are manufactured by Porter. Look at the following script:

```
SELECT *
FROM Tools
WHERE Manufacturer = 'Porter';
```

This script uses a simple SELECT statement to retrieve every column (SELECT *) from the Tools table where the Manufacturer is Porter. Take a look at the results in Figure 13-2.

ToolID ▾	ToolName ▾	Manufacturer ▾	Type ▾	Location ▾	Price ▾
8	Pliers	Porter	Hand Tool	C	$9.00
10	Tool Belt	Porter	Accessories	D	$15.00

Figure 13-2. Results (output)

As you can see, the result shows all of the tools that were manufactured by Porter.

Creating a Parameter Query

The query in Example 1 is used to retrieve tools that are manufactured by Porter. Say you wanted to use the query to retrieve tools made by a manufacturer other than Porter. In fact, say you wanted to prompt the user to change the manufacturer name on the fly. Take a look at Example 2.

Example 2

In this example we will switch from SQL view to Design view to customize the query from Example 1 to prompt the user to enter a manufacturer name.

Let's begin by switching from SQL view to Design view. To do this, click the **View** button and select **Design View**.

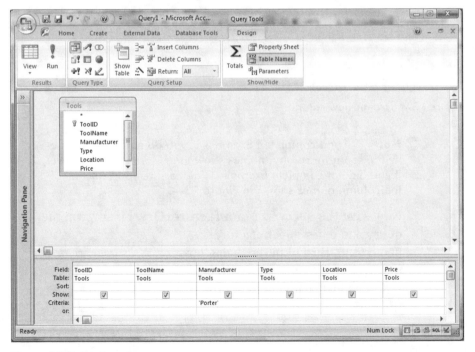

Figure 13-3. Design view

In Figure 13-3, notice the criteria in the Manufacturer field. As you can see, the criteria is specified as 'Porter'. To prompt the user to enter a manufacturer name you must change the criteria from 'Porter' to [x], as shown in Figure 13-4.

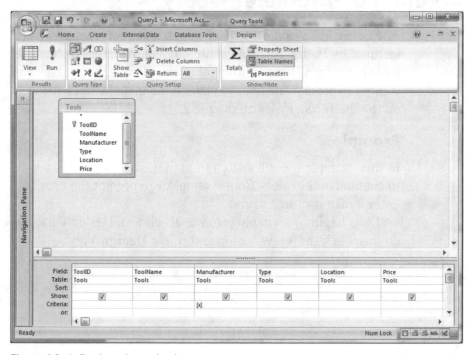

Figure 13-4. Design view criteria

➲ **Note:** If you completed Example 1, you do not have to specify the separate column names shown in Figure 13-4. However, if you did not complete Example 1, make sure you select all of the column names shown in Figure 13-4.

Now save the query as **ManufacturerQry**. Finally, run the query and enter a manufacturer name (e.g., Bosch) in the dialog box that appears (Figure 13-5), then click **OK**. It is just that simple to prompt the user.

Figure 13-5. Enter Parameter Value dialog box

The above example works because of the variable you typed between the brackets ([ ]). Make sure that you always include the brackets.

When Microsoft Access detects a variable during the execution of a query, it tries to bind the variable to a value. If Access cannot find a value (i.e., the name of a column or a calculated field in the query, the value on an open form) to bind the variable to, it asks the user for the value of the parameter using the Enter Parameter Value dialog box.

The dialog box contains an "x" because we typed an "x" between the brackets. You can edit the "x" to whatever you want. Customizing your prompts will make them more user-friendly. Take a look at Example 3.

Customizing Your Dialog Box

Example 3

In this example you will customize the Enter Parameter Value dialog box that the user sees when prompted.

In Example 2, the user saw a very simple and somewhat cryptic dialog box. Generally you will want to make things a bit easier for the user by providing prompts that are meaningful.

So, let's change the "x" in the dialog box to "Type the name of a Manufacturer." To accomplish this, select Design view and change the criteria from [x] to **[Type the name of a Manufacturer]**. Now run the query. Your dialog box should now look like Figure 13-6.

Figure 13-6. Updated dialog box

Type **Porter** in the updated dialog box and click **OK**. Look at the results in Figure 13-7.

ToolID ▾	ToolName ▾	Manufacturer ▾	Type ▾	Location ▾	Price ▾
8	Pliers	Porter	Hand Tool	C	$9.00
10	Tool Belt	Porter	Accessories	D	$15.00

Figure 13-7. Results (output)

The result shows all of the records for which the manufacturer is Porter.

You can type whatever you want in place of the "x" as long as you enclose your variables in brackets. Unfortunately, you need to make the prompt meaningful enough to be useful and short enough that the variable name does not become too unwieldy. More on this later.

Creating Multiple Prompts

In some cases you may need to prompt the user for information more than once. For example, you may want the user to be able to retrieve a range of values or to obtain multiple criteria. In Example 4 we will prompt the user for two values (a lower and an upper value).

Example 4

ToolID ▾	ToolName ▾	Manufacturer ▾	Type ▾	Location ▾	Price ▾
1	Jigsaw	Dewalt	Power Tool	A	$60.00
2	Hand Drill	Dewalt	Power Tool	A	$30.00
3	Router	Dewalt	Power Tool	A	$40.00
4	Nail Gun	Bosch	Power Tool	A	$60.00
5	Sandpaper	Bosch	Sanding	B	$4.00
6	Scrapers	Bosch	Sanding	B	$8.00
7	Hammer	Makita	Hand Tool	C	$14.00
8	Pliers	Porter	Hand Tool	C	$9.00
9	Screwdriver	Makita	Hand Tool	C	$4.00
10	Tool Belt	Porter	Accessories	D	$15.00
11	Battery Charger	Dewalt	Accessories	D	$20.00

Figure 13-8. Tools table

Say you want to use the Tools table in Figure 13-8 to prompt the user to retrieve tool IDs between two specified values.

To prompt the user to enter a lower and an upper value, complete the following steps:

1. In Design view, select the **ToolID**, **ToolName**, **Manufacturer**, **Type**, **Location**, and **Price** fields.

2. Select the **Tools** table.

3. Type the following in the Criteria cell of the **ToolID** column:

    ```
    >[Type the first number:] AND <[Type the second number:]
    ```

    Take a look at Figure 13-9.

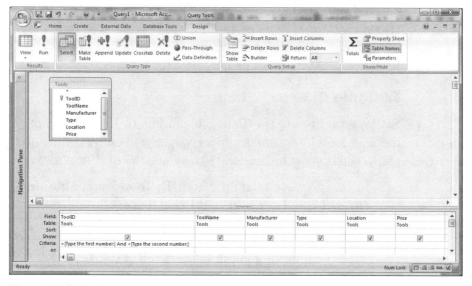

Figure 13-9. Design view

⊃ **Note:** In Design view, if you do not see specific column names in the Design view grid, double-click the column name in the appropriate table located above the Design view grid.

4. Run the query and you will be prompted twice. In the first dialog box, enter the number **1** (lower limit) and click **OK**. In the second dialog box, enter the number **4** (upper limit) and click **OK**. Look at the results in Figure 13-10.

ToolID	▾	ToolName	▾	Manufacturer	▾	Type	▾	Location	▾	Price	▾
2		Hand Drill		Dewalt		Power Tool		A		$30.00	
3		Router		Dewalt		Power Tool		A		$40.00	

Figure 13-10. Results (output)

The results from the preceding query only include the values (2, 3) between the lower and upper values specified by the user. It does not include records that match the values entered into the dialog box. To additionally include the values the user entered you must use the BETWEEN keyword or replace the criteria with >=[Type the first number:] AND <=[Type the second number:]. Refer to Example 5 for more on this.

Make sure you save the query for future use.

Example 5

Say you want to use the Tools table in Figure 13-8 to prompt the user for a lower and an upper value, yet you want the output to additionally include the two values the user specifies.

1. In Design view, select the **ToolID**, **ToolName**, **Manufacturer**, **Type**, **Location**, and **Price** fields.

2. Select the **Tools** table.

3. Type the following in the Criteria cell of the **ToolID** column:

```
BETWEEN [Type the first number:] AND [Type the second number:]
```

4. Run the query. In the first dialog box enter the number **1** (lower limit) and click **OK**. In the second dialog box enter the number **4** (upper limit) and click **OK**. Look at the results in Figure 13-11.

ToolID ▾	ToolName ▾	Manufacturer ▾	Type ▾	Location ▾	Price ▾
1	Jigsaw	Dewalt	Power Tool	A	$60.00
2	Hand Drill	Dewalt	Power Tool	A	$30.00
3	Router	Dewalt	Power Tool	A	$40.00
4	Nail Gun	Bosch	Power Tool	A	$60.00

Figure 13-11. Results (output)

The results include the values between the lower and upper values as well as the values entered by the user.

Make sure you save the query for future use.

Using the LIKE Keyword to Prompt the User

Example 6

Suppose you want to prompt the user to enter only the first character of a value. For example, say you want the user to be able to retrieve tools based on the type of tool using only the first character of a type of tool.

1. In Design view, select the **ToolID, ToolName, Manufacturer, Type, Location**, and **Price** fields.

2. Select the **Tools** table.

3. Type the following in the Criteria cell of the **Type** column:

    ```
    Like [Enter the letter the word begins with:] & "%"
    ```

➔ **Note:** If your Access database is set to SQL-89 use an asterisk (*) instead of a percent sign (%) in the above SQL script.

4. Next, run the query and type the letter **s** in the dialog box. Look at the results in Figure 13-12.

ToolID ▾	ToolName ▾	Manufacturer ▾	Type ▾	Location ▾	Price ▾
5	Sandpaper	Bosch	Sanding	B	$4.00
6	Scrapers	Bosch	Sanding	B	$8.00

Figure 13-12. Results (output)

The result shows all of the records that have a value in the Type column beginning with the letter s.

Prompting the User for Dates

You can also use a parameter query to prompt a user for a date. Take a look at Example 7.

Example 7

SalesID	ProductID	CustomerID	DateSold
1	BN200	2	3/3/2008
2	CT200	3	2/5/2008
3	ET100	5	2/6/2007
4	PO200	1	7/8/2008
5	TH100	3	2/8/2008
6	RX300	4	2/10/2007
7	CT200	2	2/22/2008
8	ET100	6	2/20/2008
9	LF300	6	2/18/2008
10	BN200	1	2/17/2008

Figure 13-13. Sales table

Suppose you want to use the Sales table in Figure 13-13 to prompt the user to enter the date an item was sold. Follow these steps:

1. Click the **Design** tab from the top menu; click the **Show table** button to add the Sales table to Query Design view. After you add the Sales table to Query Design view, click **Close.**

2. In the Query Design Grid, select the **SalesID,** **ProductID**, **CustomerID**, and **DateSold** fields.

3. Select the **Sales** table.

4. Next, type the following in the Criteria cell of the **DateSold** column:

```
[Enter a date (mm/dd/yyyy):]
```

⟲ **Note:** We included the format of the dates stored in the database so that the user types the date in the correct format.

5. Next, run the query and type the following date in the dialog box:

03/03/2008

6. Click the **OK** button and review the results.

SalesID ▾	ProductID ▾	CustomerID ▾	DateSold ▾
1	BN200	2	3/3/2008

Figure 13-14. Results (output)

The results in Figure 13-14 show one product that was sold on 03/03/2008.

Creating a Button to Prompt the User

Parameter queries can also be used within forms. A common practice is to create a button that when clicked prompts the user for information. Take a look at Example 8, which does exactly that.

Example 8

Suppose you wanted to create a button on a form that when clicked implements the query created in Example 2. That query uses the Tools table to prompt the user to enter a manufacturer name.

To create a button that prompts the user in Microsoft Access 2007, use the following steps:

1. Highlight (click) the **Tools** table under Tables from the Navigation pane.

2. Click **Create** from the menu running across the top of the Microsoft Access interface.

3. Click the **Form** button.

4. Save the form as **ToolsFrm** by clicking the **Microsoft Office** button and selecting **Save** from the drop-down menu.

5. Switch to Design view by clicking the **View** button and selecting **Design View**.

6. Click the **Button** form control in the Controls section.

➲ **Note:** Your cursor will change to a plus sign and a rectangle after you click on the Button control.

7. Click anywhere on the form. A Command Button Wizard will appear.

8. Select **Miscellaneous** under Categories.

9. Select **Run Query** under Actions, as shown in Figure 13-15.

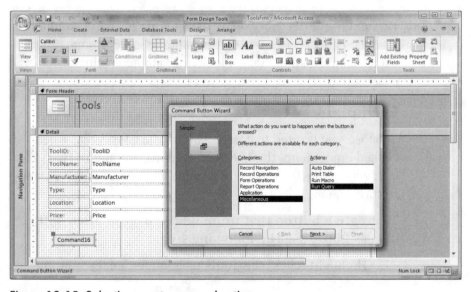

Figure 13-15. Selecting a category and action

10. Click the **Next** button.

11. Select the **ManufacturerQry** query and click **Next**, as shown in Figure 13-16.

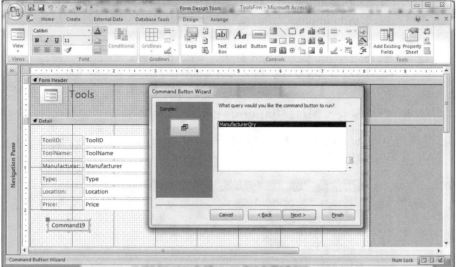

Figure 13-16. Selecting a query

12. Choose **Text** and type the following text: **Query by Manufacturer.**

13. Click **Next** and type the following text: **Query by Manufacturer.**

14. Click **Finish**.

To create a button that prompts the user in Microsoft Access 2003, complete the following steps:

1. Create a simple form in Design view. (Double-click **Create form in Design View** under Forms on the main interface of Access.)

2. Save the form as **ToolsFrm**.

3. Click the **Command** button on the toolbar.

⊃ **Note:**   Your cursor will change to a plus sign and a rectangle after you click on the Command button.

4. Click anywhere on the form. A Command Button Wizard will appear.

⊃ **Note:**   If the Command Button Wizard does not appear, you need to first click/select the Control Wizards button on the toolbar.

5. Select **Miscellaneous** under Categories.

6. Select **Run Query** under Actions, as shown in Figure 13-17.

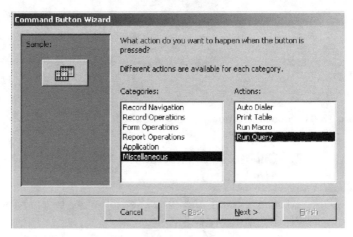

Figure 13-17. Selecting a category and action

7. Click the **Next** button.

8. Select the **ManufacturerQry** query and click **Next**, as shown in Figure 13-18.

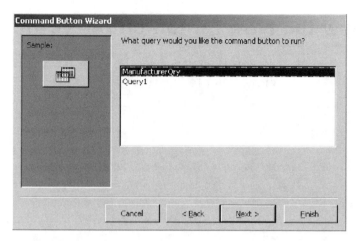

Figure 13-18. Selecting a query

9. Choose **Text** and type the following text: **Query by Manufacturer.**

10. Click **Next** and type the following text: **Query by Manufacturer.**

11. Click **Finish.**

View the New Button on the Form

1. To view the form, click the **View** button and select **Form View**. Refer to Figure 13-19.

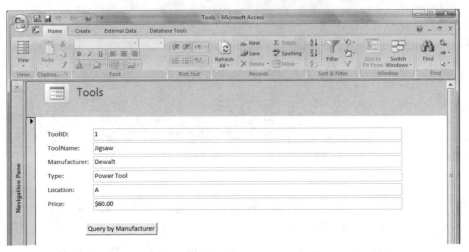

Figure 13-19. Form view

Now we can use the newly created button on the form.

2. Click the **Query by Manufacturer** button and type **Bosch** in the dialog box, then click **OK**.

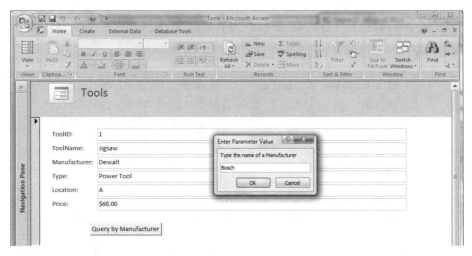

Figure 13-20. Query by Manufacturer

Look at the results in Figure 13-21, which shows all of the tools that were manufactured by Bosch.

ToolID ▾	ToolName ▾	Manufacturer ▾	Type ▾	Location ▾	Price ▾
4	Nail Gun	Bosch	Power Tool	A	$60.00
5	Sandpaper	Bosch	Sanding	B	$4.00
6	Scrapers	Bosch	Sanding	B	$8.00

Figure 13-21. Results (output)

SQL Syntax for a Parameter Query in SQL View

Although we created all of the criteria for each of our parameter queries in Design view, you can also create parameter queries in SQL view. Take a look at the following example, which shows the SQL view equivalent of Example 3.

Example 9

This example shows the SQL script created when you wrote the criteria in Example 3. Remember that even if you use Design view to specify the criteria, you can click the View button and select SQL view to view the SQL script. Take a look at the following scripts, which are equivalent to Example 3.

```
SELECT *
FROM Tools
WHERE (((Tools.Manufacturer)=[Type the name of a Manufacturer]));
```

OR

```
SELECT *
FROM Tools
WHERE Tools.Manufacturer=[Type the name of a Manufacturer];
```

Either of the above queries will run. Microsoft Access tends to add additional brackets and parentheses.

The brackets enclose the text that will be displayed on the dialog box. Whenever you create a parameter you must include the brackets.

Example 10

SalesID ▾	ProductID ▾	CustomerID ▾	DateSold ▾
1	BN200	2	3/3/2008
2	CT200	3	2/5/2008
3	ET100	5	2/6/2007
4	PO200	1	7/8/2008
5	TH100	3	2/8/2008
6	RX300	4	2/10/2007
7	CT200	2	2/22/2008
8	ET100	6	2/20/2008
9	LF300	6	2/18/2008
10	BN200	1	2/17/2008

Figure 13-22. Sales table

Suppose you want to use the Sales table in Figure 13-22 to create a query in SQL view that accepts two input date ranges. The following query will display customer order information (SalesID, ProductID, CustomerID, DateSold) that is based on two dates entered by the user:

```
SELECT SalesID, ProductID, CustomerID, DateSold
FROM Sales
WHERE DateSold BETWEEN [Type the first date (mm/dd/yyyy):] AND [Type
the second date (mm/dd/yyyy):];
```

This query prompts the user to enter two dates. The dates are used to pinpoint orders placed between the two dates specified. The WHERE clause specifies the criteria for the two input date ranges. It uses the DateSold column, the BETWEEN and AND operators, and text in brackets to prompt the user to enter two dates.

If the user entered 01/04/2007 for the first date and 12/29/2007 for the second date, the following results would be displayed:

SalesID ▾	ProductID ▾	CustomerID ▾	DateSold ▾
3	ET100	5	2/6/2007
6	RX300	4	2/10/2007

Figure 13-23. Results (output)

247

While parameter queries are extremely useful, many programmers (including one of the authors) tend to shy away from them. The main reason is that you are extremely limited in your ability to check the user input when you let the system handle things. Usually it is better to have the user input the desired parameters into a text field on a form, then validate the input before the query is processed. This prevents strange error messages from popping up and allows the designer to handle errors in a manner appropriate to the program.

We have shown in a previous chapter that it is possible to dynamically create a query before its execution. This same logic can be applied here as an alternative to a parameter query.

With that said, there is a variation of the parameter query that is extremely useful. As you will see in Chapter 16, it is possible to create a stored procedure with a passed parameter. The advantage of this parameter query over a dynamically built query is that the code for the query can be preprocessed on the server. This results in faster query execution and a generally happier user.

Non-parameter Parameter Queries

One of the more interesting situations that can occur in the SQL world is when you do not have the ability to build a true parameter query to work with your data. In fact, there often comes a time when you cannot directly build queries that allow you to set up parameters. An instance of this is when you have stored procedures on an SQL server that you cannot change either because of system limitations of where you are working or simply because you want maximum speed and do not want the overhead of building a new query and then compiling it. There is a way around this problem that might not be obvious to the casual user.

Remember that a parameter query is just a filter. Up to this point we have discussed the placement of the filter value in the WHERE clause, but there is another way to create a filter that does not require you to rebuild the query.

Let's go back to our first query in this section where we wanted to find all the tools manufactured by Porter. This time, though, let's assume that we can't change the query after it is built. So, instead of changing the existing query we construct one that is slightly different and includes a join between our current table Tools and a new table tempTools (Figure 13-24).

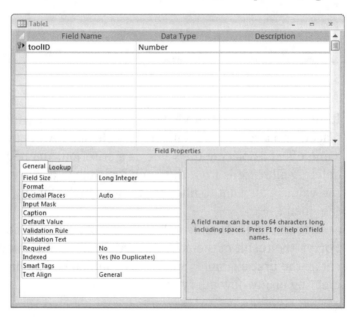

Figure 13-24. Temporary tools table

Now build a query that joins this table to the primary Tools table (Figure 13-25).

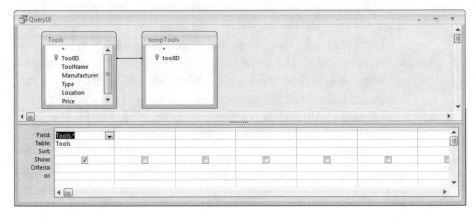

Figure 13-25. Join query

It might not seem intuitive, but any value used as a filter can be placed into a row in the tempTools table and it will have the same effect as placing the value as a criterion. You begin by deleting all records from the tempTools table. Next, you add the values you want to filter for to tempTools. Finally, you run the query.

If the tempTools table only consists of a single record with Porter, the result of the above query would be the same record-set as the first example. Simple, elegant, and no modifying or creating of any new query would be needed.

Summary

In this chapter, you learned what a parameter query is and how it can be used in Access to create customized queries. You learned how to create a parameter query, customize a dialog box, create multiple prompts to the user, use the LIKE keyword to prompt the user, prompt the user for dates, and create a button that prompts the user. You also learned how to create and view parameter queries in SQL view.

Quiz 13

1. True or False. A parameter query is a query that enables the user to set the criteria for selecting records at run time by filling in a dialog box.

2. True or False. When you use the BETWEEN keyword in a parameter query, it does not include records that match the values entered by the user.

3. True or False. Parameter queries can be used within forms.

4. True or False. The use of brackets in a parameter query is optional.

5. True or False. The asterisk is used with the LIKE keyword to match characters in a parameter query.

Project 13

Use the Sales table in Figure 13-13 to create a parameter query that prompts the user for two dates.

Chapter 14

Integrating SQL Script in VBA Code

Introduction

Why SQL? We have demonstrated in this book how much of SQL script writing can be done through the Access query grid. In fact, the query grid is so easy to use that Microsoft has incorporated it into SQL Server and is indicating that it is going to be the major way most future SQL will be done. Despite this trend, there is much still going for raw, text-based SQL. For starters, SQL is far easier to handle and manipulate than query grids. It also provides a degree of functionality that is not available to the query grid developer. In this chapter we will show how SQL is critical for Visual Basic development. The next chapter will continue this theme with a demonstration of how the coding of web Active Server pages can be enhanced using SQL.

Definitions

Recordset — A collection of records in Visual Basic programming.

VBA — Visual Basic for Applications. The flavor of Visual Basic incorporated in Access and in much of the Microsoft Office suite.

This chapter will assume that you are familiar with Access programming and that you know your way around modules and basic Visual Basic code. It also assumes that you have a good understanding of items and properties of those items. In particular, we will be concentrating on the properties of forms and combo boxes and how you can set some of these properties dynamically using code. Before some of you begin to panic, we promise to keep things as simple as possible to make our points. On the other hand, if you have made it this far, you have a desire to learn SQL, and what better reason for this than to improve your Visual Basic programming ability?

Fixed Queries vs. "On-the-Fly" Queries

The first reason for developing queries dynamically rather than building them in the query grid and storing them is a simple matter of logistics and aesthetics. Access is a very powerful program. It permits the user to develop queries to do just about anything. Unfortunately, as powerful as the query development tools are, the management and organization of the queries leaves much to be desired. To see how far we should have come in Access, we need to go back to the early days of DOS. In those early days, all files on storage media were kept in a single list on the media. In the case of floppy disks, each floppy would have a single directory and all files would be in the directory. While simple and straightforward, the lone directory could have hundreds of files, which in turn could be associated with multiple applications. It was the responsibility of the operator to know which files were associated with each application and to keep things straight. Generally the operator did not keep up with this responsibility, which resulted in chaos.

This problem was alleviated with the introduction of cascading directory trees. With directories, files could be grouped and put together with related files separate from nonrelated files. For example, a data directory could be set up to contain data. A template directory could be set up to hold all the templates associated with a program. Finally, a program directory could be set up to contain the actual program files. Directories could be placed in other directories, establishing a hierarchal system to manage all files on the media.

Unfortunately, Access has never gotten past the initial stage of putting forms in one container, modules in a second container, tables in a third container, and so on. There is no provision to group queries based on function or tables based on contents. The net effect is that if you have a hundred queries, they will all be in a single list. There could be a dozen queries that are performing similar tasks, but just like in the early days of computers, there is no real way to organize the queries other than by careful user-managed naming conventions. Until Access provides a better way of organizing queries, one of the tricks that the programmer can implement is to reduce the number of needed queries, thereby simplifying the organization of the remaining queries.

Now, some astute reader will be remarking at this point "What about groups?" While groups are a convenient way to organize objects, they are really only shortcuts and only provide a visual link to the object. In some ways they actually make things messier since you not only still have all the original objects in a single long list but now you have multiple virtual copies of the object.

This is where SQL enters the picture. One of the easiest ways to avoid having queries appear in the list of queries is to build the queries dynamically in code rather than by having each query stored in the query list. By entering query operations as inline code rather than as separate, unique queries, you have fewer queries, which are far easier to manage.

This is just the first of many reasons for building queries dynamically in code and creating them on the fly rather than to have them permanently saved in the query list. But this is by far the most important reason. We will introduce a few more reasons as this chapter progresses.

The following shows a simple example of this (see Figure 14-1).

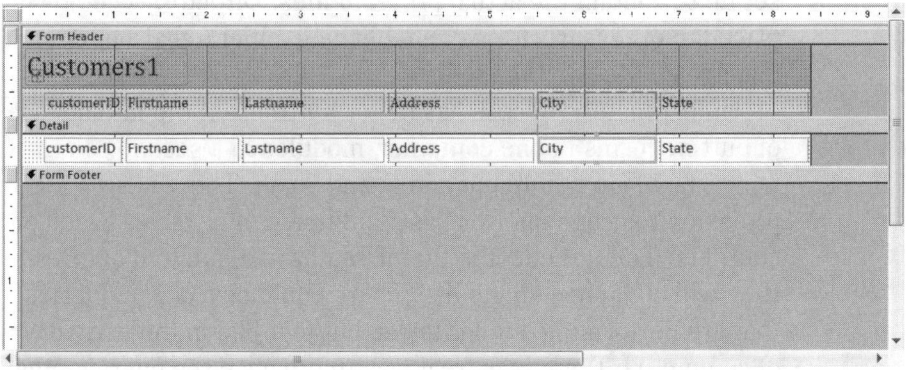

Figure 14-1

Using our earlier example of the Customers table (last accessed in Chapter 10), let's first add a few records to the table to give us a larger number of records with which to work. This will provide us with additional filtering capabilities and show off a few additional features of filter parameters. (Note that we've skipped record 7 to separate the new ones a bit.)

```
INSERT INTO Customers
VALUES (8, 'Henry', 'George', '1000 East West St',
        'Jacksonville', 'FL', 32211, 904, '444-2323');

INSERT INTO Customers
VALUES (9, 'Alice', 'George', '1000 East West St',
        'Jacksonville', 'FL', 32211, 904, '444-2323');
INSERT INTO Customers
VALUES (10, 'Bill', 'George', '1812 Hemingway',
        'Jacksonville', 'FL', 32213, 904, '421-3246');

INSERT INTO Customers
VALUES (11, 'Mary', 'Wilson', '13120 N 15th East',
        'Ogden', 'UT', 84102, 919, '321-9443');
```

Now that we have added these records, assume that you want to display only those people who are in Florida. One method of addressing this requirement is to build and save a special query where the state equals Florida. A second method of doing this is to build the recordsource for the form using the Query Builder, which is accessed with the builder button (the ellipsis that appears to the right of the drop-down arrow). Using the Query Builder you can select the recordsource as the Customers table and add your filter for the state (Florida) as shown in Figure 14-2.

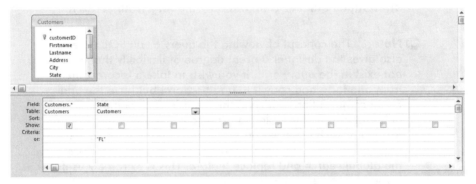

Figure 14-2

What happens when you save this query is interesting. Access evaluates what you have entered in the query grid and automatically saves it in the recordsource as an SQL query.

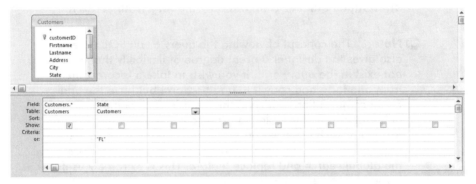

Figure 14-3

This brings up several other possible uses for Access SQL. The first is that you can type the SQL directly into the recordsource instead of going to the Query Builder, as shown in Figure 14-3. Sometimes this is a far faster way of entering the recordsource. Second, if you have a form that already has the recordsource that you want to use for your current form, copy the SQL code from the first form and paste it into the second form. This is often much quicker than building a query from scratch.

⊃ **Note:**   The concept of viewing the query as an SQL statement also gives the designer a great degree of flexibility that does not exist in the query grid. If you wish to take a recordsource from one form and copy it to another form but have the additional complication of having the recordsource being a different but similar table, you can copy the SQL string into a text editor such as Microsoft Word. You can then use search and replace to change the initial table to the new table using the global search and replace feature. This is extremely useful if you have a very complex query and don't wish to recreate everything. A quick search and replace followed by cutting and pasting the result back into Access completes the operation. Unfortunately, Access does not have a convenient way of doing this. The Access text editing capabilities are more primitive than even those of Notepad. And while it is possible to get a larger window for viewing your SQL (the Zoom window, accessed by pressing the Shift+F2 keyboard shortcut) the larger window is still relatively small and provides no functionality except data entry.

⊃ **Note:**   Microsoft has an interesting feature in the Zoom window that significantly improves its usefulness. You can select your font in the Zoom window so you are not limited to a microscopic font size. You can select the font to be any font on your computer at any size; however, the larger the font, the less you can see on the screen. Refer to Figure 14-4.

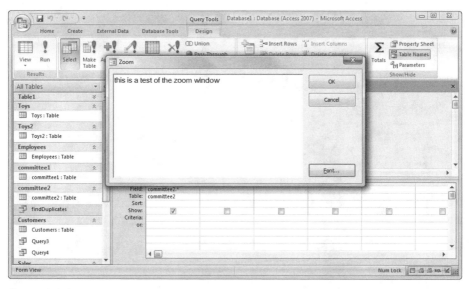

Figure 14-4

Filtered Recordsets for Forms

Now that we have shown that the recordsource of a form is just an SQL statement, we can make the leap to dynamically set up the query as needed. Dynamic queries are extremely useful when working with a filtered recordset in a form or report.

Just like with every other task in Access, there are many ways to filter a recordset. First, you can enter the filter when opening a form. We will demonstrate this with the frmCustomers form in the sample database we've been using (see Figure 14-5). Selecting a record on the Customers form, then pressing either of the "Open with" buttons on the form will open the frmTransactions form to show the transactions for that customer. If there is only one transaction, frmTransactions will only have one record to display. If there is more than one transaction, the user is able to move forward and backward through the records.

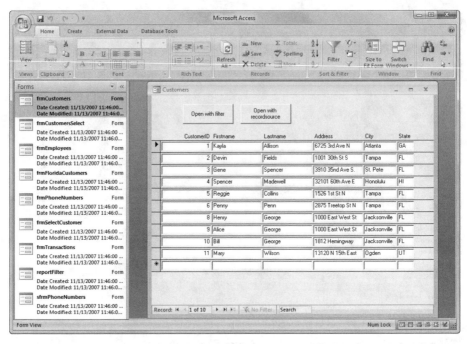

Figure 14-5

So much for the overview — now we will get into the fun stuff! The first button, Open with filter, is the equivalent of setting the filter parameter of the recordset to the entered value. Take a look at the code behind this button:

```
Private Sub cmdOpenFilter_Click()
    DoCmd.OpenForm "frmTransactions", , , "customerID= " &
        CustomerID
End Sub
```

In effect, this code opens the frmTransactions form and sets the Filter property of the form. In the example above, when the user selects the customer with the ID of 1, the filter string "customerID =1" is placed into the Filter property (see Figure 14-6).

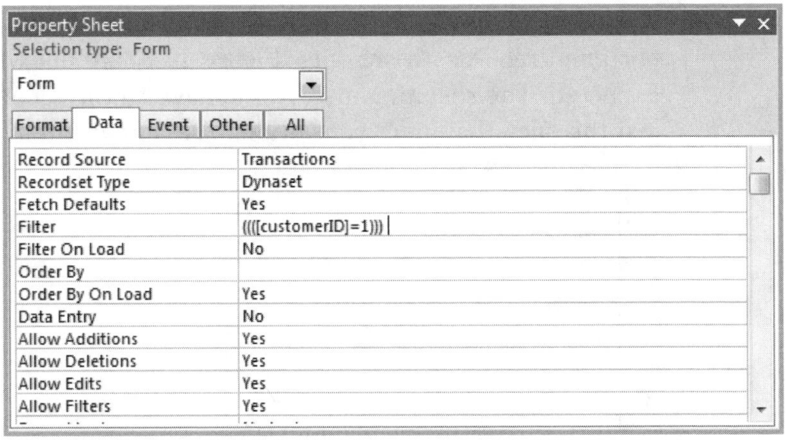

Figure 14-6

The one problem with this approach is that you generally want to allow the user to perform additional filters with the data. If the user enters a new filter via the Filter button or through "filter by form," the new filter will overwrite the one you had carefully built and will change the list of records displayed with no obvious way to get back to the initial filter set. For example, selecting "filter by selection" when the date sold of 2/8/2008 is selected produces the filter shown in Figure 14-7. You get the records that you want but you have to tread on shaky ground.

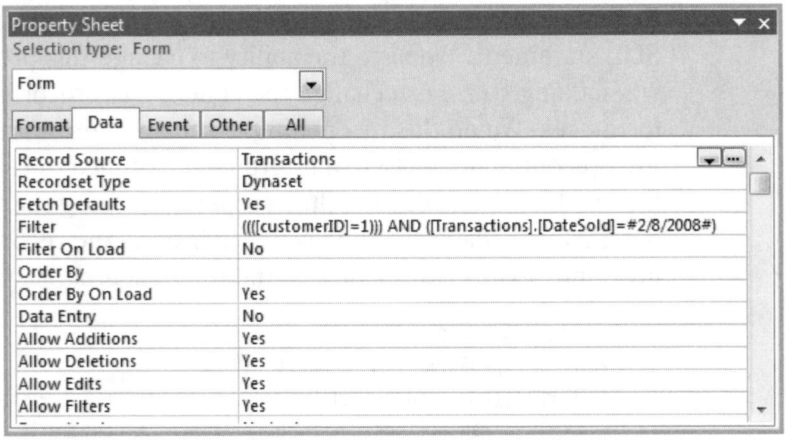

Figure 14-7

If the user removes the filter to try to go back to the full set of pertinent records, the results (Figure 14-8) are not what is expected. The resulting display will have all the records, not just the ones that meet your original customer filter.

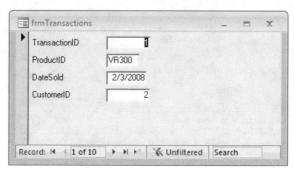

Figure 14-8

Let's take a step back for a moment and look at this problem in a bit more detail. You really don't want the user to be able to view the full set of records, no matter what filters he chooses to set up. You want the user to only have access to the records you want him to see. This is best accomplished by setting the recordsource of the form to a recordset that only has the values that you want.

Looking at the properties of our form, notice that the Recordset property is either a table or a query expressed as an SQL statement. We have the ability to change this property and when doing so we can change the collection of records that the form uses. We do this by opening the form, then setting the Recordsource property to a filtered query. Since the form is not filtered by the use of the Filter property, clearing the filter will not affect our dataset. The user is limited to the records we give him permission to view in the recordsource.

```
Private Sub cmdOpenRecord_Click()
    DoCmd.OpenForm "frmTransactions"
    Forms![frmtransactions].RecordSource = "SELECT * FROM
        Transactions WHERE customerID =" & CustomerID
End Sub
```

We can see this in the Immediate window in Visual Basic (Figure 14-9). Note that the recordset has a filter applied and the filter for the form is blank.

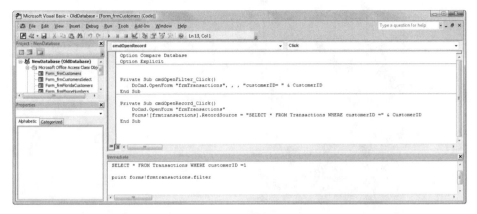

Figure 14-9

Filtered Recordsets for Combo Boxes

The second place that dynamic recordsets are commonly used is in combo boxes. In many cases you may want the combo box to have varying data depending upon the value of an option group. Take a look at the next form from the sample database, frmSelectCustomer (Figure 14-10).

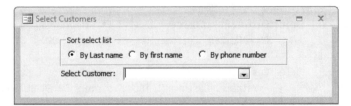

Figure 14-10

In this example, we want the contents of the combo box to be sorted by the selected option. We also want the combo box to reflect the choice of the option group. We do this by setting the Rowsource property of the combo box programmatically during

the after update event based on the value of the option box.
Depending upon the option selected, the program will set up
the rowsource to sort by the selected field (Figure 14-11).

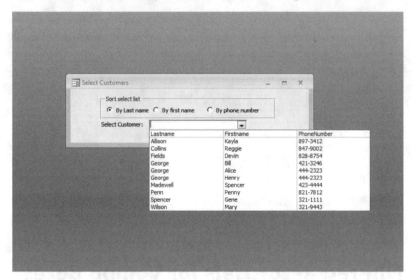

Figure 14-11

```
Private Sub selectBy_AfterUpdate()
If selectBy = 1 Then
    selectCustomer.RowSource = "SELECT Lastname, Firstname,
        PhoneNumber, CustomerID FROM Customers ORDER BY lastname"
ElseIf selectBy = 2 Then
    selectCustomer.RowSource = "SELECT Firstname, Lastname,
        PhoneNumber, CustomerID FROM Customers ORDER BY firstname"
Else
    selectCustomer.RowSource = "SELECT PhoneNumber, Lastname,
        Firstname, CustomerID FROM Customers ORDER BY phonenumber"
End If
End Sub
```

Examine the difference in the combo box when different
options are selected. The differences in the values for the
combo box are a direct result of the SQL that is placed behind
the rowsource of the combo box (Figure 14-12).

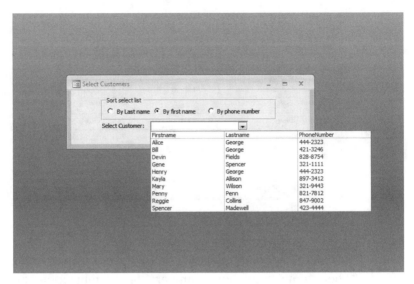

Figure 14-12

Recordsets for Subforms

The third major use of dynamic SQL statements in code is the building of the recordsource for subforms. There are three major reasons for using SQL to change the recordsource of subforms. The most common reason is identical to that of filtered recordsets for forms — it gives you control of the recordset and eliminates the possibility of the user disturbing your filter through manual action.

The second reason for using SQL to change the recordsource of a subform parallels the idea of dynamically changing the rowsource of a combo box. Sometimes the programmer needs to have different data in the subform based on other decisions made on the form. If the visual appearance of the subform does not need to change to reflect the different data, it is often advantageous to save time and effort by using one subform designed to hold both types of data and just changing the recordsource of the subform. Look at the following form, frmPhoneNumbers (Figure 14-13).

265

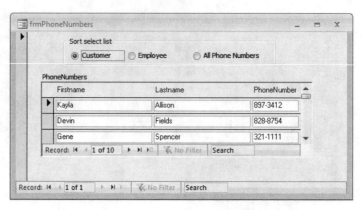

Figure 14-13

Depending upon the user's selection of customer phone numbers, employee phone numbers, or a combination of the two, the appropriate code is built and saved as the recordsource of the subform. This is far simpler and easier to maintain than it would be if there were three subforms, one for each of the options. Using this approach, if you need to change the layout of the subform or add additional information to it, you will only have to do your changes in one spot rather than three.

Let's examine the code behind this form. The key to this example is the code behind the AfterUpdate event for the option box.

```
Private Sub selectBy_AfterUpdate()
Dim srceStr As String
Select Case selectBy
    Case 1:
        srceStr = "SELECT firstname, lastname, phonenumber FROM
                Customers"
    Case 2:
        srceStr = "SELECT firstname, lastname, phonenumber FROM
                Employees"
    Case 3:
        srceStr = "SELECT firstname, lastname, phonenumber FROM
                Customers UNION " & _
                " SELECT firstname, lastname, phonenumber FROM
                Employees"
```

```
End Select
[PhoneNumbers].Form.RecordSource = srceStr
End Sub
```

In this example, we first defined a variable to hold the SQL string. We could just set the recordsource directly to the string, but adding the intermediate variable is a good idea, as it helps facilitate debugging mistakes in the SQL code. It is far easier to debug the SQL statement if we have it in a variable that can be pasted and analyzed in the debug window. The Microsoft content pop-up generally is not big enough to hold the entire SQL string and it goes away before you can really tell what has happened. The more complex the SQL, the more we are inclined to use the temporary variable. Anyway, as an indication that something is happening when the code executes, you will note that the number of records in the recordset changes to reflect the counts for the two groups of phone numbers and the combined list of phone numbers.

In the dataset for this example, if you select the Customer button, the resulting form displays 10 records (see Figure 14-14).

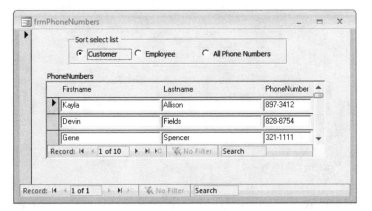

Figure 14-14

267

If we instead select the Employee button, the form displays five records (see Figure 14-15).

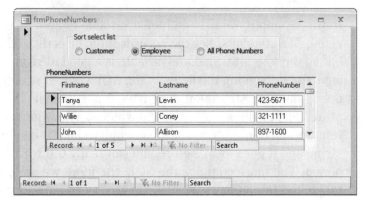

Figure 14-15

Finally, if the All Phone Numbers button is selected, the number of records increases to 16 (see Figure 14-16).

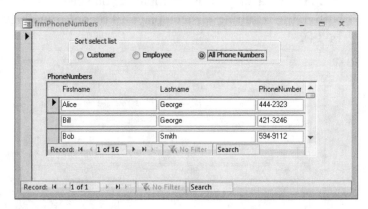

Figure 14-16

The real power to this approach is evident the moment you need to modify the layout of the subform. If you need to increase the width of the Lastname field, you can do it in one place. If you had three subforms, you would have to carefully resize each of the Lastname fields in each of the forms to ensure that they are the same size and carefully move the PhoneNumber fields so each is in the correct location. Otherwise, the form would "jump" on the screen as the different options were selected. It is far simpler to have a single form.

There is one other reason for not including the recordsource of a subform at form construction time but instead setting it during the running of the form — speed. If a form has multiple subforms on it, there will be a certain amount of processing time needed to fill each of the subforms. The more subforms on the main form and the more record searching that is required to calculate the form, the more time it takes for the form to be displayed. If instead of filling in all the recordsources of the subforms when the form is opened, the recordsource subform is filled only when actually needed, there is a perception by the viewer that the form is running faster. This is most noticeable when one has multiple tabs on a form where each tab contains a subform. If a tab is not selected while the user is viewing the form, any calculation on that tab will just be unnecessary overhead. Unfortunately there is the other side of the coin. If the user needs to constantly swap between tabs, there is the additional overhead of filling in the subform information. Of course, if you really want to totally optimize the program to get every bit of advantage out of the code, you can set the program so the recordset is loaded only the first time a tab is opened. Subsequent tab selection can then use the previously created subform. It is more work, but it will give you the fastest performance.

Report Filters

The single most important use of embedded SQL is the flexibility it provides in filtering reports. Since it is common to have many reports based on a similar set of filter parameters, it is often a good idea to have one standard form where the user can select the filters before the report is run. When the report is run, the SQL string can be constructed based on the filters established on the form. This concept is far easier to observe than it is to describe, so let's take this one step at a time. Begin by looking at the frmReportFilter form. This form is used by several reports to build the generic filtered recordsource for the reports. Looking at the basic form shown in Figure 14-17, you will see that it is user friendly and guides the user through the possible options.

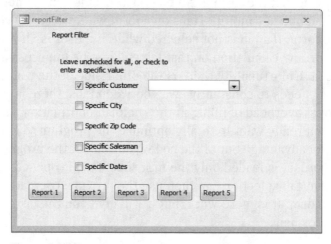

Figure 14-17

As the user selects the parameter to filter by, the corresponding field for the filter appears on the form for data entry.

When all the filters are selected, the user chooses the appropriate report. Using Report 1 as an example, we now get to examine the code behind the button.

```
Private Sub cmdReport1_Click()
On Error GoTo Err_cmdReport1_Click
    Dim stDocName As String
    Dim filter As String
    Dim rptSource As String

    filter = buildfilter()
    rptSource = "SELECT * FROM qrySalesComposite " & filter
    stDocName = "rptSalesComposite"
    DoCmd.OpenReport stDocName, acViewDesign
    Reports.rptSalesComposite.RecordSource = rptSource
    DoCmd.OpenReport stDocName, acPreview
Exit_cmdReport1_Click:
    Exit Sub
Err_cmdReport1_Click:
    MsgBox Err.Description
    Resume Exit_cmdReport1_Click
End Sub
```

The first thing you will note is that the majority of the processing for this button occurs in the buildfilter function. Generally, the block of code used to build the filter is very generic and called from several places. Rather than duplicating the code over and over, we have placed it in a function for convenience and have it returned to our main functions as a string. We have also placed the names of the recordsource and the filter into local string variables so we can verify them during the debug process.

The real meat of the operation occurs in the buildfilter function.

```
Private Function buildfilter() As String
Dim filt As String
filt = ""
If customerFiltered = True Then
    filt = "customerID = " & customerFilter
End If
If cityFiltered = True Then
    If filt <> "" Then filt = filt & " AND"
    filt = filt & "city = '" & cityFilter & " '"
End If
If zipCodeFiltered = True Then
```

271

```
      If filt <> "" Then filt = filt & " AND"
      filt = filt & "zipcode = '" & zipCodeFilter & "'"
End If
If salesmanFiltered = True Then
      If filt <> "" Then filt = filt & " AND"
      filt = filt & "ID = " & salesmanFilter
End If
If dated = True Then
      If filt <> "" Then filt = filt & " AND"
      filt = filt & "dateSold > #" & startdate & " # AND
            dateSold < #" & stopdate & "#"
End If
If filt <> "" Then
      filt = " WHERE " & filt
End If
buildfilter = filt
End Function
```

The buildfilter function is fairly straightforward. The function goes through each of the possible filter check boxes to see if the box is checked and if a filter is to occur. If checked, the code fragment is built for that specific conditional. Look at the first possible filter, which is Customer. If the user has opted to filter by customer, that customer name is appended to the filter string as "customerID = " followed by the ID of the customer. This process is repeated for each of the other possible filters. Also of interest here is the way the AND operator is added to the filter string. If something exists before the current conditional, the program inserts the " AND" operator. If there is nothing before the current condition, there is no need for the " AND" so it is not inserted.

One of the major potential trouble areas is determining when the special delimiters for strings and dates are needed and how to construct them. The process is identical for strings and dates and is illustrated with the date filter fragment above. In our case, we want the date to be between a start date and a stop date. The user enters two dates in the filter form and it is then the program's job to parse that into a valid string. The first step is to build the start date by setting up the conditional "dateSold = " followed by the date. Dates have to be preceded by the # sign. It is put inside the quotes since it is to be part of the filter string, so the string becomes "dateSold = #". To this we append the date from the text box, startdate. This value is currently a string that we want to append to our current string, so we now have "dateSold = #" & startdate. We finish off this filter fragment with a final "#" also expressed as a string, giving us the final "dateSold = #" & startdate & "#". Note that the startdate is not included in quotes since we want the value of the field startdate, not the word "startdate." Also note that the string concatenation symbol (&) is preceded and followed by a space while the # symbols are not. Let's put this through a manual code-generation process using the date 2/5/2008. Plugging in all the values and evaluating it produces the string "startdate = #2/5/2008#".

The same approach is used for strings to be inserted, but the # character is replaced by the single quote ('). If we were to use the salesman's last name instead of the ID value, that string would be "lastname = '" & lastname & "'".

➲ **Note:** If you haven't guessed, things can get very hairy if you use the #, quote, or double quote characters in field names. In those cases you have to go through the very careful gyrations of making sure the code knows how to process the characters correctly. It can easily become a mess if you are not careful. One database that we inherited used the fieldname "father's name." We spent several hours figuring out why the filter was not working properly before we realized that the quote was fouling up how the string was being handled. Sure, you can use paired double quotes, but in this case a bit of planning at the start can save you many hours of grief later.

➲ **Note:** One of the more unusual errors that popped up was when we used the last name rather than the index in a dynamic SQL query. Everything went fine until we had the name O'Brian. Access decided that the single quote in the name was a string delimiter and the programming went crazy. Besides being faster, these problems do not occur when you use indexes.

Summary

This chapter showed how SQL can be used within Access and how the developer can use SQL to simplify code development and improve ease of use.

Chapter 15

Integrating SQL
Script into ASP Code

Introduction

When you start writing web pages you generally begin with basic HTML (Hypertext Markup Language). You can write the HTML either directly or through a web page development program, but the net effect is that you get text-based code that your browser knows how to interpret. The biggest problem with HTML is that it can only be used to display static data. It cannot be used to extract data from a database. To get past this minor inadequacy (and to have more dynamic content), Microsoft introduced the concept of Active Server Pages. ASP code is not just static information. It can be used to do different things depending upon user actions and, more important, it can be used to access data from databases. Unfortunately, unless you want to tie yourself into a program with server-side extensions like FrontPage or Dreamworks, the easiest way to get data from a database is through our good friend SQL. In this chapter we will be constructing a few very simple Active Server Pages to show how SQL can interface with HTML to give the viewer database information. Some basic knowledge of HTML is required, but we will try to take things slowly, one step at a time.

Definitions

ASP — Active Server Pages. Visual Basic code used in web development for web pages that need to access a back-end database or have processing on the page.

HTML — Hypertext Markup Language.

IIS — Internet Information Services.

VBA — Visual Basic for Applications. The flavor of Visual Basic incorporated in Access and in much of the Microsoft Office suite.

Basics

The major thing to realize about Active Server Pages is that the whole concept is a bit convoluted. It is part HTML code and part Visual Basic, and it is the responsibility of the person who is writing the code to keep everything in sync. One of the authors (guess which one) goes back to the early days of Assembly language when spaghetti code was more the norm than the exception. He has often compared the basic ASP coding process to the worst days of Assembly code. With that in mind, let's begin to construct ASP.

The first requirement in writing ASP code is to have a web server that is capable of handling it. This generally means running Internet Information Services. IIS is included with Windows 2000, XP, Vista, and all flavors of Windows Server. In the case of Vista, it is no longer an automatically included component, however. You will have to install it manually. IIS functions as the middleman. It is responsible for making the inquiries to the SQL back end, formatting the data that is returned, and sending the information to the client. In short, IIS functions as the middle tier in a three-tier architecture, where SQL Server is the first tier, IIS is the second tier, and Internet Explorer on the destination computer is the third tier.

The second requirement in writing ASP code that can access a database is to have a database engine on the computer. While this can be full SQL Server, you can also use the Jet database engine that comes with Access.

Finally, you will need to have a method of joining the database engine to the IIS program. We are going to use the KISS (Keep It Simple, Stupid) principle here and just use good ol' ODBC to tie everything together.

It is, unfortunately, beyond the scope of this book to show how to set up a web server or ODBC driver installation, so we are going to assume that these components are in place.

For our development of code we will be using the HTML view of Microsoft FrontPage. While FrontPage is not a perfect tool for code development, and it is no longer a component of Office, it does color-coordinate the parts of the code and makes viewing the code a bit easier than if a pure text editor like Notepad were used. A word of caution, however: Don't try to view your web page in the FrontPage viewer and expect to see anything remotely like the final displayed page. Also, do not go back into normal mode and try entering anything. The probability of the parser destroying your work is almost at the 100 percent level. With these caveats given, let's proceed.

Building the Components

For this example we are going to take the Customers table that we used in the last chapter and show how it can be done in ASP. You will note that the SQL statements are almost identical to the ones from the previous chapter. What is different is the framework around the SQL.

ODBC Connection

The first thing that has to be done when accessing data from a database is to declare the connection. We have discovered that an ADO ODBC connection works well. Setting up the ODBC connection is partially dependent upon your operating system, but once you get past the basics the setup is straightforward.

1. Using Windows 2000, go into the Control Panel and select **Administrative Tools**. On the Administrative Tools screen, select **Data Sources (ODBC)**. This brings up the ODBC Data Source Administrator window.

    If you are using Windows Vista, go into the Control Panel, select **Administrative Tools** (choose Classic View if necessary) and then select **Data Sources (ODBC)** to bring up the ODBC Data Source Administrator window. This sounds identical to Windows 2000 in operation but the screens are totally different! Luckily, the ODBC Data Source Administrator screen is identical (see Figure 15.1).

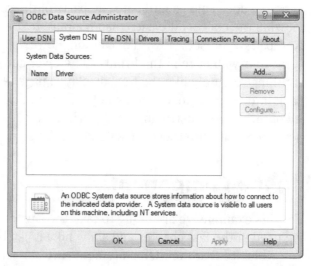

Figure 15-1. ODBC Data Source Administrator window

2. Any of the three types of DSNs can be created and all work identically. Generally we select System DSN since it can be used by anyone on the host computer. The only real advantage of creating a file DSN is that it is portable and can be copied from machine to machine. That is not an issue for this demonstration, so select **System DSN**.

3. Select **Add** to create a new DSN connection by bringing up the Create New Data Source window (see Figure 15-2).

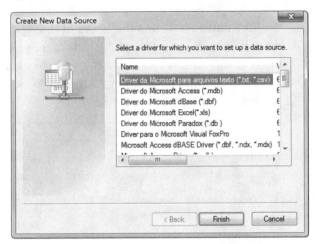

Figure 15-2. Create New Data Source window

4. Depending upon how much stuff you have installed on your machine, this may be a very short or very long list. For Access, select the Microsoft Access driver. For an SQL Server database, you would select SQL Server. Since we will be using an Access database, just select the **Access** driver and click the **Finish** button. You will now need to fill out the ODBC Microsoft Access Setup window shown in Figure 15-3.

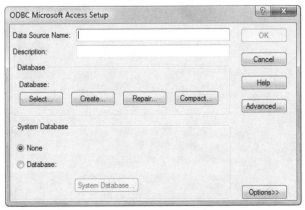

Figure 15-3. ODBC Microsoft Access Setup window

5. Any name can be given to the data source and any description can be entered. The important parts of this form are the Database and System Database sections. Click the **Select** button to enter the name of the Access database and, if you are using a system database, select the **Database** radio button and enter the system database. When completed, the ODBC Microsoft Access Setup form will look something like Figure 15-4.

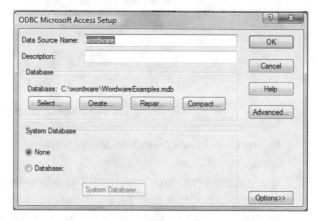

Figure 15-4. Selecting the database

6. If you have set up login names and passwords, you will need to select the Advanced button and set the appropriate advanced options (see Figure 15-5).

Figure 15-5. Set Advanced Options window

Code

The first step in accessing the data is to build the commands to create and open the ODBC connection. To do this we will use ADO to access the data.

```
set conntemp=server.createobject("adodb.connection")
conntemp.open "DSN=wordware"
```

That is the bulk of the overhead work. From this point on, all we have to do is open the appropriate SQL recordset. Once again we will build the SQL statement into a string variable, then use the ADO command to open the string.

```
mySQL = "SELECT * FROM customers"
set rstemp=conntemp.execute(mySQL)
```

Except for the slight difference in procedure calls dictated by ADO, you will note that the SQL code is identical to the code that we have used before to get all records from the Customers table.

The rest of the code is a bit different and you will note that there is quite a bit of setup to format the data that is being sent out to the browser, but the final result produces a result similar to the one we have seen before (Figure 15-6).

CustomerID	Firstname	Lastname	Address	City	State
1	Kayla	Allison	6725 3rd Ave N	Atlanta	GA
2	Devin	Fields	1001 30th St S	Tampa	FL
3	Gene	Spencer	3910 35th Ave S.	St. Pete	FL
4	Spencer	Madewell	32101 60th Ave E	Honolulu	HI
5	Reggie	Collins	1526 1st St N	Tampa	FL
6	Penny	Penn	2875 Treetop St N	Tampa	FL
8	Henry	George	1000 East West St	Jacksonville	FL
9	Alice	George	1000 East West St	Jacksonville	FL
10	Bill	George	1812 Hemingway	Jacksonville	FL
11	Mary	Wilson	13120 N 15ᵗʰ East	Ogden	UT

Figure 15-6. Display of full recordset

The first block of code that is needed is for some housekeeping. Unlike Access, which is relatively forgiving when it comes to empty recordsets, ASP is not quite so forgiving and will display nasty messages if you have not taken the no data condition into account. So, we first check to see if there is no data, and if there is no data we stop processing:

```
if  rstemp.eof then
    response.write "no data for<br>"
    response.write mySQL
    conntemp.close
    set conntemp=nothing
    response.end
else
```

If there is data, we can then call up the records in the recordset and forward them to the browser. Unfortunately, as mentioned, unlike Access you have to tell the browser everything and there is no really convenient way to do this except by brute force. We begin by setting up some header information in HTML:

```
<p align="center"><b><font size="5" face="Arial"
color="#990000"> Customers</font></b><p align="center">
<table border="0" width="781" height="462">
```

```
<tr>
    <td width="20" height="31" bgcolor="#080830"
            bordercolor="#C0B068">
        <font color="#C0B068">Customer ID </font>
    <td width="122" height="31" bgcolor="#080830"
            bordercolor="#C0B068">
        <font color="#C0B068">Firstname </font>
    <td width="114" height="31" bgcolor="#080830"
            bordercolor="#C0B068">
        <font color="#C0B068">Lastname </font>
    <td width="118" height="31" bgcolor="#080830"
            bordercolor="#C0B068">
        <font color="#C0B068">Address</font></tr>
    <td width="61" height="31" bgcolor="#080830"
            bordercolor="#C0B068">
        <font color="#C0B068">City</font>
    <td width="20" height="31" bgcolor="#080830"
            bordercolor="#C0B068">
        <font color="#C0B068">State</font>
</tr>
```

Now we can move through the records one at a time, extract the data from the fields, and format the data into an HTML format. The major thing this block of the code shows is the interaction between the HTML and the VB script. All formatting of information is done through HTML. All processing, including the looping operation and the pulling of the data from the recordset, is done in VB. This is where things get a bit messy. The system assumes that everything you are doing is HTML until you go into VB mode with the opening (<%) and termination (%>) symbols. The net effect of this movement between HTML and VB is that the system is not capable of determining where code blocks occur and stop in either the VB or the HTML segments. It becomes the job of the programmer to ensure that things start and stop in a consistent manner. For example, if you begin a loop, you have to make sure that the loop is terminated. If you begin a table row, you have to make sure that it is properly terminated, regardless of intervening VB code. The code in the above example looks like this:

```
<%  do until rstemp.eof %>
    <tr>
        <td width="20" height="1"><%=rstemp("customerID")%></td>
        <td width="122" height="1"><%=rstemp("firstname")%></td>
        <td width="114" height="1"><%=rstemp("lastname")%></td>
        <td width="118" height="1"><%=rstemp("address")%></td>
        <td width="61" height="1"><%=rstemp("city")%></td>
        <td width="20" height="1"><%=rstemp("state")%></td>
    </tr>
<%      rstemp.movenext
    loop
%>
```

Note that we have carefully indented and bracketed the <tr>
</tr> pair as well as the do.... loop statements.

One other thing in this code that is a bit unusual for Access
VB programmers is the use of the alternate form of field designation where the field name is specified in quotes rather than
by the dot notation.

Putting all the code together with a few more bits of formatting produces the final result of:

```
<html>
<head>
<meta http-equiv="Content-Language" content="en-us">
<meta http-equiv="Content-Type" content="text/html;
    charset=windows-1252">
<meta name="GENERATOR" content="Microsoft FrontPage 5.0">
<meta name="ProgId" content="FrontPage.Editor.Document">

</head>

<body>

<%

myDSN="DSN=wordware"
set conntemp=server.createobject("adodb.connection")
conntemp.open myDSN
```

```
mySQL = "SELECT * FROM customers"
set rstemp=conntemp.execute(mySQL)

if  rstemp.eof then
   response.write "no data for<br>"
   response.write mySQL
   conntemp.close
   set conntemp=nothing
   response.end
else
%>
   <p align="center"><b><font size="5" face="Arial" color=
         "#990000"> Customers</font></b><p align="center">
   <table border="0" width="781" height="462">
      <tr>
      <td width="20" height="31" bgcolor="#080830" bordercolor=
            "#C0B068">
        <font color="#C0B068">Customer ID </font>
      <td width="122" height="31" bgcolor="#080830" bordercolor=
            "#C0B068">
        <font color="#C0B068">Firstname </font>
      <td width="114" height="31" bgcolor="#080830" bordercolor=
            "#C0B068">
        <font color="#C0B068">Lastname </font>
      <td width="118" height="31" bgcolor="#080830" bordercolor=
            "#C0B068">
        <font color="#C0B068">Address</font></tr>
      <td width="61" height="31" bgcolor="#080830" bordercolor=
            "#C0B068">
        <font color="#C0B068">City</font>
      <td width="20" height="31" bgcolor="#080830" bordercolor=
            "#C0B068">
        <font color="#C0B068">State</font>
      </tr>
<% do until rstemp.eof %>
   <tr>
      <td width="20" height="1"><%=rstemp("customerID")%></td>
      <td width="122" height="1"><%=rstemp("firstname")%></td>
      <td width="114" height="1"><%=rstemp("lastname")%></td>
      <td width="118" height="1"><%=rstemp("address")%></td>
```

```
            <td width="61" height="1"><%=rstemp("city")%></td>
            <td width="20" height="1"><%=rstemp("state")%></td>
        </tr>
    <%    rstemp.movenext
        loop
    %>
        </table>
    <%
    end if
    %>
     
    </body>
```

Building SQL Statements

In the previous chapter we had an example of how conditional statements could be used with SQL statements to build record-sources for Access forms. The same process can be used to build data sources for web pages. Using our phone number example, we will show how an ASP page can be built with code and SQL to alleviate the need of having several queries and to reduce the number of web pages.

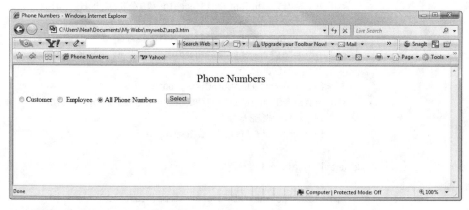

Figure 15-7. Selection page

The web form begins with the same basic layout as the Access form. When the user selects an option button and then clicks on the Select button (Figure 15-7), information for everyone in the database who has a phone number appears, as shown in Figure 15-8.

			Phone Numbers		

○ Customer ○ Employee ● All Phone Numbers [Select]

1	Kayla	Allison	6725 3rd Ave. N	Atlanta	GA
2	Devon	Fields	1001 30th St S	Tampa	FL
3	Gene	Spencer	3910 35th Ave S	St.Pete	FL
4	Spencer	Madewrll	32101 60th Ave E	Honolulu	HI
5	Reggie	Collins	1526 1st St. N	Tampa	FL
6	Peny	Penn	2875 Treetop St N	Tampa	FL
8	Henry	George	1000 East West St	Jacksonville	FL
9	Alice	George	1000 East West St	Jacksonville	FL
10	Bill	George	1812 Hemingway	Jacksonville	FL
11	Mary	Wilson	13120 N 15th East	Ogden	UT

Figure 15-8. Selection page with results

We have cheated a bit on this code to do everything in one form. Basically the important part of the ASP code (from the standpoint of SQL) is contained in a SELECT statement similar to the one in Access.

```
allorone = request.form("allorone")
select case allorone
    case "Cust"
        mySQL = "SELECT firstname, lastname, phonenumber FROM
        Customers"
    case "Emp"
        mySQL = "SELECT firstname, lastname, phonenumber FROM
        Employees"
    case "All"
        mysql = "SELECT firstname, lastname, phonenumber FROM
        Customers UNION SELECT firstname, lastname, phonenumber FROM
        Employees"
```

287

```
    case else
        stopprocessing = true
    end select
```

The actual code to open the SQL is as follows:

```
set rstemp=conntemp.execute(mySQL)
```

To enable a single form to handle the initial form without a button selected and handle the SQL processing after a button is selected, we have added the "else" case to set a flag notifying the system to not process the remaining ASP code on the page.

The second major deviation between this code and the Access code is the overhead needed to process the radio buttons on the form. Unlike Access VBA with a plethora of events that can trigger things happening, ASP has a very limited set of events that can trigger an action. The major way to input data into ASP is to use the POST method and to trigger it with a submit command.

```
<form action="asp2.asp" method="POST"><p> </p>
<p align="left" style="margin-left: 10">
<input type="radio" checked name="allOrOne" value="Cust">Customer
<input type="radio" name="allOrOne" value="Emp">Employee
<input type="radio" name="allOrOne" value="All">All phone
            numbers       
<input type="submit" value="select" name="select">.
```

We begin by telling ASP that the POST method will be used to open a new ASP page. The page that will be opened is asp2.asp, which just happens to be the current page. The two variables on the page that will provide data to the ASP page are allOrOne and the Select button. The allOrOne variable provides the option button values "Cust," "Emp," or "All," depending upon the radio button that is selected. The button provides the value "select," which is not used in this example. The real purpose of the button is to trigger the action.

When the button is clicked, the page asp2.asp is opened with the POST value allOrOne=Cust&select=select.

Once again we have Visual Basic overhead similar to our previous example to verify that the recordset actually does have information in it, the overhead to open the ODBC connection, and the actual Visual Basic code to pull the data from the recordset. We also have the HTML overhead to set up the fields and to arrange the data in the table. When everything is combined, the final result is as follows:

```
<html>
<head>
<meta http-equiv="Content-Language" content="en-us">
<meta http-equiv="Content-Type" content="text/html;
charset=windows-1252">
<meta name="GENERATOR" content="Microsoft FrontPage 5.0">
<meta name="ProgId" content="FrontPage.Editor.Document">
</head>
<body>
<%
    myDSN="DSN=wordware"
    set conntemp=server.createobject("adodb.connection")
    conntemp.open myDSN

%>
    <p align="center"><b><font size="5" face="Arial" color=
        "#990000"> Phone Numbers</font></b><p align=
        "center"> <p align="center">
    <form action="asp2.asp" method="POST"><p> </p>

    <p align="left" style="margin-left: 10">
    <input type="radio" checked name="allorone" value="Cust">Customer
    <input type="radio" name="allorone" value="Emp">Employee
    <input type="radio" name="allorone" value="All">All phone
            numbers       
    <input type="submit" value="select" name="select">

        <%
        allorone = request.form("allorone")

        stopprocessing = false
        select case allorone
            case "Cust"
                mySQL = "SELECT firstname, lastname, phonenumber FROM
                        Customers"
```

```
        case "Emp"
            mySQL = "SELECT firstname, lastname, phonenumber FROM
                     Employees"
        case "All"
            mysql = "SELECT firstname, lastname, phonenumber FROM
                     Customers UNION SELECT firstname, lastname,
                     phonenumber FROM Employees"
        case else
            stopprocessing = true
    end select
    if stopprocessing <> true then
        set rstemp=conntemp.execute(mySQL)
        if rstemp.eof then
            response.write "no data for<br>"
            response.write mySQL
            conntemp.close
            set conntemp=nothing
            response.end
        else %>

        <table border="0" width="781" height="462">
        <tr>
        <td width="122" height="31" bgcolor="#080830" bordercolor=
                "#C0B068">
            <font color="#C0B068">Firstname </font>
        <td width="114" height="31" bgcolor="#080830" bordercolor=
                "#C0B068">
            <font color="#C0B068">Lastname </font>
        <td width="118" height="31" bgcolor="#080830" bordercolor=
                "#C0B068">
            <font color="#C0B068">Phone Number</font>
        </tr>
<%      do until rstemp.eof %>
        <tr>
            <td width="122" height="1"><%=rstemp("firstname")%></td>
            <td width="114" height="1"><%=rstemp("lastname")%></td>
            <td width="118" height="1"><%=rstemp
                                    ("phoneNumber")%></td>
        </tr>
<%          rstemp.movenext
        loop
```

```
%>
        </table>
<%
end if
end if
%>
 </body>
```

Summary

This chapter showed how SQL can be used within ASP code to facilitate writing web pages. It also showed how the use of Visual Basic code and SQL can be used to reduce the number of actual web pages needed by judiciously reusing a basic template and by modifying the SQL data source to fill in the necessary information.

Chapter 16

Access Projects

Introduction

In this chapter, you will learn about Access projects, how they are different from Access databases, and how they provide a different perspective on the concept of SQL commands. We will also go into the fundamental elements of an Access project and show some of the pitfalls in their use.

Definitions

Access database — An Access program developed with the Access Jet database engine.

Access project — An Access program that uses an SQL back end exclusively rather than local Jet elements.

Overview

We have been a bit vague in defining exactly what database engine we have been working with for the examples in this book. The reason for this is both simple and complex as it almost always is when dealing with Microsoft products. For the most part, we have simply ignored the database engine since almost all examples will work fine no matter what version of SQL or Jet you decide to run. On the other hand, there are a few instances where the engine is critical. The "fun" is in determining in which cases the engine really does matter.

Unfortunately, Microsoft has not made things easy for us. A bit of history is in order. In the early days of Access (versions prior to Access 95), Microsoft took the approach that Access was a consumer product and the internal Jet engine was all that the user would need. FoxPro and Visual Basic were the tools to access big databases, not Access. However, as Access became more popular, Microsoft did add ODBC drivers to Access to pull data from other sources including Microsoft SQL Server and Oracle. While Jet was still the fastest and easiest way to build a database, the other back-end databases were now an additional option. Still, Access and Jet were considered light-weight consumer products that lacked the security and stability of the heavy-duty commercial products. But as Access grew in popularity and the FoxPro market continued to shrink, Micro-soft had to rethink its positioning of Access. With Access 2000, Access finally entered the "big leagues" when Microsoft intro-duced Personal SQL, a product that tried to combine the strengths of SQL Server with the convenience of Jet. We now had Access functioning as a front end to Jet, Personal SQL, and Microsoft SQL Server.

"Why three different database engines?" you might ask. It is easy to give a simple answer. Jet is easy to use, transparent to implement, and does a good job with most applications. It does, however, bog down with more than a dozen concurrent users, lacks real security, and does not have the robustness of a "real" database engine.

Microsoft SQL Server is at the other end of the spectrum. It is a true multiuser system application optimized to handle the processing of large databases. Generally it is installed on a ded-icated Windows XP Server box that is loaded with memory and has very fast hard disk access. Microsoft SQL Server has true security built into it and has true transaction processing where all data gets recorded before it is incorporated into the data-base. This allows for fallback operation and selective restoration of data, ensuring total data integrity. SQL Server also requires constant support to ensure that all operations are optimized and that data backup and system maintenance take place. One database administration consultant says that most of her business comes from companies that try to use SQL without having an administrator at hand. The databases usually work but inevitably they all seem to fail without maintenance.

The third product, Personal SQL, is a compromise and tries to combine the best aspects of Jet with the best features of SQL Server. It provides the data integrity of SQL Server but does not have the need for dedicated system maintenance. It is optimized for efficient data access but does not have the multiuser capabilities of SQL Server. It also does not have all of the support that its big brother has, so you cannot fine-tune it or perform most of the maintenance functions manually. Most important to the user, Personal SQL is a lot cheaper than full-blown SQL Server.

Programmatically, there are differences between SQL and Jet that differentiate the programs. Jet uses the old Microsoft DAO programming to access data. DAO is quick, simple, fast to implement, and relatively easy to debug. SQL generally uses the newer ADO technology. ADO is generally considered the "preferred" method of database manipulation since it is more generic and can be used for other interfaces as well as reaching SQL back ends. It also has many more features than DAO and is considered by Microsoft to be a newer and better technology. On the other hand, it is definitely more temperamental, far more difficult to program, and far more difficult to debug.

Which database engine the user should use is obviously not a simple choice. And much of the time Microsoft does not seem to have a definitive answer. Initially, Microsoft's position was that Jet was the only engine that should be used with Access. For heavy-duty database crunching SQL Server was better but one should use FoxPro as the tool to get to the data. With the relative demise of FoxPro and the increasing dependence on Access to get to all types of data, Microsoft began providing simple methods of getting SQL data to Access via ODBC drivers and new ways of referencing the data with pass-through queries. The waters were definitely getting a bit muddied on what to use and where to use it.

In the mid-'90s one of the standard questions at Microsoft seminars was "When should a database be in Jet and when should it be in SQL Server?" The answer was more often than not, "When it is too big for Jet, move it to SQL Server." A definite hedge since they made a point of not defining what "too big for Jet" really meant. They did admit that it was dependent on the size of the database, the number of users, the complexity of the queries, and the load on the network, but even these definitions were left intentionally vague.

Microsoft even tried to make it easier to migrate from Jet to SQL during this time with upsizing tools to migrate databases from Jet to SQL. While good in theory, most of these early tools were more flair than real substance. While tables would upsize, unless the designer had originally thought in terms of SQL, the upsized tables performed slower rather than faster. The tool merely moved the tables over to SQL, leaving all of the query processing local to the machine where the Access program resided. The net effect was that you had all of the overhead of SQL and all of the overhead of Jet. Most people were extremely disappointed when there was no speed increase when their databases were upsized. In all fairness, however, the tools did get better as subsequent versions were released and Microsoft's teaching tools began to introduce "better" ways of designing queries and table links.

The migration to SQL improved to the point that with the introduction of Office XP, the official Microsoft line was that Jet was dead and people should start moving to Personal SQL, which was included with Office. Microsoft did stress, however, that Personal SQL was not to be confused with its big brother, Microsoft SQL, although most of the features were identical. Personal SQL was designed for smaller systems and while the features were identical, it had not been optimized and tweaked the way Microsoft SQL had been and was definitely not a database engine for anything but the smallest environments. To further encourage the migration away from Jet and to offset the fact that Personal SQL did not come with tools to build tables or queries for server-side operations, Microsoft included a new type of Access database: the Access project that exclusively used SQL Server-like tables accessed by the SQL engines. A new method of programmatically accessing the data was also developed called ADO. ADO incorporated access to many SQL features that were not available with DAO. Features like constraint checking and altering Unicode compression will produce error messages if attempted in DAO or through the Access query grid. They work fine in ADO.

All was not perfect, however. When Microsoft declared Personal SQL was not a replacement for Microsoft SQL, they meant it. While easy to use, Personal SQL had one critical flaw: It could not be used concurrently by more than five people. In short, if you wanted to use SQL with more than a handful of people, you had to get SQL Server and pay that program's much higher price. Most people reacted to this limitation with a general decision to stick with Jet.

Then along came Access 2003. It appeared that Microsoft, which had been apparently abandoning Jet, was now embracing it again with a new version. ADO, while highly touted in most of the Microsoft literature for Access XP, was almost nonexistent in Office 2003. People continued using DAO.

This brings us back to the topic of which version of SQL we have used in this book. For the most part, we have stuck with "good old" Jet. But the Access projects feature does deserve additional mention since it provides an easier bridge to true SQL.

At least it did until Access 2007 came out and Microsoft took yet another about-face. After dealing with a lackluster reception to projects and an effort to try to move people off Access entirely and to .NET and SQL Server Reporting Services, Microsoft has abandoned projects (at least for right now). While you can still open a project in Access 2007, you cannot do anything to it in the way of making edits. The author still likes projects, however, and finds them very useful — just not in Access 2007. So, for the rest of this chapter, we will drop back to Access 2003.

Differences between Access Projects and Access Databases

The first thing you will note about Access projects is that they are a totally different entity from Access databases. When you want an Access receptacle you can create a database or you can create a project — you cannot create a hybrid between the two designs.

○ **Note:**   One other thing you will quickly see in this discussion of projects is that all the examples are done in Access 2003 on an XP system. This accounts for the different format of everything from the style of the windows and toolbars to the verbose instructions for doing everything.

A project is created when Access is opened and the user selects **New** and then **Project using new data**. See Figure 16-1.

The next dialog box that appears allows you to name the file and select the location. This process should be very familiar to the user since it is the same process used to create a traditional Access database. See Figure 16-2.

Figure 16-1. New project menu selection

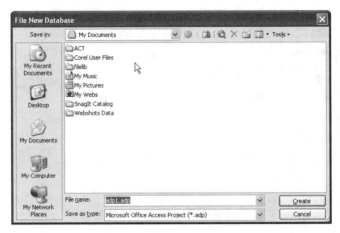

Figure 16-2. File New Database dialog

You need to specify that the file is of type **Microsoft Office Access Project (*.adp)**, but the process is identical to creating an Access database.

The next window is new for projects. Since projects depend on SQL Server or Personal SQL for the database engine, you will next have to select the location of the SQL database through the SQL Server Database Wizard. It is assumed that you either have installed Personal SQL on your machine or have a network connection to an SQL Server. If you don't, you will not be able to proceed past this step. Microsoft has made it very difficult to mess up this step!

Figure 16-3. SQL Server Database Wizard screen

The first thing you will need to do is select an SQL Server from the drop-down (Figure 16-3). All SQL Servers available to your computer should appear in this drop-down list. We have noticed that once in a while, SQL gets confused and does not include the local server in this list. Just entering the name of the local server is often enough to get the wizard to go out and find the server. Next, fill in the Login ID and Password boxes. If you have set up the SQL Server or Personal SQL to use system passwords, you might be able to skip entering the ID and password. Finally, enter the name of the new SQL Server database or enter the name of an existing database that you plan on using. Clicking on the Next button completes the connection process and you will return to the project window.

Project Window

You will notice that this window is very similar to the one that you have for an Access database, but there are a few differences. The first big difference is the inclusion of Database Diagrams in the Objects list, as shown in Figure 16-4.

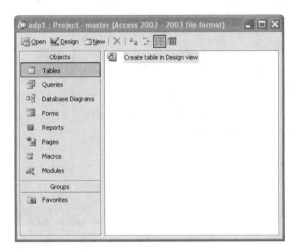

Figure 16-4. Project window

The second difference is a bit more subtle but even more important. Note that the SQL database is included in the title bar. If you have just loaded an Access project, you do not have the link to the SQL back end until you log in to it. This can be noted by the "disconnected" indicator in the title bar as shown in Figure 16-5.

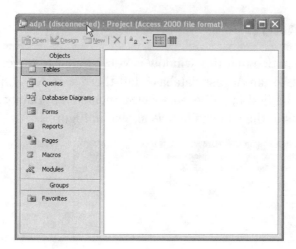

Figure 16-5. Not connected

Tables

The real differences between a project and a database appear when you begin working with objects, beginning with tables. The layout of a project table is slightly different from a database table, as Figure 16-6 shows. Nulls are indicated as a primary attribute, not just a property. Second, there is no special data type for autonumbers. Instead, an autonumbering index is built by selecting the data type as int (integer), then selecting the Identity property of Yes. Also note that the identity seed and identity increment can be set directly in the Table view.

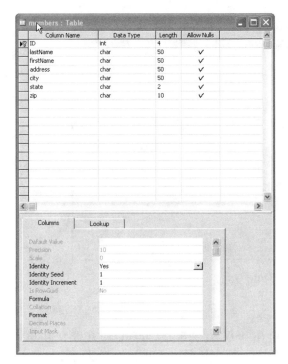

Figure 16-6. Table view

The Table view also gives you the full spectrum of data types, unlike database tables. Some of the possibilities are shown in Figure 16-7.

Figure 16-7. Data types

We have previously shown the various types of data available to Jet and how the Jet data types map to SQL. Here is the same information from Microsoft Office Online presented with an SQL perspective.

Table 16-1. Data types

ANSI SQL Data Type	Microsoft Jet SQL Data Type	Synonym	Microsoft SQL Server Data Type
BIT, BIT VARYING	BINARY (See Notes)	VARBINARY, BINARY VARYING, BIT VARYING	BINARY, VARBINARY
Not supported	BIT (See Notes)	BOOLEAN, LOGICAL, LOGICAL1, YESNO	BIT
Not supported	TINYINT	INTEGER1, BYTE	TINYINT
Not supported	COUNTER (See Notes)	AUTO-INCREMENT	(See Notes)
Not supported	MONEY	CURRENCY	MONEY

ANSI SQL Data Type	Microsoft Jet SQL Data Type	Synonym	Microsoft SQL Server Data Type
DATE, TIME, TIMESTAMP	DATETIME	DATE, TIME (See Notes)	DATETIME
Not supported	UNIQUEIDEN-TIFIER	GUID	UNIQUE-IDENTIFIER
DECIMAL	DECIMAL	NUMERIC, DEC	DECIMAL
REAL	REAL	SINGLE, FLOAT4, IEEESINGLE	REAL
DOUBLE PRECISION, FLOAT	FLOAT	DOUBLE, FLOAT8, IEEEDOUBLE, NUMBER (See Notes)	FLOAT
SMALLINT	SMALLINT	SHORT, INTEGER2	SMALLINT
INTEGER	INTEGER	LONG, INT, INTEGER4	INTEGER
INTERVAL	Not supported	Not supported	Not supported
Not supported	IMAGE	LONGBINARY, GENERAL, OLEOBJECT	IMAGE
Not supported	TEXT (See Notes)	LONGTEXT, LONGCHAR, MEMO, NOTE, NTEXT (See Notes)	TEXT
CHARACTER, CHARACTER VARYING, NATIONAL CHARACTER, NATIONAL CHARACTER VARYING	CHAR (See Notes)	TEXT(n), ALPHA-NUMERIC, CHARACTER, STRING, VARCHAR, CHARACTER VARYING, NCHAR, NATIONAL CHARACTER, NATIONAL CHAR, NATIONAL CHARACTER VARYING, NATIONAL CHAR VARYING (See Notes)	

Notes

- The ANSI SQL BIT data type does not correspond to the Microsoft Jet SQL BIT data type. It corresponds to the BINARY data type instead. There is no ANSI SQL equivalent for the Microsoft Jet SQL BIT data type.
- TIMESTAMP is no longer supported as a synonym for DATETIME.

- NUMERIC is no longer supported as a synonym for FLOAT or DOUBLE. NUMERIC is now used as a synonym for DECIMAL.

- A LONGTEXT field is always stored in the Unicode representation format.

- If the data type name TEXT is used without specifying the optional length, such as TEXT(25), a LONGTEXT field is created. This enables CREATE TABLE statements to be written that will yield data types consistent with Microsoft SQL Server.

- In Jet databases, the AUTONUMBER data type is a specific data type separate from LONG. In SQL, the same attributes are set up by declaring a variable of type INT and assigning its identity properties.

- A CHAR field is always stored in the Unicode representation format, which is the equivalent of the ANSI SQL NATIONAL CHAR data type.

- If the data type name TEXT is used and the optional length is specified, such as TEXT(25), the data type of the field is equivalent to the CHAR data type. This preserves backward compatibility for most Microsoft Jet applications, while enabling the TEXT data type without a length specification to be aligned with Microsoft SQL Server.

Database Diagrams

Another difference between a project and a database appears in the database diagram object type. This is the equivalent of the Relationship window that is opened via the Tools | Relationships toolbar item.

The database diagrams are built in the same way that the relationship screen is with one major exception: Unlike the relationship screen, each table can be added to a diagram only once. See Figure 16-8.

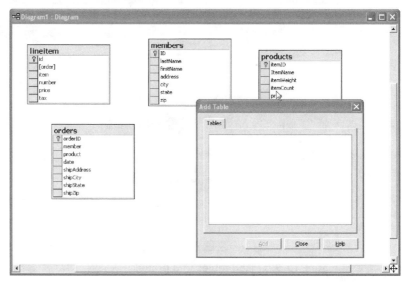

Figure 16-8. Database diagram

Once the tables are added to a diagram, joins can be constructed just like in the relationship screen. The display of the
table relationships is a bit different from that of the relationship
screen (Figure 16-9.). For example, the fields that compose the
link are not apparent on the database diagram unless you wait
for the pop-up. On the other hand, if you go into the properties
of each table within the database diagram, there is far more
information available than can be pulled from the relationship
screen.

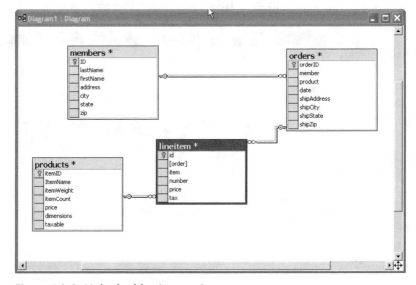

Figure 16-9. Linked tables in a project

One of the biggest improvements of the database diagram over
the relationship screen is that Microsoft has provided a signifi-
cant amount of control over how the tables appear on the
screen. Figure 16-10 shows the pop-up menu for this window.
With a single click of the mouse, the tables can be rearranged,
moved around on the screen, and formatted for printing.

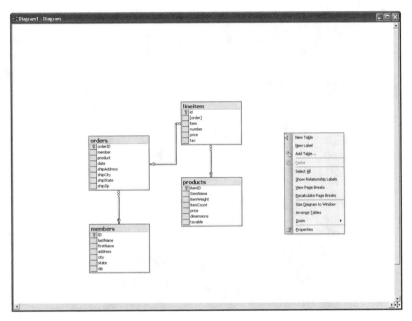

Figure 16-10. Database diagram pop-up menu

The other area of major improvement is the Properties menu. A tremendous amount of information about every table, field, index, and relationship can be derived from the Properties menu. And to go even further, selections made in the combo boxes on the Properties pages are immediately reflected in the database diagram. Select a different table and the highlight shifts to the newly selected table. See Figure 16-11.

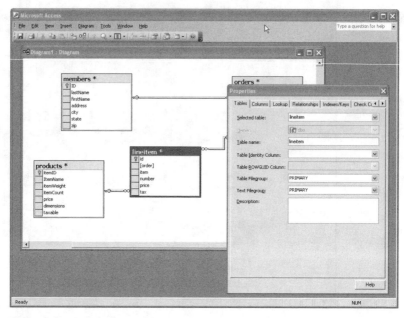

Figure 16-11. Database diagram Properties window

Queries

While tables and database diagrams have many cosmetic changes that make them different from the Access database equivalents, the real differences between projects and databases lie in the area of queries. Projects are designed with SQL back ends in mind, and the fundamental concepts of project queries highlights this. The Queries tab shows the three primary types of SQL queries: functions, views, and stored procedures (Figure 16-12). Unlike the Access database, you can design each query based on how it will function in the SQL environment.

Figure 16-12. Project query creation selection

Notice that there is a definite separation in the classification of queries. Views are basically the linked combination of tables and other views. They can best be compared with select queries in Access databases. Stored procedures are the equivalent of make-table queries, update queries, delete queries, and append queries. Functions are similar to views but allow parameters to be passed and get preprocessed in SQL rather than Access.

Views

Views are the Access project equivalent of select queries with the same basic functionality and limitations. Like select queries, views do not occupy space as an independent collection but reference the underlying dataset of the tables. The net effect is that anything you do to the data in the view gets reflected in the underlying table. Views are great for predefined slicing and dicing of a database but are rather inflexible since they do not permit run-time parameters.

311

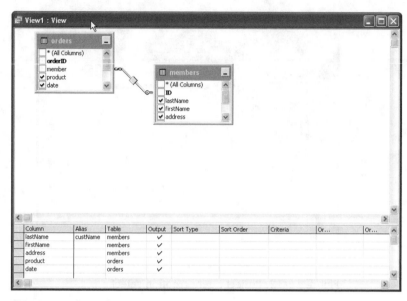

Figure 16-13. Project view

Note that the view shown in Figure 16-13 presents the join
between the tables in a slightly more informative manner than
does the Access database.

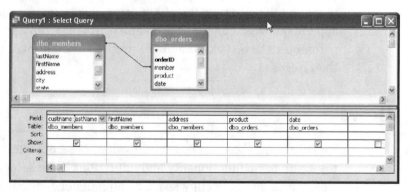

Figure 16-14. Database select query

While databases allow you to enter alias names, displaying these aliases is a bit cumbersome. In an Access database the way to construct an alias is to place the alias name on the field line separated from the field source by a colon. See the custname field in Figure 16-14 for an example of this. This is definitely harder to read than the format for views, which have a distinct column for the alias names.

The second big difference in the layout of the view is that you can tell immediately if a field is present in the view by noting whether the check box in front of the field name is checked or not checked. You can also add fields to the query grid by checking the boxes next to the field names. This is a minor feature but one that is extremely valuable when the query consists of many fields.

The next big difference between views and select queries is the ordering of fields: Views have fields in a vertical format; select queries are in a horizontal arrangement. This is another minor difference but one that makes the query a lot more readable.

The joins have been enhanced in projects with a few new features that can be entered from the query grid. These can be observed by noting that the connector between the two tables now has a symbol that graphically describes the join. In Access projects, when you have a join between records in one table that match records in a second table, the line is a solid line. When the join includes all the records from one table and only the matching records from the second table, the line is replaced with an arrow. The tail of the arrow represents the table from which all records are taken and the head of the arrow represents the table from which only matching records are present. The Access project represents this by the diamond shape in the middle of the join, as shown in Figure 16-15.

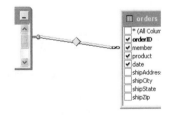

Figure 16-15. Join representation

To show that all records are to be taken from the orders table, the center diamond is modified as shown in Figure 16-16.

Figure 16-16. Right outer join

In a similar manner, all records from the members table are represented by the symbol pointing the opposite direction as shown in Figure 16-17.

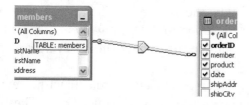

Figure 16-17. Left outer join

The new addition is when you wish to take all records from both tables regardless of whether they have a corresponding record in the other table. See Figure 16-18.

Figure 16-18. Full outer join

The join is built in the same manner as a join is built in an Access database. Right-clicking on the join brings up the pop-up window from which properties can be selected. In the

Properties window are two check boxes for which records to include. See Figure 16-19.

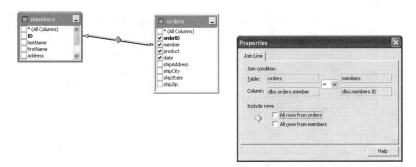

Figure 16-19. Properties window

The Properties window also allows the user to set up the join condition (Figure 16-20). In Access databases, it is assumed that the join is going to be an equal join where the join field in the first table is equal to the join field in the second table. An Access project allows you to set the condition in the Properties window to other comparisons including not equal, greater than, less than, less than or equal, and greater than or equal.

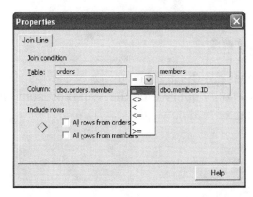

Figure 16-20. Properties window options

Selecting not equal (< >) for the join condition changes the SQL statement as expected, as shown in Figure 16-21.

315

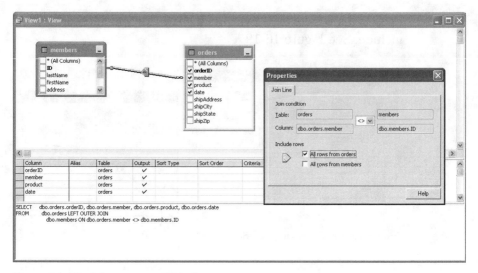

Figure 16-21. Join property SQL view

Functionally, views and select queries are identical with the primary difference being that views are stored on the server and queries are calculated locally. In the case of a remote SQL Server, the view calculations take place on the server and produce far less transfer of data.

Stored Procedures

Stored procedures are the action queries of the Access project realm and are the only query type that can represent an update, append, make-table, or delete query.

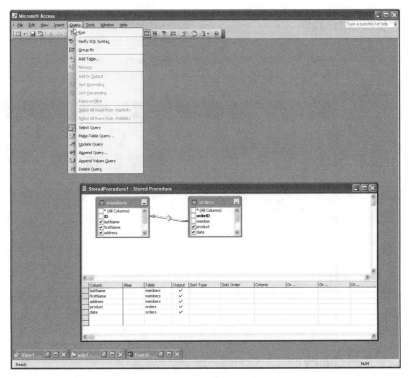

Figure 16-22. Database project stored procedures

As Figure 16-22 shows, the stored procedure allows the user to set up the initial query, then determine what type of action is going to take place. Here are several interesting observations on stored procedures. First, while a standard select query format is possible, the recordset that is derived from the stored procedure is not editable. Second, when a stored procedure is used to construct an update query, only one item can be in the upper portion of the query grid. This is easily handled, however, by making a view composed of several tables as the source. The view can have as its source whatever you wish, but from the standpoint of Access, it is a single entity.

Functions

Visually, functions appear identical to views as Figure 16-23 shows.

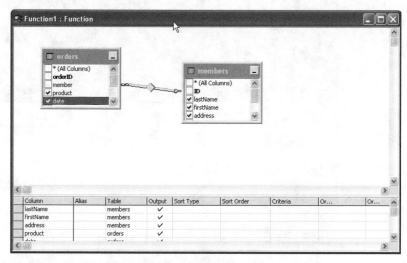

Figure 16-23. Database project functions

The data grid view is very deceptive, however, since there is a great deal that is not revealed. To get under the covers, so to speak, we have to look at the SQL view for both types of queries. If you display the SQL equivalent of the view, you get a standard select query as shown in Figure 16-24.

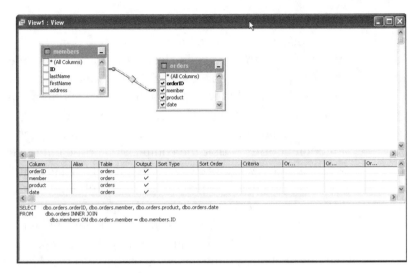

Figure 16-24. View with SQL

The SQL produced by a function is a little bit different. Notice that it actually returns a value, in this case a table. In short, a query function is just like all other functions in programming. It can take a variety of parameters and generate a single result as the output. In the case of the function query, the output result is a table.

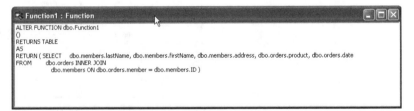

Figure 16-25. Function as SQL

What makes the function far more powerful than the view is what appears in the second line of the function shown in Figure 16-25. Notice the open and close parentheses. Just like any other function, you can add parameter values for the function to process. Generally these parameters are such things as filter values, but one can be extremely creative in defining a function query through parameters. Another important aspect of these function queries is that the compilation of the query occurs when the query is stored, not when it is run. This can lead to far faster processing since the elements of the query do not have to be evaluated every time the query is run.

Now we get into the fun stuff that we have been hinting at. Instead of building a new query from the three options given in the query display, build a new query by selecting New from the menu bar. Notice that there are a few different options, as shown in Figure 16-26.

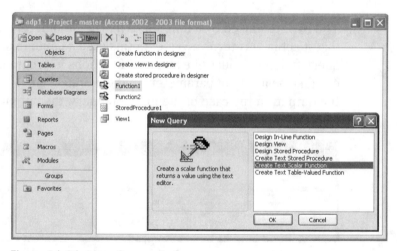

Figure 16-26. New Query window

Selecting Create Text Scalar Function produces the following function template.

```
Function3 : Function                                    _ □ ✕
CREATE FUNCTION "Function3"
        (
        /*
        @parameter1 datatype = default value,
        @parameter2 datatype
        */
        )
RETURNS /* datatype */
AS
        BEGIN
                /* sql statement ... */
        RETURN /* value */
        END
```

Figure 16-27. Function query template

Notice that what we end up with is a skeleton layout for producing a query. It is here that we can define our parameters and build our SQL statements. When complete and stored away, Access takes the input and creates a function from our input. In short, we have come full circle. We began our discussion of Access projects by showing how they were like Access databases and provided complete graphical tools for building database elements. Our final example uses the graphical elements to once again go back to simple text for entering SQL statements.

Summary

The Access project is a powerful tool for building SQL interfaces. It makes the transition from the Access Jet database model to the more powerful SQL Server engine by providing a familiar interface. While there are some subtle (and not so subtle!) differences, the overall effect is to provide the user with a comfortable way to enter the world of true SQL.

321

Personally, we are sorry to see that Microsoft has discontinued projects. It did provide a very simple and convenient way of accessing MS/SQL databases and it was very easy to use. But who is to say that they are gone permanently. Like everything at Microsoft, there are no definites.

Quiz 16

1. What are the major differences between a project and a database?

2. True or False. The only way to include an SQL table in Access is with an Access project.

Project 16

The best way to see the advantages and disadvantages of an Access project is to take an existing Access database and rebuild it in the project template. Take some of the examples in the previous chapters and create them in a new Access project. Especially note the differences mentioned in this chapter.

As an additional exercise, populate the database and project with identical data and note the differences in the speeds of the two data sources.

Chapter 17

Concluding Thoughts

Introduction

In this chapter we will be adding those thoughts that do not fit in anywhere else in the book. We will also be adding a few concluding remarks on what we consider to be the big picture regarding SQL.

Common Rules

One of the most important rules to follow when designing any query or table is to consider how the information will be used. While we have shown that there is a lot of power in SQL, we have glossed over the important aspects of table and query optimization. **The most important thing about SQL is that its only purpose is to access data.** It is a tool, not the end result. If a query runs slowly because of poor design or because table linkages are not thought out, the user will become frustrated with the amount of effort needed to get the information and will be less inclined to use the program. It doesn't matter if you have a beautiful query if the user does not use it. Remember that the user does not see the code, just the end result.

To this end, there are a few basic rules about query design that need to be stressed. First, it is always better to filter first, then perform needed calculations on the data. There is no need to perform the calculations and waste time when the calculation is not going to be used.

Second, filter first, then link secondary tables. The thoughts regarding calculations apply here, too.

Third, temporary tables and views are extremely powerful when you are using a subset of the data over and over. Why bother to rerun filters and calculations when you can have the data put away in a temporary location for very quick access?

Fourth, just because you can grab all the fields in all the tables does not mean you should grab all the fields. If you only need one field from a 200-column table, it makes far more sense to only take the field you need and reduce your overhead by an order of magnitude. Sure, you can use the * shorthand to grab all the fields, but you will find that what you save in laziness will cost you in processing.

Fifth, if you need to do a calculation more than once, store the result and don't repeat the calculation. For example, if you need the first occurrence of a particular string after a specific character and you use this same value more than once, set a temporary field to the value and keep using it rather than recalculating it every time. It is amazing how much faster queries go with this type of optimization.

Summary

In this book we have covered the basics of SQL and how it can be used in Access. But there is far more to the SQL story. Microsoft and Oracle have developed versions of SQL that are designed to get every possible degree of speed out of accessing data. While most of the optimization tricks and special features of Oracle and Microsoft SQL are beyond the scope of this book, there is a wealth of power in these programs that we have not begun to address. This book can be used to reach a good plateau of expertise that will greatly improve your skill with databases. It can also be used as a stepping-stone to additional knowledge.

➲ **Note:**   Some people might be curious about the software we used to write this book and what we have on our systems. Neal is currently running two systems on his desk. His old system is a P4 1.7 GHz with 512 MB of memory and approximately 400 GB of hard disk space. This old system is running a dual boot Windows 2000 and Windows XP Pro and is used primarily for those times when he gets frustrated with Vista or needs non-Vista compatible programs like his old Micrografx software. His new system is a dual core 2.0 GHz with 2 GB of memory and 1.4 TB of storage. It is a Vista system. He is currently bouncing between Access 2000, Access XP, Access 2003, and Access 2007 but he prefers Access 2002. He uses SQL Server 2000 as his SQL back end. Cecelia used mainly Access 2007 but experimented with Access 2003 as well. Most sections of the book were written using Word 2003. Our graphic program for screen captures and picture manipulation is primarily SnagIt by TechSmith.

Appendix A

Answers to Quizzes and Projects

This appendix provides answers to the quizzes and assignments found at the end of each chapter throughout the book.

Quiz 1

1. True or False. Normalization is a three-step technique used to ensure that all tables are logically linked together and that all fields in a table directly relate to the primary key. Answer: TRUE

2. True or False. A relational database is a collection of one or more tables that are related by key values. Answer: TRUE

3. True or False. A table is a two-dimensional column that contains files and fields. Answer: FALSE

4. True or False. A foreign key is a record in a table that links records of one database with those of another database. Answer: FALSE

5. True or False. A primary key is a column in a table that uniquely identifies every record in that table. Answer: TRUE

Project 1

Use the ERD model to diagram a one-to-many relationship showing one student who takes many courses and a many-to-one relationship showing many students in a single course. Compare this to the many-to-many model.

Answer:

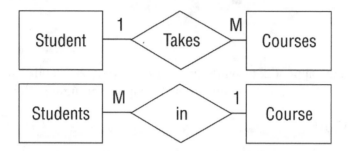

There are many courses with many students.

Quiz 2

1. What does SQL stand for? Answer: Structured Query Language

2. What was SQL called before it was called SQL? Answer: SEQUEL

3. Which SQL component is used to create tables and establish relationships among tables? Answer: Data Definition Language (DDL)

4. True or False. SQL is a procedural database programming language used within DBMSs to create, manage, and secure relational databases. Answer: FALSE

5. True or False. Microsoft Access refers to SQL as PLSQL. Answer: FALSE

Project 2

Practice locating SQL view without looking at the instructions for doing so.

Answer:

For Microsoft Access 2007

1. Click **Create** from the menu at the top of the screen.

2. Next, click the **Query Design** button near the top-right side of the screen.

3. Click **Close** on the Show Table dialog box without selecting any tables.

4. Locate the View drop-down button near the top left of the screen.

5. Use the View button to select **SQL View**. (Click the down arrow and scroll to the SQL View option.)

For Microsoft Access 2003

1. Click **Queries** on the left, and then click the **New** button located near the top of the screen.

2. When the New Query dialog box appears, select **Design View** and click **OK**.

3. Click **Close** in the Show Table dialog box (do not select any tables).

4. Locate the View button near the top of the screen.

5. Use the View button to select **SQL View**. (Click the down arrow located on the View button to locate the SQL View option.)

Quiz 3

1. True or False. NOT NULL means no value. Answer: FALSE

2. True or False. A data type specifies the maximum number of characters that a cell in a column can hold. Answer: FALSE

3. What constraint is used to link the records of one table to the records of another table? Answer: FOREIGN KEY

4. True or False. The WHERE keyword is used to insert a record into a table. Answer: FALSE

5. True or False. The UPDATE statement is used to update table names. Answer: FALSE

Project 3

Use the following values to insert a record into the Manufacturers table created earlier in the chapter:

Column Name	Value
ManufacturerID	1
ToyID	1
CompanyName	Matel
Address	2892 23rd Ave S
City	St. Petersburg
State	FL
PostalCode	33710
AreaCode	727
PhoneNumber	324-5421

Answer:

```
INSERT INTO Manufacturers
VALUES (1, 1, 'Matel','2892 23rd Ave S', 'St. Petersburg', 'FL',
        33710, 727, '324-5421');
```

Quiz 4

1. What two keywords must be used in the SELECT statement? Answer: SELECT and FROM

2. Records retrieved from the database are often referred to as what? Answer: The result set

3. True or False. The TOP keyword is used to display records that fall in the middle of a range specified by an ORDER BY clause. Answer: FALSE

4. True or False. The AS keyword is used to create an alias. Answer: TRUE

5. True or False. The DISTINCT keyword is used to display the duplicate values in a column. Answer: FALSE

Project 4

Use the Committee2 table in Figure 4-23 to create a query that displays the following output:

Name	FullAddress	TelephoneNumber
Brown, Debra	1900 12th Ave S Atlanta, GA 98718	301-897-0987
Cole, Leonard	1323 13th Ave N Atlanta, GA 98718	301-897-1241
Coney, Panzina	9033 Colfax Loop Tampa, FL 33612	813-223-6754
Fields, Kayla	2211 Peachtree St S Tampa, FL 33612	813-827-4532
London, Jerru	6711 40th Ave S Honolulu, HI 96820	808-611-2341

Answer:

```
SELECT Lastname& ', ' &Firstname AS Name, Address& ' ' &Zipcode
    AS FullAddress, Areacode& '-' &PhoneNumber AS
    TelephoneNumber
FROM Committee2
ORDER BY Lastname;
```

Quiz 5

1. True or False. An expression is a special character used to match parts of a value. Answer: FALSE

2. True or False. The following queries are equivalent:

   Query 1:

   ```
   SELECT *
   FROM Tools
   WHERE ToolID > 3 AND ToolID <10;
   ```

   Query 2:

   ```
   SELECT *
   FROM Tools
   WHERE ToolID BETWEEN 3 AND 10;
   ```

   Answer: FALSE

3. Using the Friends table in Figure 5-16, what will the following query return?

   ```
   SELECT FriendsID
   FROM Friends
   WHERE Lastname = 'Jones' AND Email IS NULL;
   ```

   Answer: 2

4. True or False. The exclamation mark (!) in the following WHERE clause means NOT:

   ```
   WHERE Location LIKE '[!A-C]';
   ```

   Answer: TRUE

5. True or False. The OR operator is processed before the AND operator in the order of evaluation. Answer: FALSE

Project 5

Use the Friends table in Figure 5-16 to write a query that returns records for individuals who live in Florida (FL).

Answer:

```
SELECT *
FROM Friends
WHERE Address LIKE '*FL*';
```

Quiz 6

1. True or False. The divide (/) operator is used to return the remainder in division. Answer: FALSE

2. True or False. Aggregate functions operate on only one row at a time. Answer: FALSE

3. True or False. The ddd date format displays the full names of days. Answer: FALSE

4. True or False. The CURRENTTIME () function is used to return the current time. Answer: FALSE

5. True or False. The numeric representation of dates is called a Julian (or serial) date. Answer: TRUE

Project 6

Use the Computers table in Figure 6-13 to display today's date and time, the SerialNum column, and the last five numbers from each serial number in the SerialNum column.

Answer:

```
SELECT NOW () AS DateAndTime, SerialNum, RIGHT (SerialNum, 5)
      AS LastFiveChars
FROM Computers;
```

Quiz 7

1. True or False. The GROUP BY clause can only be used in queries that contain at least two aggregate functions. Answer: FALSE

2. Will the following query work?

```
SELECT DATE () AS TodaysDate
FROM Transactions
GROUP BY CustomerID;
```

Answer: No. The query does not require a GROUP BY clause since there is no aggregate function in the query.

3. True or False. When using the GROUP BY clause with a WHERE clause, the GROUP BY clause must appear before the WHERE clause. Answer: FALSE

4. True or False. The GROUP BY clause must appear before the ORDER BY clause. Answer: TRUE

5. True or False. The HAVING clause filters rows before any data is grouped. Answer: FALSE

Project 7

Use the Transactions table in Figure 7-2 to display the customer IDs and the total number of products purchased by customers who only purchased one product.

Answer:

```
SELECT CustomerID, COUNT (ProductID) AS TotalProductsPurchased
FROM Transactions
GROUP BY CustomerID
HAVING COUNT (ProductID) = 1;
```

Quiz 8

1. True or False. A join enables you to use a single SELECT statement to query two or more tables simultaneously. Answer: TRUE

2. True or False. The following shows the correct syntax to qualify a table and column name: Tablename,Columnname. Answer: FALSE

3. True or False. Table aliases are created just like column aliases. Answer: TRUE

4. True or False. The UNION ALL keyword is used to combine records from two queries while excluding duplicate records. Answer: FALSE

5. True or False. A left outer join is used to select every record from the table specified to the left of the LEFT JOIN keywords. Answer: TRUE

Project 8

Use the Products table in Figure 8-12 and the Transactions table in Figure 8-14 to create an outer join that will display product IDs with customer IDs and purchase dates for customers who purchased a product (product ID). Additionally, display product IDs of products that have not been purchased yet.

Answer:

```
SELECT P.ProductID, T.CustomerID, T.DateSold

FROM Transactions AS T RIGHT JOIN Products AS P

ON T.ProductID = P.ProductID;
```

Quiz 9

1. True or False. A correlated subquery executes once for each record a referenced query returns. Answer: TRUE

2. True or False. The NOT operator is used to instruct Microsoft Access to match any condition opposite of the one defined. Answer: TRUE

3. True or False. The IN predicate is often used with the following comparison operators: =, <>, <, >, <=, and >=. Answer: FALSE

4. True or False. A subquery linked by the IN predicate can return two columns. Answer: FALSE

5. True or False. Subqueries nested within other queries are processed first, working outward. Answer: TRUE

Project 9

Use the Products table in Figure 9-21 to create a subquery that retrieves the ProductID and ProductName columns for products that have 30 or more items on order.

Answer:

```
SELECT ProductID, ProductName
FROM Products
WHERE OnOrder >= ALL
(SELECT OnOrder
FROM Products
WHERE OnOrder = 30);
```

Quiz 10

1. True or False. Updating data in views does not affect data stored in tables. Answer: FALSE

2. Views are commonly referred to as what? Answer: Virtual tables

3. True or False. Views are deleted using the DELETE keyword. Answer: FALSE

4. True or False. Views are created in SQL-92 using the CREATE VIEW keywords. Answer: TRUE

5. True or False. Deleting a table on which a view is dependent does not affect the view. Answer: FALSE

Project 10

Use the ComputerBrandLoc view in Figure 10-7 to update the Computers table in Figure 10-1. Update the office number for serial number X8276538101 from 311 to 136.

Answer:

```
UPDATE ComputerBrandLoc
SET OfficeNumber = 136
WHERE OfficeNumber = 311
AND SerialNum = 'X8276538101';
```

Quiz 11

1. True or False. The DISALLOW NULL option is used in the WITH clause. Answer: TRUE

2. Which option is used in the WITH clause to cause null data in a table to be ignored for an index? Answer: IGNORE NULL

3. True or False. The DELETE TABLE keywords are used to delete or remove an index. Answer: FALSE

4. True or False. The ALTER TABLE keywords are used to modify columns in an existing table. Answer: TRUE

5. What keywords are used in the ALTER TABLE statement to change a column's data type or field size? Answer: ALTER COLUMN

Project 11

1. Add a column named NewColumn to the Numbers table in Figure 11-1. Additionally, add a CHAR data type with a field size of 3.

   Answer:

   ```
   ALTER TABLE Numbers
   ADD NewColumn CHAR (3);
   ```

2. Create a unique index named NewColumnIdx for the NewColumn column you created in the Numbers table.

   Answer:

   ```
   CREATE UNIQUE INDEX NewColumnIdx
   ON Numbers (NewColumn);
   ```

Quiz 12

1. True or False. Updating data in temporary tables does not affect data stored in tables. Answer: TRUE

2. True or False. Temporary tables are automatically dropped when you log off or close Access. Answer: FALSE

3. True or False. Temporary tables are deleted using the DELETE keyword. Answer: FALSE

4. True or False. You must use the INTO keyword to create a temporary table in Access. Answer: TRUE

5. True or False. Temporary tables store the most current, up-to-date data. Answer: FALSE

Project 12

Create a temporary table named Temp2 that selects all the information from a table named Flowers with the following column names: FlowerID, Type, Color, Size.

Answer:

```
SELECT * INTO Temp2
FROM Flowers;
```

Quiz 13

1. True or False. A parameter query is a query that enables the user to set the criteria for selecting records at run time by filling in a dialog box. Answer: TRUE

2. True or False. When you use the BETWEEN keyword in a parameter query, it does not include records that match the values entered by the user. Answer: FALSE

3. True or False. Parameter queries can be used within forms. Answer: TRUE

4. True or False. The use of brackets in a parameter query is optional. Answer: FALSE

5. True or False. The asterisk is used with the LIKE keyword to match characters in a parameter query. Answer: TRUE

Project 13

Use the Sales table in Figure 13-13 to create a parameter query that prompts the user for two dates.

Answer:

```
SQL View:
SELECT *
FROM Sales;
```

Design view criteria:

```
BETWEEN [Type the first date:] AND [Type the second date:]
```

Quiz 16

1. What are the major differences between a project and a database? Answer: Review Chapter 16 for the answers.

2. True or False. The only way to include an SQL table in Access is with an Access project. Answer: FALSE

Appendix B

Frequently Used SQL Keywords in Microsoft Access

This appendix lists the most frequently used keywords in Access SQL. Most of the following keywords are used throughout the chapters. Some of the keywords are only available in version SQL-92 and later, while others are available in all versions of SQL. Keep in mind that there is a wide range of keywords in the SQL language and new keywords are continually being added.

ABS ()	CHAR
ADD	COLUMN
ALL	CONSTRAINT
ALTER COLUMN	COUNT (*)
ALTER TABLE	COUNT (*ColumnName*)
AND	COUNTER
ANY	CREATE INDEX
AS	CREATE TABLE
ASC	CREATE VIEW
AVG ()	DATE ()
BETWEEN	DATEPART (*interval,*
BINARY	*date* [*firstweekday*]
BIT	[, *firstweek*])
CCUR	DATETIME

DAY ()
DECIMAL
DEFAULT
DELETE
DELETE TABLE
DESC
DISALLOW NULL
DISTINCT
DISTINCTROW
DROP INDEX
DROP VIEW
EXISTS
FIRST ()
FLOAT
FOREIGN KEY
FORMAT (*ColumnName,*
  DateFormat)
GROUP BY
HAVING
HOUR ()
IGNORE NULL
IMAGE
IN
INDEX
INNER JOIN
INSERT INTO
INSERT INTO SELECT
INSTR (*Start,*
  SourceString,
  SearchString)
INT ()
INTEGER
INTO
IS NOT NULL
IS NULL
LAST ()

LCASE ()
LEFT (*StringExpression, n*)
LEFT JOIN
LEN ()
LIKE
LTRIM ()
MAX ()
MID (*StringExpression,*
  Start, Length)
MIN ()
MINUTE ()
MONEY
MONTH ()
NCHAR
NOT
NOT EXISTS
NOT NULL
NOW ()
NTEXT
NULL
NUMBER
NUMERIC
Nz (*Variant* [, *ValueIfNull*])
ON
ON DELETE CASCADE
ON UPDATE CASCADE
OR
ORDER BY
OUTER JOIN
PRIMARY KEY
REAL
RIGHT (*StringExpression,*
  n)
RIGHT JOIN
ROUND (*Fieldname,*
  DecimalValue)

RTRIM ()
SECOND ()
SELECT
SELECT INTO
SET
SMALLINT
SOME
SPACE ()
STDEV ()
STDEVP ()
SUM ()
TABLE
TIME ()
TIMESERIAL (*hour,*
minute, second)
TINYINT
TOP
TOP PERCENT

TRANSFORM
TRIM ()
TRUNCATE (*Fieldname,*
DigitValue)
UCASE ()
UNION
UNION ALL
UNIQUE
UNIQUEIDENTIFIER
UPDATE
VAR ()
VARCHAR
VARP ()
VIEW
WEEKDAY ()
WHERE
WITH
YEAR ()

Appendix C

Terms and Definitions

This appendix provides the terms and definitions discussed throughout the book.

Access database — An Access program developed with the Access Jet database engine.

Access project — An Access program that uses an SQL back end exclusively rather than local Jet elements.

Aggregate functions — Used to return a single value based on calculations on values stored in a column.

Alias — An alternate name for a table or column.

ALL — Keyword used to retrieve records from the main query that match all of the records in the subquery.

ALTER TABLE — Keywords used to modify table definitions in an existing table.

ANY — Keyword used to retrieve records from the main query that match any of the records in the subquery.

Arithmetic operators — Used to perform mathematical calculations.

AS — Keyword used to assign an alternate name to a column or table.

ASC — Keyword used to sort column values in ascending order.

ASP — Active Server Pages. Visual Basic code used in web development for web pages that need to access a back-end database or that have processing on the page.

Attribute — The characteristics of an entity.

Cartesian product — When each row in one table is multiplied by the total number of rows in another table.

Clause — A segment of an SQL statement that assists in the selection and manipulation of data.

Client — A single-user computer that interfaces with a multiple-user server.

Client/server database system — A database system that divides processing between client computers and a database server.

Column — A field within a table.

Comparison operators — Used to perform comparisons among expressions.

Concatenation — Merging values or columns together.

Constraints — Used to restrict values that can be inserted into a field and to establish referential integrity.

Correlated subquery — Executes once for each record a referenced query returns.

CREATE TABLE — Keywords used to instruct the database to create a new table.

CREATE VIEW — Keywords used to instruct the DBMS to create a new view.

Data modeling — The process of organizing and documenting the data that will be stored in a database.

Data type — Specifies the type of data a column can store.

Database — A collection of electronically stored organized files that relate to one another.

Database management system (DBMS) — Used to create, manage, and secure relational databases.

Date and time functions — Used to manipulate values based on the time and date.

DELETE — Used to remove records from a table.

DESC — Keyword used to sort column values in descending order.

DISALLOW NULL — Keywords used to prevent null data from being inserted into a column.

DISTINCT — Keyword used to display unique values in a column.

DISTINCTROW — Keyword used to exclude records based on the entire duplicate records, not just duplicate fields.

DROP VIEW — Keywords used to delete a view.

Entity — Any group of events, persons, places, or things used to represent how data is stored.

ERD model — The representation of data in terms of entities and relationships.

EXISTS — Keyword used to check for the existence of a value in the subquery.

Expression — Any data type that returns a value.

Field — Equivalent to a column.

Field size — Specifies the maximum number of characters that a cell in a column can hold.

File — A collection of similar records.

Foreign key — A column in a table that links records of the table to the records of another table.

GROUP BY clause — Used with aggregate functions to combine groups of records into a single functional record.

HAVING clause — Used with the GROUP BY clause to set conditions on groups of data calculated from aggregate functions.

HTML — Hypertext Markup Language.

IGNORE NULL — Used to cause null data in a table to be ignored for an index.

IIS — Internet Information Services.

IN — Keyword used to compare values in a column against column values in another table or query.

INDEX — Keyword used to sort and save the values of a column in a different location on the computer with a pointer pointing to the presorted records.

INNER JOIN — Keywords used to instruct the DBMS to combine matching values from two tables.

INSERT statement — Used to add records to a table.

Keys — Columns of a table with record values that are used as a link from other tables.

Keywords — Reserved words used within SQL statements.

LEFT JOIN — Keywords used to select every record from the table specified to the left of the LEFT JOIN keywords.

Logical operators — Used to test for the truth of some condition.

Microsoft Access — A desktop database management system used to create, manage, and secure relational databases.

Non-correlated subquery — Executes once since it contains no reference to an outside query.

Normalization — A three-step technique used to ensure that all tables are logically linked together and that all fields in a table directly relate to the primary key.

NOT — Keyword used to match any condition opposite of the one defined.

NULL — Keyword used to indicate no value.

ON — Keyword used to specify a condition.

ORDER BY clause — Used to sort retrieved records in descending or ascending order.

Parameter query — A query that enables the user to set the criteria for selecting records at run time by filling in a dialog box.

PRIMARY — Keyword used to designate a column as a primary key.

Primary key — A column in a table that uniquely identifies every record in a table.

Qualification — Used to match a column with a specific table.

Query — A question or command posed to the database.

Recordset — A collection of records in Visual Basic programming.

Referential integrity — A system of rules used to ensure that relationships between records in related tables are valid.

Relational database — A collection of two or more tables related by key values.

Relationship — An association between entities.

Result set — Records retrieved from the database.

RIGHT JOIN — Keyword used to select every record from the table specified to the right of the RIGHT JOIN keywords.

Row — A record within a table.

SELECT statement — Used to retrieve records from the database.

Self join — Used to join a table to itself.

Server — A multiple-user computer that provides shared database connection, interfacing, and processing services.

SOME — Keyword used to retrieve records from the main query that match any of the records in the subquery.

Statements — Keywords combined with data to form a database query.

String functions — Used to manipulate strings of character(s).

Structured Query Language (SQL) — A nonprocedural database programming language used within DBMSs to create, manage, and secure relational databases.

Subquery — A query linked to another query enabling values to be passed among queries.

Syntax — A series of rules that state how SQL script must be scripted.

Table — A two-dimensional file that contains rows and columns.

Temporary table — A table that encompasses the result of a saved SELECT statement.

TOP — Keyword used to display records that fall at the top or bottom of a range that is specified by an ORDER BY clause.

TOP PERCENT — Keywords used to display a percentage of records that fall at the top or bottom of a range that is specified by an ORDER BY clause.

UNION — Keyword used to combine records from two queries while excluding duplicate records.

UNION ALL — Keywords used to combine records from two queries while including duplicate records.

UNIQUE — Keyword used to ensure that only unique, non-repeating values are inserted in an indexed column.

UPDATE statement — Used to update records in a table.

VBA — Visual Basic for Applications. The flavor of Visual Basic incorporated in Access and in much of the Microsoft Office suite.

View — A saved query that queries one or more tables.

WHERE clause — Used to filter retrieved records.

Wildcard characters — Special characters used to match parts of a value.

Appendix D

Microsoft Access Data Types

This appendix provides the data types most commonly used in Microsoft Access.

➲ **Note:** Some of the following data types are used in Design view and some are used in SQL view.

Numeric Data Types:

AUTONUMBER — Used for indexing records in tables.

CURRENCY — Used for monetary calculations.

DECIMAL — An exact numeric data type that holds values from $-10 \wedge 28 - 1$ to $10 \wedge 28 - 1$.

FLOAT — Stores double-precision floating-point values.

INTEGER — Also called INT. Stores a long integer from −2,147,483,648 to 2,147,483,647.

NUMBER — Numerical data that can be used in all forms of calculations except those dealing with money. The Field size property determines the number of bytes used to store the number and, subsequently, the number range.

REAL — Stores single-precision floating-point values.

SMALLINT — Stores an integer from −32,768 to 32,767.

TINYINT — Stores an integer from 0 to 255.

String Data Types:

CHAR — Stores a combination of text and numbers up to 255 characters.

MEMO — Variable-length text fields from 1 to 65,536 characters in length.

TEXT — Stores a combination of text and numbers up to 255 characters.

Miscellaneous Data Types:

BINARY — Enables you to store any type of data in a field. No transformation of the data is made in this type of field.

BIT — Used to store one of two types of values. For example, true/false, yes/no, or on/off.

COUNTER — Stores a long integer value that automatically increments whenever a new record is inserted.

DATETIME — Stores date and time values for the years 100 through 9999.

HYPERLINK — Links to a file, web address, or other location. Just like Internet links, the hyperlink is a stored string which, when clicked, will redirect the program to the address referenced by the hyperlink.

IMAGE — Used to store Object Linking and Embedding (OLE) objects, such as pictures, audio, and video.

MONEY — Stores currency values and numeric data used in mathematical calculations.

OLE OBJECT — Any linked or embedded object including such things like images, Excel spreadsheets, Word documents, or virtually anything else.

UNIQUEIDENTIFIER — A unique identification number used with remote procedure calls.

YES/NO — Boolean values that have only two states like yes/no, true/false, or on/off.

SQL Script to Create the Tables in This Book

This appendix provides the SQL script to create and populate 16 of the tables used in the examples throughout the book. To create and populate a single table, run the Create Table script. Next, delete the Create Table script and copy, paste, and run each INSERT statement *one at a time*.

⊃ **Note:** In Microsoft Access, each time you insert a new record, a message will display telling you that you are about to append one record. Click Yes in response to this message.

Create and Populate the Activities Table

```
CREATE TABLE Activities
(
ActivityID NUMBER CONSTRAINT ActID PRIMARY KEY,
ActivityName CHAR (50) NOT NULL,
StartDate DATE,
EndDate DATE
);

INSERT INTO Activities (ActivityID, ActivityName, StartDate,
        EndDate)
VALUES (1, 'Aerobics', '01/1/08', '01/9/08');
```

```
INSERT INTO Activities (ActivityID, ActivityName, StartDate,
    EndDate)
VALUES (2, 'Games', '01/2/08', '01/10/08');

INSERT INTO Activities (ActivityID, ActivityName, StartDate,
    EndDate)
VALUES (3, 'Outdoor activities', '01/3/08', '01/10/08');

INSERT INTO Activities (ActivityID, ActivityName, StartDate,
    EndDate)
VALUES (4, 'Trips and tours', '01/1/08', '01/17/08');

INSERT INTO Activities (ActivityID, ActivityName, StartDate,
    EndDate)
VALUES (5, 'Arts and crafts', '01/17/08', '01/27/08');

INSERT INTO Activities (ActivityID, ActivityName, StartDate,
    EndDate)
VALUES (6, 'Resident discussion groups', '01/9/08', '01/17/08');

INSERT INTO Activities (ActivityID, ActivityName, StartDate,
    EndDate)
VALUES (7, 'Coffee or cocktail hours', '01/1/08', NULL);
```

Create and Populate the Committee1 Table

```
CREATE TABLE Committee1
(
CommitteeID INTEGER CONSTRAINT Com1ID PRIMARY KEY,
Firstname CHAR (50) NOT NULL,
Lastname CHAR (50) NOT NULL,
Address CHAR (50) NOT NULL,
Zipcode CHAR (10) NOT NULL,
Areacode CHAR (3) NULL,
PhoneNumber CHAR (8) NULL
);

INSERT INTO Committee1
VALUES (1, 'Yolanda', 'Cole', '3466 42nd Ave E. St. Pete, FL',
    33711, 727, '321-1111');
```

```
INSERT INTO Committee1
VALUES (2, 'John', 'Allison', '2345 40th Ave N Honolulu, HI', 96820,
       808, '423-4222');

INSERT INTO Committee1
VALUES (3, 'Kayla', 'Fields', '2211 Peachtree St S Tampa, FL',
       33612, 813, '827-4532');

INSERT INTO Committee1
VALUES (4, 'Debra', 'Brown', '1900 12th Ave S Atlanta, GA', 98718,
       301, '897-0987');

INSERT INTO Committee1
VALUES (5, 'Leonard', 'Miles', '400 22nd Ave N Atlanta, GA', 98718,
       301, '897-1723');
```

Create and Populate the Committee2 Table

```
CREATE TABLE Committee2
(
CommitteeID INTEGER CONSTRAINT Com2ID PRIMARY KEY,
Firstname CHAR (50) NOT NULL,
Lastname CHAR (50) NOT NULL,
Address CHAR (50) NOT NULL,
Zipcode CHAR (10) NOT NULL,
Areacode CHAR (3) NULL,
PhoneNumber CHAR (8) NULL
);

INSERT INTO Committee2
VALUES (1, 'Leonard', 'Cole', '1323 13th Ave N Atlanta, GA', 98718,
       301, '897-1241');

INSERT INTO Committee2
VALUES (2, 'Panzina', 'Coney', '9033 Colfax Loop Tampa, FL', 33612,
       813, '223-6754');

INSERT INTO Committee2
VALUES (3, 'Kayla', 'Fields', '2211 Peachtree St S Tampa, FL',
       33612, 813, '827-4532');
```

```
INSERT INTO Committee2
VALUES (4, 'Jerru', 'London', '6711 40th Ave S Honolulu, HI', 96820,
        808, '611-2341');

INSERT INTO Committee2
VALUES (5, 'Debra', 'Brown', '1900 12th Ave S Atlanta, GA', 98718,
        301, '897-0987');
```

Create and Populate the Computers Table

```
CREATE TABLE Computers
(
SerialNum CHAR (11) CONSTRAINT CompIDPk PRIMARY KEY,
Brand CHAR (20) NOT NULL,
Department CHAR (20) NOT NULL,
OfficeNumber NUMBER NOT NULL
);

INSERT INTO Computers
VALUES ('M6289288289', 'Dell', 'Accounting', 134);

INSERT INTO Computers
VALUES ('G9277288282', 'Dell', 'HR', 122);

INSERT INTO Computers
VALUES ('X8276538101', 'Dell', 'HR', 311);

INSERT INTO Computers
VALUES ('W2121040244', 'Gateway', 'CustomerService', 22);

INSERT INTO Computers
VALUES ('R2871620091', 'Dell', 'Information Systems', 132);
```

Create and Populate the Customers Table

```
CREATE TABLE Customers
(
CustomerID NUMBER CONSTRAINT CusID PRIMARY KEY,
Firstname CHAR (50) NOT NULL,
Lastname CHAR (50) NOT NULL,
Address CHAR (50) NOT NULL,
City CHAR (20) NOT NULL,
```

```
State CHAR (2) NOT NULL,
Zipcode CHAR (10) NOT NULL,
Areacode CHAR (3) NULL,
PhoneNumber CHAR (8) NULL
);

INSERT INTO Customers
VALUES (1, 'Kayla', 'Allison', '6725 3rd Ave N', 'Atlanta', 'GA',
        98700, 301, '897-3412');

INSERT INTO Customers
VALUES (2, 'Devin', 'Fields', '1001 30th St S', 'Tampa', 'FL',
        33677, 813, '828-8754');

INSERT INTO Customers
VALUES (3, 'Gene', 'Spencer', '3910 35th Ave S.', 'St. Pete', 'FL',
        33700, 727, '321-1111');

INSERT INTO Customers
VALUES (4, 'Spencer', 'Madewell', '32101 60th Ave E', 'Honolulu',
        'HI', 96822, 808, '423-4444');

INSERT INTO Customers
VALUES (5, 'Reggie', 'Collins', '1526 1st St N', 'Tampa', 'FL',
        33622, 813, '847-9002');

INSERT INTO Customers
VALUES (6, 'Penny', 'Penn', '2875 Treetop St N', 'Tampa', 'FL',
        33621, 813, '821-7812');
```

Create and Populate the Customers2 Table

```
CREATE TABLE Customers2
(
CustomerID INTEGER NOT NULL PRIMARY KEY,
Firstname CHAR (50) NOT NULL,
Lastname CHAR (50) NOT NULL,
Address CHAR (50) NOT NULL,
City CHAR (20) NOT NULL,
State CHAR (2) NOT NULL,
Zipcode CHAR (10) NOT NULL,
Areacode CHAR (3) NULL,
```

```
PhoneNumber CHAR (8) NULL
);

INSERT INTO Customers2
VALUES (1, 'Tom', 'Evans', '3000 2nd Ave S', 'Atlanta', 'GA', 98718,
       301, '232-9000');

INSERT INTO Customers2
VALUES (2, 'Larry', 'Genes', '1100 23rd Ave S', 'Tampa', 'FL',
       33618, 813, '982-3455');

INSERT INTO Customers2
VALUES (3, 'Sherry', 'Jones', '100 Free St S', 'Tampa', 'FL', 33618,
       813, '890-4231');

INSERT INTO Customers2
VALUES (4, 'April', 'Jones', '2110 10th St S', 'Santa Fe', 'NM',
       88330, 505, '434-1111');

INSERT INTO Customers2
VALUES (5, 'Jerry', 'Jones', '798 22nd Ave S', 'St. Pete', 'FL',
       33711, 727, '327-3323');

INSERT INTO Customers2
VALUES (6, 'John', 'Little', '1500 Upside Loop N', 'St. Pete', 'FL',
       33711, 727, '346-1234');

INSERT INTO Customers2
VALUES (7, 'Gerry', 'Lexington', '5642 5th Ave S', 'Atlanta', 'GA',
       98718, 301, '832-8912');

INSERT INTO Customers2
VALUES (8, 'Henry', 'Denver', '8790 8th St N', 'Holloman', 'NM',
       88330, 505, '423-8900');

INSERT INTO Customers2
VALUES (9, 'Nancy', 'Kinn', '4000 22nd St S', 'Atlanta', 'GA',
       98718, 301, '879-2345');
```

Create and Populate the Departments Table

```
CREATE TABLE Departments
(
DepartmentID INTEGER CONSTRAINT DepID PRIMARY KEY,
SocialSecNum CHAR (50) NOT NULL,
DepartmentName CHAR (50) NOT NULL
);

INSERT INTO Departments
VALUES (01, '444-57-3892', 'Human Resources');

INSERT INTO Departments
VALUES (02, '666-15-3392', 'Finance');

INSERT INTO Departments
VALUES (03, '165-35-4892', 'Information Systems');

INSERT INTO Departments
VALUES (04, '111-10-1029', 'Customer Service');

INSERT INTO Departments
VALUES (05, '452-72-0123', 'Human Resources');
```

Create and Populate the Employees Table

```
CREATE TABLE Employees
(
SocialSecNum CHAR (11) CONSTRAINT SocID PRIMARY KEY,
Firstname CHAR (50) NOT NULL,
Lastname CHAR (50) NOT NULL,
Address CHAR (50) NOT NULL,
Zipcode CHAR (10) NOT NULL,
Areacode CHAR (3) NULL,
PhoneNumber CHAR (8) NULL
);

INSERT INTO Employees
VALUES ('444-57-3892', 'John', 'Allison', '1400 22nd Ave N Atlanta,
        GA', 98700, 301, '897-1600');
```

```
INSERT INTO Employees
VALUES ('666-15-3392', 'Rosa', 'Coney', '4399 Center Loop Tampa,
        FL', 33677, 813, '898-0001');

INSERT INTO Employees
VALUES ('165-35-4892', 'Willie', 'Coney', '3900 35th Ave S. St.
        Pete, FL', 33700, 727, '321-1111');

INSERT INTO Employees
VALUES ('111-10-1029', 'Tanya', 'Levin', '2001 40th Ave S Honolulu,
        HI', 96822, 808, '423-5671');

INSERT INTO Employees
VALUES ('452-72-0123', 'Yolanda', 'Cole', '9021 Peachtree St N
        Tampa, FL', 33622, 813, '827-4411');
```

Create and Populate the Friends Table

```
CREATE TABLE Friends
(
FriendsID NUMBER CONSTRAINT FrdID PRIMARY KEY,
Firstname CHAR (50) NOT NULL,
Lastname CHAR (50) NOT NULL,
Address CHAR (50) NOT NULL,
Zipcode CHAR (10) NOT NULL,
Areacode CHAR (3) NULL,
PhoneNumber CHAR (8) NULL,
Email CHAR (20) NULL
);

INSERT INTO Friends
VALUES (1, 'John', 'Hill', '2322 3rd Ave S Atlanta, GA', 98753, 301,
        '822-1600', 'jhill@juno.com');

INSERT INTO Friends
VALUES (2, 'Gina', 'Jones', '7123 Kendle Rd Tampa, FL', 33673, 813,
        '811-0001', NULL);

INSERT INTO Friends
VALUES (3, 'Timothy', 'Jones', '1000 6th Ave N. St. Pete, FL',
        33700, 727, '366-1111', 'tjones@aol.com');
```

```
INSERT INTO Friends
VALUES (4, 'Reginald', 'Coney', '3210 7th Ave E Honolulu, HI',
        96111, 808, '423-0022', NULL);

INSERT INTO Friends
VALUES (5, 'Otis', 'Rivers', '2400 Ferry Rd N Tampa, FL', 33623,
        813, '321-1432', 'orivers@hotmail.com');
```

Create and Populate the Manufacturers Table

```
CREATE TABLE Manufacturers
(
ManufacturerID INTEGER CONSTRAINT ManfID PRIMARY KEY,
ToyID INTEGER NOT NULL,
CompanyName CHAR (50) NOT NULL,
Address CHAR (50) NOT NULL,
City CHAR (20) NOT NULL,
State CHAR (2) NOT NULL,
PostalCode CHAR (5) NOT NULL,
AreaCode CHAR (3) NOT NULL,
PhoneNumber CHAR (8) NOT NULL UNIQUE,
CONSTRAINT ToyFk FOREIGN KEY (ToyID) REFERENCES Toys (ToyID)
);

INSERT INTO Manufacturers (ManufacturerID, ToyID, CompanyName,
        Address, City, State, PostalCode, AreaCode, PhoneNumber)
VALUES (1, 1, 'Matel', '2892 23rd Ave S', 'St. Petersburg', 'FL',
        33710, 727, '324-5421');

INSERT INTO Manufacturers (ManufacturerID, ToyID, CompanyName,
        Address, City, State, PostalCode, AreaCode, PhoneNumber)
VALUES (2, 2, 'Jurnes', '1231 Lindsay Ave N', 'Tampa', 'FL', 33618,
        813, '234-3982');

INSERT INTO Manufacturers (ManufacturerID, ToyID, CompanyName,
        Address, City, State, PostalCode, AreaCode, PhoneNumber)
VALUES (3, 3, 'Radae', '1872 3rd Ave N', 'Baltimore', 'MD', 21210,
        240, '713-0011');

INSERT INTO Manufacturers (ManufacturerID, ToyID, CompanyName,
        Address, City, State, PostalCode, AreaCode, PhoneNumber)
```

```
VALUES (4, 4, 'Winnies', '6000 16th Ave N', 'San Diego', 'CA',
        92101, 213, '981-8745');

INSERT INTO Manufacturers (ManufacturerID, ToyID, CompanyName,
        Address, City, State, PostalCode, AreaCode, PhoneNumber)
VALUES (5, 5, 'Lenar', '1230 9th Ave N', 'Baltimore', 'MD', 21202,
        301, '321-0987');
```

Create and Populate the Numbers Table

```
CREATE TABLE Numbers
(
ColumnOne INTEGER NOT NULL,
ColumnTwo INTEGER NOT NULL,
ColumnThree INTEGER NOT NULL
);

INSERT INTO Numbers
VALUES (5, 2, 98);

INSERT INTO Numbers
VALUES (1, 8, 11);

INSERT INTO Numbers
VALUES (10, 1, 22);

INSERT INTO Numbers
VALUES (90, 6, 12);

INSERT INTO Numbers
VALUES (40, 27, 6);

INSERT INTO Numbers
VALUES (90, 7, 4);

INSERT INTO Numbers
VALUES (70, 43, 3);

INSERT INTO Numbers
VALUES (70, 61, 144);
```

Create and Populate the Products Table

```
CREATE TABLE Products
(
ProductID CHAR (7) NOT NULL PRIMARY KEY,
ProductName CHAR (50) NOT NULL,
Price MONEY NOT NULL,
SalePrice MONEY NOT NULL,
InStock INTEGER NOT NULL,
OnOrder INTEGER NOT NULL
);

INSERT INTO Products
VALUES ('VR300', 'China Doll', 20.00, 13.00, 100, 0);

INSERT INTO Products
VALUES ('CT200', 'China Puppy', 15.00, 13.50, 20, 40);

INSERT INTO Products
VALUES ('ET100', 'Wooden Clock', 11.00, 9.90, 100, 0);

INSERT INTO Products
VALUES ('PO200', 'Glass Rabbit', 50.00, 45.00, 50, 20);

INSERT INTO Products
VALUES ('TH100', 'Crystal Cat', 75.00, 67.50, 60, 20);

INSERT INTO Products
VALUES ('RX300', 'Praying Statue', 25.00, 22.50, 3, 40);

INSERT INTO Products
VALUES ('CE300', 'Miniature Train Set', 60.00, 54.00, 1, 30);

INSERT INTO Products
VALUES ('OT100', 'Dancing Bird', 10.00, 9.00, 10, 20);

INSERT INTO Products
VALUES ('LF300', 'Friendly Lion', 14.00, 12.60, 0, 30);

INSERT INTO Products
VALUES ('BN200', 'Animated Rainbow', 20.00, 18.00, 10, 20);
```

```
INSERT INTO Products
VALUES ('AN200', 'Animated Picture', 20.00, 18.00, 10, 20);
```

Create and Populate the Sales Table

```
CREATE TABLE Sales
(
SalesID INTEGER NOT NULL PRIMARY KEY,
ProductID CHAR (7) NOT NULL,
CustomerID INTEGER NOT NULL,
DateSold DATETIME NOT NULL
);

INSERT INTO Sales
VALUES (1, 'BN200', 2, '3/3/08');

INSERT INTO Sales
VALUES (2, 'CT200', 3, '2/5/08');

INSERT INTO Sales
VALUES (3, 'ET100', 5, '2/6/07');

INSERT INTO Sales
VALUES (4, 'PO200', 1, '7/8/08');

INSERT INTO Sales
VALUES (5, 'TH100', 3, '2/8/08');

INSERT INTO Sales
VALUES (6, 'RX300', 4, '2/10/07');

INSERT INTO Sales
VALUES (7, 'CT200', 2, '2/22/08');

INSERT INTO Sales
VALUES (8, 'ET100', 6, '2/20/08');

INSERT INTO Sales
VALUES (9, 'LF300', 6, '2/18/08');

INSERT INTO Sales
VALUES (10, 'BN200', 1, '2/17/08');
```

Create and Populate the Tools Table

```
CREATE TABLE Tools
(
ToolID NUMBER CONSTRAINT ToolIDPk PRIMARY KEY,
ToolName CHAR (40) NOT NULL,
Manufacturer CHAR (40) NOT NULL,
Type CHAR (40) NOT NULL,
Location CHAR (40) NOT NULL,
Price MONEY NOT NULL
);

INSERT INTO Tools
VALUES (1, 'Jigsaw', 'Dewalt', 'Power Tool', 'A', 60.00);

INSERT INTO Tools
VALUES (2, 'Hand Drill', 'Dewalt', 'Power Tool', 'A', 30.00);

INSERT INTO Tools
VALUES (3, 'Router', 'Dewalt', 'Power Tool', 'A', 40.00);

INSERT INTO Tools
VALUES (4, 'Nail Gun', 'Bosch', 'Power Tool', 'A', 60.00);

INSERT INTO Tools
VALUES (5, 'Sandpaper', 'Bosch', 'Sanding', 'B', 4.00);

INSERT INTO Tools
VALUES (6, 'Scrapers', 'Bosch', 'Sanding', 'B', 8.00);

INSERT INTO Tools
VALUES (7, 'Hammer', 'Makita', 'Hand Tool', 'C', 14.00);

INSERT INTO Tools
VALUES (8, 'Pliers', 'Porter', 'Hand Tool', 'C', 9.00);

INSERT INTO Tools
VALUES (9, 'Screwdriver', 'Makita', 'Hand Tool', 'C', 4.00);

INSERT INTO Tools
VALUES (10, 'Tool Belt', 'Porter', 'Accessories', 'D', 15.00);
```

```
INSERT INTO Tools
VALUES (11, 'Battery Charger', 'Dewalt', 'Accessories', 'D', 20.00);
```

Create and Populate the Toys Table

```
CREATE TABLE Toys
(
ToyID INTEGER CONSTRAINT ToyPk PRIMARY KEY,
ToyName CHAR (30) NOT NULL,
Price MONEY NOT NULL,
Description CHAR (40) NULL
);

INSERT INTO Toys (ToyID, ToyName, Price, Description)
VALUES (1, 'ToyTrain1', 11.00, 'Red/blue battery powered train');

INSERT INTO Toys (ToyID, ToyName, Price, Description)
VALUES (2, 'ToyTrain2', 11.00, 'Green/red/blue battery powered
        train');

INSERT INTO Toys (ToyID, ToyName, Price, Description)
VALUES (3, 'ElectricTrain', 15.00, 'Red/white AC/DC powered train');

INSERT INTO Toys (ToyID, ToyName, Price, Description)
VALUES (4, 'LivingDoll1', 12.00, 'Asian American Doll');

INSERT INTO Toys (ToyID, ToyName, Price, Description)
VALUES (5, 'LivingDoll2', 12.00, 'African American Doll');

INSERT INTO Toys (ToyID, ToyName, Price, Description)
VALUES (6, 'DollHouse', 17.00, 'Grand Town House');

INSERT INTO Toys (ToyID, ToyName, Price, Description)
VALUES (7, 'Doll/TownHouse', 15.00, 'Town House');
```

Create and Populate the Transactions Table

```
CREATE TABLE Transactions
(
TransactionID INTEGER NOT NULL PRIMARY KEY,
ProductID CHAR (7) NOT NULL,
CustomerID INTEGER NOT NULL,
DateSold DATETIME NOT NULL
);

INSERT INTO Transactions
VALUES (1, 'VR300', 2, '2/3/08');

INSERT INTO Transactions
VALUES (2, 'CT200', 2, '2/5/08');

INSERT INTO Transactions
VALUES (3, 'ET100', 5, '2/6/08');

INSERT INTO Transactions
VALUES (4, 'PO200', 1, '2/8/08');

INSERT INTO Transactions
VALUES (5, 'TH100', 3, '2/8/08');

INSERT INTO Transactions
VALUES (6, 'RX300', 4, '2/10/08');

INSERT INTO Transactions
VALUES (7, 'CE300', 2, '2/22/08');

INSERT INTO Transactions
VALUES (8, 'OT100', 6, '2/20/08');

INSERT INTO Transactions
VALUES (9, 'LF300', 6, '2/18/08');

INSERT INTO Transactions
VALUES (10, 'BN200', 1, '2/17/08');
```

Index

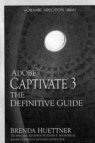

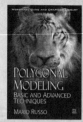